INVESTING ONLINE FOR DUMMIES®

2ND EDITION

by Kathleen Sindell, Ph.D.

Foreword by Charles R. Schwab
Chairman, The Charles Schwab Corporation

IDG Books Worldwide, Inc.
An International Data Group Company

Foster City, CA ♦ Chicago, IL ♦ Indianapolis, IN ♦ New York, NY

Investing Online For Dummies® 2nd Edition

Published by
IDG Books Worldwide, Inc.
An International Data Group Company
919 E. Hillsdale Blvd.
Suite 400
Foster City, CA 94404
www.idgbooks.com (IDG Books Worldwide Web site)
www.dummies.com (Dummies Press Web site)

Library of Congress Catalog Card No.: 98-89941

ISBN: 0-7645-0509-2

Printed in the United States of America

10 9 8 7 6 5 4

2B/QT/QT/ZZ/IN

Distributed in the United States by IDG Books Worldwide, Inc.

Distributed by CDG Books Canada Inc. for Canada; by Transworld Publishers Limited in the United Kingdom; by IDG Norge Books for Norway; by IDG Sweden Books for Sweden; by Woodslane Pty. Ltd. for Australia; by Woodslane (NZ) Ltd. for New Zealand; by TransQuest Publishers Pte Ltd. for Singapore, Malaysia, Thailand, Indonesia, and Hong Kong; by ICG Muse, Inc. for Japan; by Norma Comunicaciones S.A. for Colombia; by Intersoft for South Africa; by Le Monde en Tique for France; by International Thomson Publishing for Germany, Austria and Switzerland; by Distribuidora Cuspide for Argentina; by Livraria Cultura for Brazil; by Ediciones ZETA S.C.R. Ltda. for Peru; by WS Computer Publishing Corporation, Inc., for the Philippines; by Contemporanea de Ediciones for Venezuela; by Express Computer Distributors for the Caribbean and West Indies; by Micronesia Media Distributor, Inc. for Micronesia; by Grupo Editorial Norma S.A. for Guatemala; by Chips Computadoras S.A. de C.V. for Mexico; by Editorial Norma de Panama S.A. for Panama; by American Bookshops for Finland. Authorized Sales Agent: Anthony Rudkin Associates for the Middle East and North Africa.

For general information on IDG Books Worldwide's books in the U.S., please call our Consumer Customer Service department at 800-762-2974. For reseller information, including discounts and premium sales, please call our Reseller Customer Service department at 800-434-3422.

For information on where to purchase IDG Books Worldwide's books outside the U.S., please contact our International Sales department at 317-596-5530 or fax 317-596-5692.

For consumer information on foreign language translations, please contact our Customer Service department at 1-800-434-3422, fax 317-596-5692, or e-mail rights@idgbooks.com.

For information on licensing foreign or domestic rights, please phone +1-650-655-3109.

For sales inquiries and special prices for bulk quantities, please contact our Sales department at 650-655-3200 or write to the address above.

For information on using IDG Books Worldwide's books in the classroom or for ordering examination copies, please contact our Educational Sales department at 800-434-2086 or fax 317-596-5499.

For press review copies, author interviews, or other publicity information, please contact our Public Relations department at 650-655-3000 or fax 650-655-3299.

For authorization to photocopy items for corporate, personal, or educational use, please contact Copyright Clearance Center, 222 Rosewood Drive, Danvers, MA 01923, or fax 978-750-4470.

About the Author

Kathleen Sindell has more than 20 years of financial services experience and is the founder of a firm that provides management consulting to the financial services industry and authoritative publications about new ways of conducting business and managing finances in the emerging electronic economy. She and her colleagues are specialists in business, finance, real estate and e-commerce and work with organizations to deliver effective business solutions that enable financial institutions to chart a course through a rapidly changing financial services market place. She is the former Associate Director of the Financial Management and Commercial Real Estate Programs for the University of Maryland, University College Graduate School of Management & Technology.

Dr. Sindell recently completed the second edition of *A Hands-On Guide to Mortgage Banking Internet Sites,* a separate directory published by *Mortgage Banking* magazine (August 1998 and July 1997). She is the author of *The Handbook of Real Estate Lending* (McGraw-Hill Professional Publishing, 1996), and she edited a book titled *Essentials of Financial Management Kit* (Dryden Press, 1993).

Dr. Sindell developed the *Lending Solutions Decision Support Program* to identify, assess, monitor, and mitigate the credit quality of real estate loans. This software application is based on her hands-on experience as a Real Estate Vice President for American Savings & Loan and as the Construction Lending Services Manager for Perpetual Federal Savings Bank.

Dr. Sindell has taught 20 graduate-level courses in financial management; she lectures for the New York Institute of Finance; and she is a well-known speaker for regional and national conferences. Dr. Sindell is on the adjunct faculty of the Johns Hopkins University School of Continuing Studies, where she teaches graduate-level financial management courses. She has provided seminars to senior bank examiners from the Federal Reserve and various other regulatory agencies.

She received her BA in Business from Antioch University, an MBA with a concentration in finance from the California State University at San Jose, and a Ph.D. in Administration and Management from Walden University, Institute for Advanced Studies.

Dr. Sindell lives and writes in Alexandria, Virginia. She is interested in your comments about this book and can be contacted at her Web site www.kathleensindell.com or send e-mail to ksindell@kathleensindell.com.

ABOUT IDG BOOKS WORLDWIDE

Welcome to the world of IDG Books Worldwide.

IDG Books Worldwide, Inc., is a subsidiary of International Data Group, the world's largest publisher of computer-related information and the leading global provider of information services on information technology. IDG was founded more than 30 years ago by Patrick J. McGovern and now employs more than 9,000 people worldwide. IDG publishes more than 290 computer publications in over 75 countries. More than 90 million people read one or more IDG publications each month.

Launched in 1990, IDG Books Worldwide is today the #1 publisher of best-selling computer books in the United States. We are proud to have received eight awards from the Computer Press Association in recognition of editorial excellence and three from Computer Currents' First Annual Readers' Choice Awards. Our best-selling *...For Dummies*® series has more than 50 million copies in print with translations in 31 languages. IDG Books Worldwide, through a joint venture with IDG's Hi-Tech Beijing, became the first U.S. publisher to publish a computer book in the People's Republic of China. In record time, IDG Books Worldwide has become the first choice for millions of readers around the world who want to learn how to better manage their businesses.

Our mission is simple: Every one of our books is designed to bring extra value and skill-building instructions to the reader. Our books are written by experts who understand and care about our readers. The knowledge base of our editorial staff comes from years of experience in publishing, education, and journalism — experience we use to produce books to carry us into the new millennium. In short, we care about books, so we attract the best people. We devote special attention to details such as audience, interior design, use of icons, and illustrations. And because we use an efficient process of authoring, editing, and desktop publishing our books electronically, we can spend more time ensuring superior content and less time on the technicalities of making books.

You can count on our commitment to deliver high-quality books at competitive prices on topics you want to read about. At IDG Books Worldwide, we continue in the IDG tradition of delivering quality for more than 30 years. You'll find no better book on a subject than one from IDG Books Worldwide.

John Kilcullen
Chairman and CEO
IDG Books Worldwide, Inc.

Steven Berkowitz
President and Publisher
IDG Books Worldwide, Inc.

Eighth Annual Computer Press Awards ≥1992

Ninth Annual Computer Press Awards ≥1993

Tenth Annual Computer Press Awards ≥1994

Eleventh Annual Computer Press Awards ≥1995

IDG is the world's leading IT media, research and exposition company. Founded in 1964, IDG had 1997 revenues of $2.05 billion and has more than 9,000 employees worldwide. IDG offers the widest range of media options that reach IT buyers in 75 countries representing 95% of worldwide IT spending. IDG's diverse product and services portfolio spans six key areas including print publishing, online publishing, expositions and conferences, market research, education and training, and global marketing services. More than 90 million people read one or more of IDG's 290 magazines and newspapers, including IDG's leading global brands — Computerworld, PC World, Network World, Macworld and the Channel World family of publications. IDG Books Worldwide is one of the fastest-growing computer book publishers in the world, with more than 700 titles in 36 languages. The "...For Dummies®" series alone has more than 50 million copies in print. IDG offers online users the largest network of technology-specific Web sites around the world through IDG.net (http://www.idg.net), which comprises more than 225 targeted Web sites in 55 countries worldwide. International Data Corporation (IDC) is the world's largest provider of information technology data, analysis and consulting, with research centers in over 41 countries and more than 400 research analysts worldwide. IDG World Expo is a leading producer of more than 168 globally branded conferences and expositions in 35 countries including E3 (Electronic Entertainment Expo), Macworld Expo, ComNet, Windows World Expo, ICE (Internet Commerce Expo), Agenda, DEMO, and Spotlight. IDG's training subsidiary, ExecuTrain, is the world's largest computer training company, with more than 230 locations worldwide and 785 training courses. IDG Marketing Services helps industry-leading IT companies build international brand recognition by developing global integrated marketing programs via IDG's print, online and exposition products worldwide. Further information about the company can be found at www.idg.com.   1/24/99

Dedication

To my husband, Ivan Sindell. His enthusiasm added a lot to this work.

Author's Acknowledgments

My thanks to Joyce Pepple, acquisitions editor, for her thoughtful guidance and support. Thanks to my literary agent, Carole McClendon and all the folks at Watershide Productions for their encouragement. My appreciation to Andrea Boucher for her dedication to high quality. Thanks also to Rowena Rappaport for her fine editing. My appreciation to everyone who worked behind the scenes, especially all the people who are listed on the credits page. Thank you for making this book happen.

My thanks to the IDG Books media development group (Heather Dismore, Carmen Krikorian, Marita Ellixson, and Megan Roney) for making the companion CD-ROM so great.

A very special thank you and note of appreciation to my brother-in-law, Gerald Sindell, for his profound counsel on everything relating to the business of publishing.

And finally, my thanks to the folks who put investing information online for the public. They have changed the financial community forever.

Publisher's Acknowledgments

We're proud of this book; please register your comments through our IDG Books Worldwide Online Registration Form located at http://my2cents.dummies.com.

Some of the people who helped bring this book to market include the following:

Acquisitions, Editorial, and Media Development

Project Editor: Andrea C. Boucher

Acquisitions Editor: Joyce Pepple

Copy Editor: Rowena Rappaport

Technical Editor: Bill Karow, Adam B. Bergman

Media Development Editor: Marita Ellixson

Associate Permissions Editor: Carmen Krikorian

Media Development Coordinator: Megan Roney

Editorial Manager: Kelly Ewing

Media Development Manager: Heather Heath Dismore

Editorial Assistant: Paul E. Kuzmic

Production

Project Coordinator: E. Shawn Aylsworth

Layout and Graphics: Daniel Alexander, Linda M. Boyer, Angela F. Hunckler, Brent Savage, Jacque Schneider, Kate Snell, Brian Torwelle

Proofreaders: Kelli Botta, Nancy Reinhardt, Janet M. Withers

Indexer: Donald Glassman

Special Help

Electric Library ® is a registered trademark of Infonautics, Inc. or its subsidiaries © 1999 Infonautics Corporation. All rights not granted herein are reserved by Infonautics Corporation. © SmartMoney is a joint venture of Hearst Communication Inc. and Dow Jones & Company, Inc. J. Leonard Dury, Joe Harper, Stacey Mickelbart; Billie A. Williams

General and Administrative

IDG Books Worldwide, Inc.: John Kilcullen, CEO; Steven Berkowitz, President and Publisher

IDG Books Technology Publishing: Brenda McLaughlin, Senior Vice President and Group Publisher

Dummies Technology Press and Dummies Editorial: Diane Graves Steele, Vice President and Associate Publisher; Mary Bednarek, Director of Acquisitions and Product Development; Kristin A. Cocks, Editorial Director

Dummies Trade Press: Kathleen A. Welton, Vice President and Publisher; Kevin Thornton, Acquisitions Manager

IDG Books Production for Dummies Press: Michael R. Britton, Vice President of Production and Creative Services; Cindy L. Phipps, Manager of Project Coordination, Production Proofreading, and Indexing; Kathie S. Schutte, Supervisor of Page Layout; Shelley Lea, Supervisor of Graphics and Design; Debbie J. Gates, Production Systems Specialist; Robert Springer, Supervisor of Proofreading; Debbie Stailey, Special Projects Coordinator; Tony Augsburger, Supervisor of Reprints and Bluelines

Dummies Packaging and Book Design: Patty Page, Manager, Promotions Marketing

♦

The publisher would like to give special thanks to Patrick J. McGovern, without whom this book would not have been possible.

♦

Contents at a Glance

Cartoons at a Glance

By Rich Tennant

The 5th Wave By Rich Tennant

"I don't know—my spreadsheet tells me I should put more monthly income into my 401K, my broker says I need to be more aggressive when buying and selling, and my psychologist tells me I depend too much on outside input and should trust my instincts more."

page 9

The 5th Wave By Rich Tennant

"Hold on— our stocks haven't plummeted. It's just a booger in the loss column."

page 49

The 5th Wave By Rich Tennant

"The book value of our stocks went way down when I discovered missing pages."

page 145

The 5th Wave By Rich Tennant

"Who added my portrait of Elvis to my retirement portfolio?"

page 283

The 5th Wave By Rich Tennant

"I've never seen an adjustment to a fluctuating stock market made with a paperweight before."

page 239

Fax: 978-546-7747 • E-mail: the5wave@tiac.net

Table of Contents

Foreword

Smart, forward-thinking investors have a new partner — the Internet. Along with delivering travel information, sports scores, breaking news, and online shopping, the Internet provides some of the best financial tools and resources available. Such Internet resources can assist you in determining your investment objectives, deciding how to allocate your personal wealth, and obtaining high-level performance data for mutual funds, stocks, and bonds. In addition to providing online trading and tracking of your investments, the Internet allows you to do all this rationally, effectively, and faster than ever before.

Internet resources can provide the knowledge you need for getting the edge on investors who rely on paper-based publications. As an online investor, you have the time to plan intelligently, get the facts you need quickly, and make high-level investment decisions.

Although you can find lots of investing information out there on the Internet, not all of it is trustworthy. You may need some direction on using the Internet. What's required is more than a directory (although this book shows you some of the best Internet investment tools, links, and resources). *Investing Online For Dummies,* 2nd Edition, provides clear instructions and ample illustrations so that you don't get lost in cyberspace. The author, Dr. Kathleen Sindell, draws on her considerable experience as the Financial Management Program Director for the University of Maryland, University College Graduate School of Management & Technology. She also draws from her experience from lectures for the New York Institute of Finance and from the graduate-level financial management courses she teaches for the Johns Hopkins University, School of Continuing Studies. She has organized this book to be a comprehensive guide to online investing that explains the basics and shows how to build wealth for investors of all ages and income levels.

While you're gathering the tools you require for becoming a successful online investor, please visit Schwab's Web site at www.schwab.com or one of our 280 branch offices throughout the United States, or call us anytime, 24 hours a day. At Schwab, our goal is to bring you the latest in interactive computer technology and information delivery systems to meet the specialized needs of online investors. We can assist you in managing your trading and account services online. You'll enjoy the security and reliability that comes with trading with the acknowledged leader in electronic brokerage.

Whether you access your account in person, over the telephone, or through the Web, Schwab gives you everything you need to manage your investments online, including real-time quotes, news and research, interactive planning tools, and trading at some of Schwab's lowest commission rates.

Charles R. Schwab
Chairman of the Board
The Charles Schwab Corporation

Introduction

Welcome to *Investing Online For Dummies,* 2nd Edition. The Internet offers an astounding amount of financial information, and *Investing Online For Dummies,* 2nd Edition, provides clear instructions and ample illustrations so that you don't get lost in cyberspace. With the assistance of this book, you can develop personalized investment strategies and start investing online.

Plenty of books are available about online investing, but most assume that you are a practiced investor who enjoys talking in "Wall Street-speak." This book is different; it doesn't include statements like "Our goal is to maximize after-tax returns at a controlled risk level" or "Even though the stock has done well, it remains cheap at midyear, trading at 40 cents on the dollar of net worth and a third of the market's P/E." In other words, this book is a comprehensive guide to online investing that explains the basics and shows how to build wealth for beginning investors of all ages and income levels.

In this book, I show you how to get started, what you really need to know, and where to go on the Internet for additional information. You don't need to memorize complex commands or formulas. I describe everything in plain English, and I leave the Wall Street-speak out in the street.

Who Are You?

In writing this book, I assumed that:

- You would like to take advantage of all the timely investment information available on the Internet.
- You want to get some work done with the Internet. (Online selecting, evaluating, and monitoring of investments can be time-consuming — online investing really is work.)
- You are not interested in becoming the next Warren Buffett — at least not this week.

About This Book

Many online investing books are written by individuals who maintain Web sites, and these books often promote their authors' investment systems, products, and services. Other investment books are written by professional money managers to promote their newsletters or mutual funds. This book, however, has no hidden agenda. It focuses on commonsense ways to create and build wealth with the Internet.

I've designed *Investing Online For Dummies,* 2nd Edition, for beginning online investors, but it can also benefit so-called financial professionals and planners. Each chapter stands alone and provides all the instructions and information you need for solving an investment problem or making an investment decision.

Most online investors will read this book in chunks, diving in long enough to solve a particular investment problem ("Hmmm, I thought I knew how to contact an electronic brokerage, but I don't seem to remember . . .") and then putting it aside. However, the book is structured in such a way that if you want to read it through from beginning to end (even though the book's primary function is as a reference tool), you can do so. I discuss online investment topics in a logical way, from checking your bank balance online through bond transactions to trading stocks online.

Here's a quick rundown on some of the topics I cover:

- Using the Internet to help you make money
- Getting up-to-the-minute quotes and company data 24 hours a day
- Finding the best savings rates and treasury securities data on the Internet
- Locating Internet resources for the selection of mutual funds
- Working with Internet tools for analyzing and selecting stocks and bonds
- Trading online and paying the lowest commissions possible
- Keeping track of your portfolio
- Discovering down-to-earth strategies that can build wealth with small investments

Additionally, I offer warnings to help you avoid dangerous or costly traps, and I point out excellent online investment resources. *Investing Online For Dummies,* 2nd Edition, is your road map to cyberspace. It provides the Internet knowledge that you need to get the edge on investors who rely on newspapers and magazines.

How to Use This Book

If you have a question about an online investing topic, just look up that topic in the table of contents at the beginning of the book or in the index at the end of the book. You can get the help you're seeking immediately or find out where to look for expert advice.

Investing has evolved into a specialized field and isn't particularly easy for normal people. Don't feel bad if you have to use the table of contents and the index quite a bit. Luckily, the Internet offers plenty of sites that let you practice before you buy or trade.

If you want to experience electronic trading and are concerned that a mistake may cost you money, try practicing at the Virtual Stock Exchange (www.virtualstockexchange.com). The Virtual Stock Exchange is a free fantasy stock market game. You can compete with tens of thousands of online investors in a realistic stock trading simulation where you can buy and sell shares of stocks from NYSE, AMEX, and NASDAQ.

If you're new to investing on the Internet, check out the first three chapters in Part I. They give you an overview of the Internet and some important investor tips. To get more familiar with the Internet, try some of the activities that I detail in these chapters.

If you are new to the Internet, I recommend getting a copy of *The Internet For Dummies,* 5th Edition, by John R. Levine, Carol Baroudi, and Margaret Levine Young (IDG Books Worldwide, Inc.). This book is great for anyone who needs help getting started with the Internet. *The Internet For Dummies* can assist you in hooking up with local Internet providers, surfing the Net, downloading free software, and joining mailing lists or user groups.

If you're a new investor, check out Chapter 3 in Part I of this book, which offers warnings about online frauds, schemes, and deceptions. When you start subscribing to investor newsgroups, mailing lists, or online publications, you're likely to receive e-mail stock tips and investment offers. Treat these messages as you would any telephone cold call. Thoroughly examine the investment and get a second opinion from an independent investment expert you respect before you purchase.

How This Book Is Organized

This book has five parts. Each part stands alone — that is, you can begin reading anywhere and get the information you need for investment decision-making. Or you can read the entire book from cover to cover. If you do, you find that the simplest financial transactions come first, and I cover the more complex transactions later.

Here are the parts of the book and what they contain.

Part I: Online Investing Fundamentals

In Part I, you find out what investor tools are available on the Internet. The chapters in Part I discuss important investor uses of the Internet: searches for financial topics, electronic mail, newsgroups, and access to databases that until recently were only available to large financial institutions. You also find out how to download interesting and useful stuff. Part I also offers warnings about online frauds, schemes, and deceptions.

Part II: Finding the Right Investments

The chapters in Part II show you how to find the right investments. This part of the book discusses online banking, mutual funds, stocks, and bonds on the Internet. It cuts through the jargon and gets to the heart of what investments are (and what they're not). Discover how the Internet can help you make your money work harder. Move from saver to investor. These chapters help you understand rates of return and what mutual funds, stocks, and bonds are all about. You clearly see how online investing can fit into your personal financial aspirations. You can start anywhere in the book, but I suggest beginning with the type of investment that intrigues you the most.

Part III: Paying the Right Price

Part III includes chapters that detail how to evaluate a mutual fund's performance and buy or sell a mutual fund online. This part of the book covers online trading and portfolio management, and includes instructions on how to open a cash account with an electronic broker. It also covers how to research and analyze stocks and bonds online. It points you to many online sources for annual reports, economic data, analyst recommendations, industry standards, and more.

Part IV: Making More Money on the Internet

Part IV shows how you can pay the lowest commission rates possible and track your portfolio online. No more guessing about what to hold and when to fold. Figure I-1 shows a good example of an online portfolio management tool at Thomson Investors Network, located at www.thomsoninvest.net. Part IV also provides extra support for online investment initiatives, how to get your financial house in order before you start investing, retirement planning, and online money-saving tax tips.

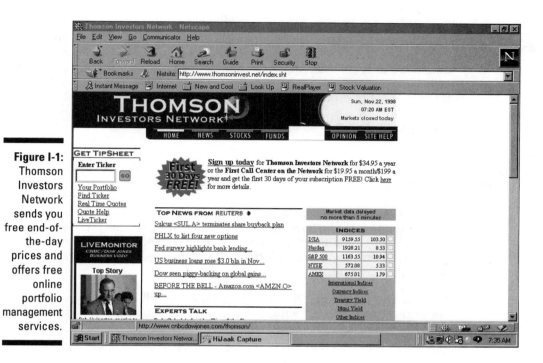

Figure I-1:
Thomson
Investors
Network
sends you
free end-of-
the-day
prices and
offers free
online
portfolio
management
services.

Part V: The Part of Tens

Part V provides handy top-ten lists packed full of ready online references. The chapters in this part cover such essentials as getting ready for online investing, planning for a comfortable retirement, and finding tax help online.

Special features

Check out this book's Internet Directory, which includes the latest and greatest investor sites on the Internet. The focus of this directory is on the sites you're most likely to use when you try to allocate your capital among mutual funds, stocks, and bonds.

The Internet is constantly changing. Thousands of new Web pages are added each day. Some sites listed in this directory (and elsewhere in the book) may have changed or gone away due to mergers with larger sites. Some Web sites just vanish for no reason. If a site has moved, you may find a link to the new location. If not, try a search engine (such as Alta Vista or Infoseek) to locate the resource you need.

The companion CD-ROM packaged with this book contains a selection of the finest Internet investment software tools and demos available for investors. You also get Microsoft Internet Explorer 4.0, and a complete Web version of the book's Internet Directory. (You don't have to type in the Web addresses of sites you want to visit; just launch your browser program, access the Internet Directory on this book's companion CD-ROM, connect to the Internet, and click on a site's name.) In addition to all of this, the CD also contains four bonus chapters.

What's New

In this second edition of *Investing Online for Dummies,* I describe dozens of the latest and greatest Internet resources that are available for assisting you in your wealth-building efforts. These Web sites include the newest online investing information, research sources, calculators, spreadsheets, shareware, freeware, and product demonstrations.

The content of *Investing Online for Dummies,* 2nd Edition, is bigger and better than ever with new chapters and more information on hot topics, such as:

- Moving from saver to investor
- Bullet-proofing your online investing
- Picking a rising star: Introducing new online tools for analyzing stocks
- Checking out technical analysis, market timing, and other online methods of analyzing stocks
- More online information about fixed income securities and bonds
- Increasing profits by selling short
- Squeezing profits: New online approaches for trading stock options
- Trading strategies for futures and commodities that you can practice (cost-free) with online simulations
- Daytrading online for beginning investors
- The big buy and sell signals

And so much more . . .

Technical Requirements

The following list details the minimum system requirements for connecting to the Internet. This list describes all the computer hardware and software you need:

- ✔ An IBM PC-compatible computer with a minimum of 8MB of RAM, 6MB available hard disk space, a 486 or faster processor, and Windows 3.*x*, Windows 95, or Windows NT operating systems. Or . . . a Macintosh or Mac clone with a minimum of 8MB of RAM, 5MB available hard disk space, a 68030 or faster processor, and System 7 or higher.
- ✔ Any Internet browser (such as Netscape Navigator 4.0 or Internet Explorer 4.0).
- ✔ A SLIP or PPP Internet connection, with a modem that runs 14.4 Kbps (28.8 Kbps is preferred), or a direct connection.

Icons Used in This Book

Throughout *Investing Online For Dummies,* 2nd Edition, I use icons to help guide you through all the suggestions, solutions, cautions, and World Wide Web sites. I hope you find that the following icons make your journey through online investment strategies smoother.

This icon indicates an explanation for a nifty little shortcut or time-saver.

This icon points out riskier investment strategies plus other things to watch out for.

This icon points out a resource on the World Wide Web that you can access with Netscape Navigator, Microsoft Internet Explorer, or other Web software.

The Technical Stuff icon lets you know that some particularly nerdy, technoid information is coming up so that you can skip it if you want. (On the other hand, you may want to read it.)

Feedback, Please

If you have any comments, suggestions, or questions, I'd love to hear from you. Please feel free to contact me in care of IDG Books Worldwide, 7260 Shadeland Station, Suite 100, Indianapolis, IN 46256. Better yet, visit my Web site at www.kathleensindell.com, and send me an e-mail message at ksindell@kathleensindell.com.

Part I
Online Investing Fundamentals

In this part . . .

The chapters in this part help you discover why the Internet should be your starting point for researching investments. These chapters point you to a variety of online investor resources and data. The chapters in this part also detail the Internet tools you need for successful online investing, and they offer timely advice about how you can tell a good deal from a scam.

Chapter 1

Why Look to the Internet for Investment Information?

*T*imely, high-quality information has always made the difference between making money and not making money. In the past, big-time investors had ticker tape machines in their offices tapping out the latest Wall Street stock prices. Now you can have a ticker automatically run on your desktop computer. You even have the option of running a ticker that shows just the stocks in your personal portfolio.

In this chapter, I help you get started with investing online by showing a short example of how the Internet can help you with each step in the investing process:

1. **Selecting assets that meet your financial objectives.**

2. **Analyzing investment candidates.**

3. **Buying securities online.**

4. **Monitoring your investments.**

5. **Selling your investments to harvest your profits.**

To help you get started, I point you toward some helpful online investment resources, and I offer examples of the types of investment information you can find on the Internet. (I assume that you're already connected to the Internet at work, at school, or at home.)

If you need help getting started on the Internet, pick up a copy of *The Internet For Dummies,* 5th Edition, by John R. Levine, Carol Baroudi, and Margaret Levine Young (IDG Books Worldwide, Inc.). *The Internet For Dummies* shows what the Internet is (and what it is not), introduces you to Internet terminology and concepts, explains different Internet services, shows you how to navigate the Web, and provides details about how to download software and other types of files from sites on the Internet.

Can You Earn Big Bucks by Investing on the Internet?

Imagine that it's Monday around 7:00 a.m. You have more than enough time to read the newspaper and check your e-mail before you head out to work. With your cup of coffee in hand, you go to your computer and read your morning e-mail newspapers: *The New York Times* interactive edition (www.nyt.com), Individual Newspage (www.newspage.com), and *Barron's Online* (www.barrons.com).

You're interested in the banking industry and have watched the large banks consolidate over the last five years. You notice that XYZ Bank's stock has taken a tumble. You find news about disappointing earnings at XYZ Bank but no speculation about additional problems. The share price has declined from $30 per share to $21, and it's now in your price range. Is XYZ Bank's declining stock price an investment opportunity for you? If you're an online investor, here's what you do:

1. **Go to the Dow Jones News Retrieval Service and The Wall Street Journal Interactive Edition (**bis.dowjones.com **and** www.wsj.com, **respectively) and get more information about XYZ Bank.**

   You find more news about the disappointing earnings but no speculation about additional problems.

2. **Go to Hoover's Online (**www.hoovers.com**) and get an in-depth company report.**

   The report indicates that the company hasn't experienced any recent management or financial problems.

3. **Go to XYZ Bank's home page and get a copy of the bank's most recent annual report.**

   You look over the ten-year summary of financial figures, stock prices, and dividends.

4. **Compare XYZ Bank's performance to the industry average at Individual Investor Online (www.iionline.com/guest/industry).**

   The company's *return on equity* (ROE) is 19 percent. That's better than most banks.

   Note: ROE is the shareholder's bottom line. It measures an investor's gain or loss for a particular stock. However, this should not be confused with rate of return, which is defined in Chapter 13.

5. **Check what Value Line and Standard & Poors has to say about XYZ Bank at www.valueline.com and www.stockinfo.standardpoor.com.**

   Value Line and Standard & Poors indicates that XYZ Bank's growth in profits and operating income has consistently improved.

6. **Check what the experts have to say at Zack's (www.zacks.com).**

   They recommend buying the stock and expect earnings to jump ahead early next year.

7. **Crunch a few numbers, perform your fundamental analysis with the help of the Internet (as I discuss in Chapter 12), and decide that future returns will pay for the risk you're taking now.**

8. **Contact your online brokerage and place your order.**

   When the market opens, you want to purchase 100 shares of XYZ Bank stock. Your online broker will e-mail you notification later in the day that your trade was executed. You can check on it at lunch.

So does online investing sound complicated? It's not, and thousands of people invest online every day — men and women in all walks of life. If you have a computer and Internet access, you can do it, too. This book shows you how.

Picking a Winning Investment Online

You may be a beginning investor who is unsure about how to leap into the finance world, or you may be an experienced investor looking for an extra edge or something new. Whatever category you fall into, the Internet can provide you with the tools and resources you need.

You don't have to be a technical genius to access all the available Internet tools, research sources, and financial data. You don't even have to be an experienced investor. This book can help you pick winning investments that match your financial objectives. Here are just a few of the many ways the Internet can assist you in picking winning investments:

✔ You can use the Internet to find investment opportunities in the news, user groups, and mailing lists you subscribe to.

✔ *Push technology* can send you the information you want each day by using such services as BackWeb (www.backweb.com) and PointCast (www.pointcast.com). (I explain push technology in Chapter 2.)

✔ You can use Internet *updatebots* (small programs) to monitor the Internet for Web site revisions that may indicate changes in investment conditions. (See Chapter 2 for more information about updatebots.)

✔ You can subscribe to investor supersites to study specific industries and general conditions of the market and to watch what professionals say and do. (I offer examples of these supersites later in this chapter. For even more information, see Chapters 11 and 12.)

✔ You can study the past-performance data and review earnings estimates of investment candidates online (see Chapter 13).

✔ You can create your own analyses and make decisions based on your own online research (see Chapter 8).

✔ You can take advantage of opportunities that you didn't even know about before you became an online investor. (For example, you can find information about reinvestment and direct stock purchase plans, as I detail in Chapter 15.)

What Can Investors Find on the Net?

I believe that the Internet is the greatest single source ever placed in the hands of the individual investor. With the Internet, you don't need to be a Wall Street insider to build your small savings into a solid investment portfolio. All you need is to be online. Here are a few examples of what you can find:

✔ Company annual reports, 24-hour access to Securities and Exchange Commission (SEC) filings (reports required by securities regulators for publicly traded companies), other in-depth industry and company data, earnings estimates, and broker recommendations for companies you're considering as candidates for investment.

✔ Alerts for when the prices of your chosen stocks reach predetermined buy or sell targets.

✔ All the information you need for buying and selling Treasury securities and government, agency, and corporate bonds.

A word of caution

Some Internet investments may sound too good to be true. Well, they are. Just like any other place, the Internet has its share of frauds, schemes, and deceptions. Investments in stocks, mutual funds, and bonds are not guaranteed to $100,000 like Federal Deposit Insurance Corporation (FDIC) savings deposits. If your legitimate investment loses money or if someone deceives you in some type of "get rich quick" scheme, no FDIC insurance payments exist to cover your losses. However, the Securities Industry Protection Corporation (SIPC) insures your money should your brokerage go out of business.

- ✔ Internet programs that sort through thousands of mutual funds so that you can find those few special mutual funds that meet your investment criteria.

- ✔ Internet screening tools to sift through thousands of stocks to find the ones that meet your predefined needs and financial goals.

- ✔ Online portfolio management programs that automatically update your portfolio each evening.

- ✔ Real-time and delayed stock quotes displayed on your desktop.

- ✔ The lowest commission fees anywhere for your online trades.

Don't invest until you determine your personal financial goals and figure out how much risk you can take. You should also give some consideration to spreading your investments around to diversify your risk. After you complete these tasks, online investing allows you to take control of your finances and start building wealth.

Where Should You Start?

Picking your first investor resources is an important task. You can get a good feel for what's available on the Internet at compilation sites called investment *supersites*. Here are a few examples:

- ✔ **Cyberinvest** (www.cyberinvest.com) is a collection of links and guides to online resources, such as online banking, electronic brokerages, investor education, interest rates, news, stock prospecting, and technical analysis.

- **Individual Investor Online** (`www.iionline.com`) offers delayed quotes, stock prospecting tools and screens, recommendations, industry research, SEC reports, earnings estimates, portfolio management, and news.

- **Invest-O-Rama** (`www.investorama.com`) is a vast collection of links to online sources, such as electronic brokers, mutual funds, financial reports, and other investor sources.

- **Investorguide** (`www.investorguide.com`) features newsletters, research, 1,000 answers to frequently asked questions (FAQs), and a well-organized investor, personal finance, and educational directory with links to thousands of investor Internet sites.

- **Investools.com** (`investools.com`) provides newsletters, portfolio workshops, quotes and news, research reports, and data.

- **Microsoft Investor** (`investor.msn.com`) investment research, news and feature articles, portfolio tracking and management, stocks and mutual fund screens. Microsoft Investor offers a free stock ticker (that you can personalize). The ticker can be added to your Microsoft Active Desktop component or your Web page.

- **Personal Wealth** (`www.personalwealth.com`) is sponsored by Standard & Poors and includes quotes and research, market snapshots and news, portfolio management, financial planning, and S & P expert advice.

- **Quicken.com** (`www.quicken.com`) is an investor supersite with portfolio management, delayed quotes with graphs, prospecting tools, news and alerts, research data, and investor education. In addition, this site contains information on taxes, insurance, retirement planning, banking and borrowing, small business, home buying and selling, and mortgages.

- **Stocksite.com** (`www.stocksite.com`) provides portfolio management, delayed quotes and charts, market monitoring and company news, prospecting tools and recommendations, message boards, research data, and company profiles.

- **Wall Street Directory** (`www.wsdinc.com`) features newsletters, a bookstore, quotes, and a software mall. The site also provides Internet sources for online trading, investment data services, financial and investment information and tools, and free offers of products and services for investors.

Chapter 2

Internet, Here I Come

● ●

In This Chapter

▶ Discovering how to get a cost-free investor education online

▶ Locating beginner investor and new online investor Web sites, FAQs sources, and glossaries

▶ Getting expert advice and news from online investor news sources, newspapers, magazines, and scholarly journals

▶ Getting investment newsletters automatically sent to your e-mailbox

▶ Investing and earning profits with investment clubs

▶ Practicing what you've discovered with Internet stock simulations

● ●

*T*he Internet can assist you in getting the information you need to be a savvy investor. I suggest that you start with one of the many online tutorials for beginning investors. Following that, I show you the best Web sites for new investors. I continue with directions to online Frequently Asked Questions (FAQs), sources, and Internet glossaries to help you with those troublesome investment terms and concepts that the experts use.

This chapter points out where you can find expert advice and late-breaking financial news from online news organizations, newspapers, and magazines. You discover how you can find scholarly financial journals to research the latest stock picking methodology that your lunch buddy expounds about daily. I even show you how to get specialized investment newsletters automatically sent to your e-mailbox so that you can stay on top of current events. I often give you prices for various services, as well, but these prices may change, so check the Web site for any updated information.

I conclude this chapter by showing you how to practice what you have discovered without losing a dime. First, you can join or start an investment club, which allows you to learn and earn with other folks that are interested in maximizing their investment returns. Second, you can register for one of the many online stock simulation games (some even offer monthly prizes or cash awards).

Getting Smart Online

According to *Money* magazine, the average online investor uses the Internet about 11.6 hours each week. The average time non-online investors spend on the Internet is 8.4 hours per week. This comparison indicates that if you start using the Internet to do your own investing, you won't spend a significantly longer time in front of your computer than other people do.

Connecting to the Internet gives you access to millions of documents, a vast variety of software programs (some of the best are on this book's companion CD-ROM), and high-caliber information that in the not-too-distant past only large financial institutions could access. The World Wide Web provides an easy-to-use interface that allows you to access the Internet's many financial resources. This interface allows individual investors to: (1) acquire an education in investing, (2) frequently avoid costly financial services, and (3) conduct high-grade online research.

Online investor tutorials

If you are serious about seeing your capital grow at the fastest rate possible, you need to get smart about investing. The Internet provides many online tutorials, courses, and feature articles that can bring you up to speed. These sites are often sponsored by traditional investment bankers and brokerages that are competing with like companies for your investment dollar.

Avoiding information overload

When you're just starting out on the Internet, it's easy to become overwhelmed by the huge amount of business and finance information that's available. The best way to avoid this information overload is to divide these sources into specific categories. These categories can be added to your browser's bookmark file. For example, this chapter provides information for these bookmark categories:

- ✔ Investment Clubs
- ✔ Investment News and Market Commentary
- ✔ Investment Publications
- ✔ Investment Simulations
- ✔ Investment Tutorials and Training

Bookmarks offer a convenient way to retrieve Web pages. To bookmark a Web page, all you have to do is click the bookmark (or favorites) icon in your Internet browser, which leads you to a drop-down menu. To make a new category, just click New Folder and enter the title in the folder text box. For example, to bookmark a page, click File⇨Bookmark. If you make a mistake, just click Edit⇨Bookmark and make your correction. The bookmarks are stored in a list that's saved on your computer's hard disk. Once you add a bookmark, it stays on your list until you remove it or change lists. For more information about bookmarks, refer to *The Internet For Dummies,* by Levine, Baroudi, and Young (IDG Books Worldwide, Inc.).

These Web sites are usually 80 percent content and 20 percent sales pitch. In my opinion, the ratio makes them well worth the annoyance or inconvenience of having to complete a free registration or read an advertising banner. The following are a few examples of these informative sites:

- **Invest Wisely** (`www.sec.gov/consumer/inws.htm`) is a feature article for beginning investors from the Securities and Exchange Commission (SEC), a government regulatory agency. The SEC Web site (at `www.sec.gov`) provides this and many other feature articles to inform and protect first-time investors.

- **Investing Basics** (`www.aaii.com/invbas`) contains feature articles from the American Association of Individual Investors (see Figure 2-1). Articles show individuals how to start successful investment programs, pick winning investments, evaluate their choices, and more. The articles cost nothing with your free registration. However, higher levels of information require your annual membership ($49).

- **Investment Basics** (`www.fidelity.com`) is a site where Peter Lynch, a successful investor, former fund manager, and author, freely offers his expert advice on topics such as: (1) the key things that every investor should know, (2) how to design your investment strategy, and (3) ways to implement your investment plan.

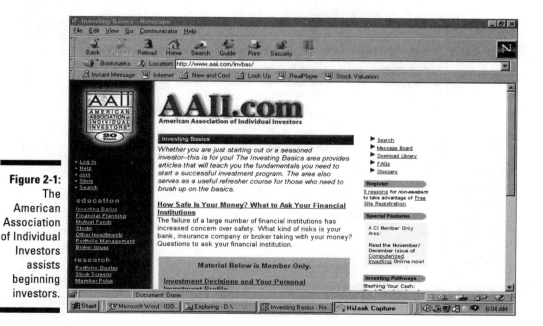

Figure 2-1: The American Association of Individual Investors assists beginning investors.

✔ **Money & Investing** (`www.eldernet.com/money.htm`) is geared for senior citizens. This site provides tutorials on the basics of investing, mutual funds, stocks, and bonds. Also includes sound advice on how to select a financial advisor.

✔ **NASD Education** (`www.investor.nasd.com/ni_module_menu.html`), provided by the National Association of Securities Dealers, is a course that's divided into six units: (1) financial decisions, (2) how financial markets work, (3) investment choices, (4) investment information, (5) investment fraud, and (6) ethics and fraud.

✔ **The New York Stock Exchange** provides a good online course called, "You & The Investment World." Go to `www.nyse.com/public` and click Education. The course is divided into small, easily digestible sections so that you won't be overwhelmed with financial jargon and technical terms.

✔ **Understanding Investment Basics** (`www.vanguard.com/educ/univ.html`), sponsored by Vanguard Mutual Funds, offers online courses that cover the fundamentals of purchasing mutual funds and retirement investing (see Figure 2-2). Go to the Web site and click Learning Center, then click University.

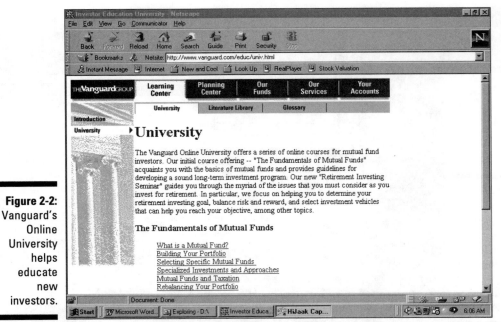

Figure 2-2:
Vanguard's
Online
University
helps
educate
new
investors.

Web sites for new investors

You can find many investor news, finance, banking, and investment organizations on the Internet. Competition is high, so they're willing to give away a large amount of high-quality information, downloadable software, and online tools for free. Many of these organizations hope that you become a fan of their great services. For those that charge fees, or those that support themselves, they want to acquire you as a steady paying customer for their products or services. The following are a few examples of investment sites for new investors:

- **Money Advisor** (www.moneyadvisor.com) provides many free online calculators and links to online government agencies and financial institutions. You may want to consider this site your online financial management tool kit.

- **MSN Investor** (investor.msn.com) is a fee-based service ($9.95 per month) that includes, among other things, investment news and features articles, interviews, strategies, and Investor Academy for your continuing investor education.

- **Quicken.com** (www.quicken.com/investments) has an extensive investment section that covers stocks, mutual funds, and bonds. A basics section with quick answers and commentary by well-known investment authors is available, in addition to columns that provide daily investment news and features.

- **Starting Point** (www.stpt.com/invest/invest.html), shown in Figure 2-3, is an uncluttered Web site that offers an investment section that has a bevy of links to high-quality investment Web sites. As an additional benefit, the links are annotated so that you don't waste your time going to Web sites that don't match their titles.

FAQs sources

The Internet is continually flooded with newbies. To keep up with the demand for beginner information, experienced online investors have developed Frequently Asked Questions (FAQ) Web sites to avoid answering the same questions over and over again. These Web sites are convenient and can often save you much time and effort (even if you are an experienced investor).

If you're seeking the answer to just one question, use your Internet browser's Find Word in Page function. For example, go to the FAQ Web site you select from the following list of sites. Click Edit at the top of your Internet browser. A drop-down menu appears. Choose Find in Page. Enter your keywords and press Enter. Your Internet browser searches the page for the words you entered, which makes your page search more efficient and shortens your research time.

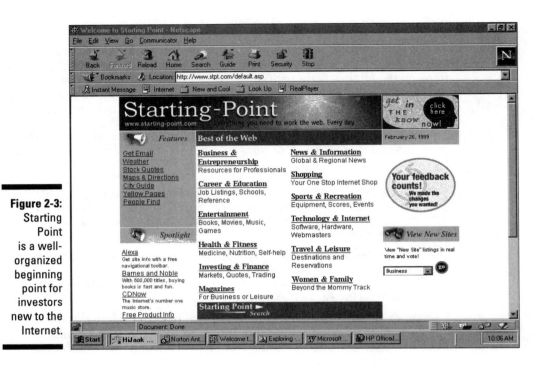

Figure 2-3:
Starting
Point
is a well-
organized
beginning
point for
investors
new to the
Internet.

Overall, the accumulated answers in these frequently asked questions (FAQs) Web sites make a solid personal finance seminar, highlighting the stock market and investing. The following is a listing of some of the best sites available at this time:

✔ **The Investment FAQ Homepage (**`invest-faq.com`**):** Enter your question to search for answers about investment and personal finance questions. Alternatively, you can browse categories for the answers you're seeking. Don't miss the regularly updated *tours* for beginning, intermediate, and experienced investors.

✔ **The Syndicate (**`www.moneypages.com/syndicate/faq`**):** Check out this list of FAQs from investment newsgroups (see Figure 2-4). The Web site is designed to help beginning or experienced investors better understand investing.

Glossaries

As you cruise the Internet, you may encounter Web sites that discuss stocks, online trading, technical analysis, and derivatives. The language may seem arcane and undecipherable. However, the Internet can help. You can find many online glossaries that can assist you in stretching your vocabulary. The following are a few examples:

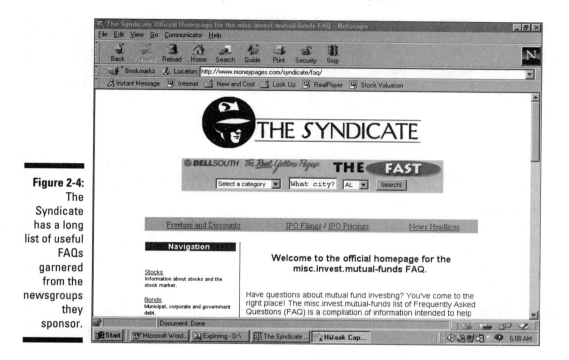

Figure 2-4:
The Syndicate has a long list of useful FAQs garnered from the newsgroups they sponsor.

✔ **Equity Analytics, Ltd.** (`www.e-analytics.com/glossary/glossar1.htm`) provides a technical analysis glossary. (Technical analysis is a statistical methodology for valuing stocks and forecasting stock prices.) Other glossaries can be found at `www.e-analytics.com/glossdir.htm`.

✔ **Prudential's Glossary of Terms** (`www.prusec.com/glos_txt.htm`) provides an online glossary for finding the definitions of financial and investment terms. This extensive glossary offers helpful examples of how investment terms are used.

✔ **Research Mag's Glossary of Investment Terms** (`www.researchmag.com/investor/glossary.htm`) features definitions for financial terms that the experts or your advisor are using. A concise and helpful online glossary.

✔ **Web Investor's Dictionary** (`www.webinvestors.com/dict.html`) provides a fast and easy way to find out investment concepts on the Web. It includes definitions, definitions with links, and new features each month.

✔ **Yahoo! Financial Glossary** (`http://biz.yahoo.com/f/g/g.html`), shown in Figure 2-5, offers a convenient glossary that includes hyperlinks that define words used in the text. For example, if a definition uses the word *option,* you can click the hyperlink and get the definition of *option.*

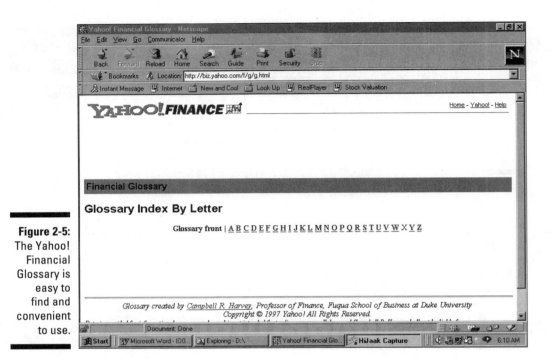

News You Can Use

Savvy investors are knowledgeable investors. The Internet is an easy way to keep informed about fast-breaking business and investment news, as well as keeping in tune to the political and economic environment that affects your investments. Hundreds of business and finance Web sites are available that provide compilations of this data, which means that by using the Internet at any time, on any day, you can discover the following:

✔ What the experts are saying about the economy

✔ Changes in industry trends

✔ What's happening at companies that interest you

✔ What the experts are saying about your investment candidates

✔ Forecasts of future earnings

✔ Historical performance data

Remember, it doesn't cost you a dime to identify investment candidates. You can track companies that interest you for several months or several years without being obligated to purchase their mutual funds, stocks, or bonds. The Internet helps you quickly and easily check out how these companies

react to a volatile market, what technological changes are affecting their industries, and how shifts in the regional or national economy affect company performance.

This section divides online investment news sources into five categories. The sources listed in this chapter are a selection of the Internet's best offerings for your daily reading. Be certain to look for features that have value to you, such as breaking news, special features, delayed stock quotes, searchable archives, and newsletters.

Large news organizations

This section contains large Internet news organizations and focuses on those that specialize in investment and financial news. I also include international news organizations that may have affiliations with newspapers, magazines, TV stations, or radio stations.

- ✔ **ABCNews.com** (`www.abcnews.com`) features business and industry news, market commentary, and personal finance articles. Catch up on the latest investment issues with the Laughing StockBroker, The Street, and S & P's Personal Wealth.

- ✔ **Bloomberg Personal Finance** (`www.bloomberg.com`) is loaded with timely news, data, and analyses of financial markets and businesses. Find data on securities, statistics, indices, and research for free. Access to the member area of the Web site is $49 per year. Additional levels of service are available, including portfolio tracking, online stock quotes, company news, mutual fund information, and at-home delivery of the monthly magazine.

- ✔ **CBS MarketWatch** (`cbs.marketwatch.com`) combines the resources of CBS News and Data Broadcasting Corporation (DBC). This Web site has many free and fee-based services. The free edition, shown in Figure 2-6, offers delayed stock quotes, feature articles, and breaking news targeted for individual investors. CBS MarketWatch RT is a $34.95/month service offering real-time quotes, company snapshots, deeper historical and fundamental data, and research tools for active investors. CBS MarketWatch LIVE is a branded version of DBC's new StockEdge Online ($79/month). This service gives the user a virtual trading desk on any or all of his or her computers. Using proprietary *active push* software (push technology pushes the information you pre-select to your desktop computer — like the price of a particular stock at intervals throughout the day), CBS MarketWatch LIVE allows the user to set up dynamically updated charts, tickers, and quote screens.

- ✔ **CNNfn** (`www.cnnfn.com`) offers news, articles on investment topics, and professional advice on money management. Major global stock indices, stock quotes, currency rates, commodities, and interest information are also available. The Research Center has links to official company Web

Figure 2-6:
Get three
levels of
investor
service
with CBS
MarketWatch.

sites, a glossary of business terms, general references, and government resources. At your request, free daily news briefings are sent to your e-mailbox.

- ✔ **Dow Jones (www.dowjones.com)** information technology has been on the Internet forever with a wide variety of products and services designed for individual investors who want to manage their own portfolios and make their own investment decisions. A few examples of its products are Smart Money (www.smartmoney.com), CNBC (www.cnbc.com), Far Eastern Economic Review (www.feer.com), Barrons Online (www.barrons.com), and The Wall Street Journal (www.wsj.com).

- ✔ **MSNBC's Investment Toolkit (www.msnbc.com/modules/commerce/ newtoolkit/default.asp)** includes market news; mutual fund, stock, and bond indexes; commodities; quotes; historical charts; corporate news; information about world markets; and personal finance features.

- ✔ **Reuters MoneyNet (http://www.moneynet.com/home/moneynet/ homepage/homepage.asp)** is sponsored by Reuters and specializes in financial data. MoneyNet is a convenient Web site for quotes, financial and company news, charts, research, and market snapshots. If you're looking for free online portfolio management, this site has Portfolio Tracker, one of the better portfolio management programs on the Web.

Newspapers

Many of the nation's daily newspapers now have online editions that provide fast-breaking news. Frequently, these sources offer online portfolio management, delayed quotes, historical stock prices, and other resources.

- ✔ **Financial Times** (`www.ft.com`) provides the latest headlines, special reports, world and company news, market and industry data, and archives with your free registration.

- ✔ **Investor's Business Daily** (`www.investors.com`) is a daily newspaper with an online edition that provides facts, figures, and objective news for investors. The online edition has an educational section and a two-week free trial.

- ✔ **Newspage** (`www.newspage.com`) lets you customize the daily news abstracts it sends to your e-mailbox for free. If you subscribe to Newspage ($3.95 per month), you have access to the full-text version of news articles and to the archives.

- ✔ **The Mercury News** (`www.mercurynews.com/business`) Business Center section presents feature articles and news, a portfolio management program, major indexes, and searchable archives ($1.95 for the full article).

- ✔ **The New York Times** (`www.nytimes.com`) Business section provides quotes and charts, an online portfolio function, breaking business and finance news, and information about the most active stocks, gainers, and losers. You can receive the daily Business Web page free by e-mail with The New York Times Direct.

- ✔ **USA Today** (`usatoday.com`) features a Money section that includes feature investment articles and news, economic and mutual fund information, calculators, and other resources. The Marketplace section includes stock quotes, market indexes, information on industry groups, currency rates, information on options and futures, and other investment information.

- ✔ **The Wall Street Journal** (`www.wsj.com`), considered the Granddaddy of all financial newspapers, is now online and better than ever. Free offers include market alerts automatically sent to your e-mailbox. The online edition includes everything the daily edition has, plus a personal journal that allows you to customize your news and track your portfolio. One excellent feature is the Company Briefing Books, which present company backgrounds, financial overviews, stock charts, company news, and press releases. Links to Zacks Research Reports, SEC filings, and the company's official Web site are also available. You can get two levels of service: free and fee-based ($59 per year for non-print edition subscribers, $29 per year for print edition subscribers).

Magazines

Like newspapers, many business and investment publications have online versions that provide the same news and feature articles that their paper-based counterparts do. Often, these online publications include additional features, such as Web-based tools for calculating your investment returns or tracking your portfolio. The following are a few examples of online magazines that are available:

- ✔ **Barrons Online** (`interactive.wsj.com/barrons`) includes This Week's Barrons, Weekday Extra, Market Lab, and a searchable archive. For a limited time, and with your free registration, you can receive This Week's Barron's at no charge.

- ✔ **Business Week** (`www.businessweek.com`) is free to all subscribers of *Business Week* magazine. Free registrants get a daily briefing, special reports, the searchable archive, banking centers, quotes, and portfolio tracking.

- ✔ **The Economist** (`www.economist.com`) offers a one-year subscription for $125 and includes full access to the online edition, which has the complete contents of the magazine. Subscriptions to the Web edition only are $48 a year and include a searchable archive. When you register, you receive five free retrievals, a downloadable The Economist's World Data Screensaver, and *Politics This Week* and *Business This Week* sent to your e-mailbox.

- ✔ **Forbes** (`www.forbes.com`) is available in an online version. Departments include technology, personal finance, startups, and e-business, in addition to conferences, publications, and the Forbes online toolbox.

- ✔ **Fortune** (`www.pathfinder.com`) includes a free subscription to *Street Life,* its irreverent e-mail newsletter, stock and fund quotes, personal finance information, and small business and special reports.

- ✔ **Kiplinger Online** (`www.kiplinger.com`) presents news, stock quotes, listings of the top performing funds, mutual fund analyses, online calculators, yield and rate information, retirement advice, Web site recommendations, personal finance information, advice, and a FAQs section.

- ✔ **Money** (`www.pathfinder.com/money`) is the online version of Time Warner's *Money* magazine. With your free registration you can access market information, stock and fund quotes, charts, track your portfolio, and receive business and finance news.

- ✔ **Mutual Funds Online** (`www.mfmag.com`) requires your free registration for access. Registrants have access to fund family guides and brokers, fund services, a load performance calculator, and related links. Your member subscription ($9 a month) includes performance rankings, profiles, screens, calculators, access to back issues, a weekly e-mail newsletter, and the monthly magazine.

✔ **Newsweek Online (**www.newsweek.com**),** shown in Figure 2-7, is the latest national magazine to go online, as of this writing. This Web site edition includes breaking news from its sister publication, the *Washington Post,* daily updates from *Newsweek,* narrated photo essays, quotes, company look-ups, market data, and personal portfolio tracking.

Scholarly journals

If you really want to check out those newfangled stock analysis methods, you can find lots of scholarly financial journals online. Some articles you can download immediately. Other Web sites only provide abstracts, and you may have to contact the author by telephone, fax, e-mail, or U.S. mail for the complete article. The following are some of the many scholarly financial journals online:

✔ **Financial Economics Network (**www.ssrn.com**, click FEN at the home-page)** is directed by Michael C. Jensen, the Jesse Isidor-Straus Professor at the Harvard Business School. The Financial Economics Network lets you search for information by topic or author. You can download abstracts published in the last 60 days, and subscribers regularly receive e-mailed abstracts of journal articles and working papers.

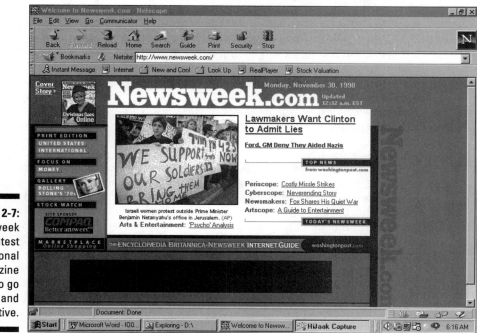

Figure 2-7: Newsweek is the latest national magazine to go online and interactive.

The tone of the site is such that journal readers are encouraged to communicate with other subscribers concerning their and others' research. Membership fees are $15 for students, $25 for non-students, and $50 for professionals. The cost per journal is $5 for students, $10 for non-students, and $20 for professionals. A free trial offer is available.

✔ **FINweb** (www.finweb.com) is a Web site managed by James R. Garven, the William H. Wright, Jr. Endowed Chair for Financial Services in the Department of Finance at the E. J. Ourso College of Business Administration at Louisiana State University. The site provides Internet sources that have substantive information concerning economics and finance-related topics. FINweb supports electronic publishing and has a long list of links to journals and working papers.

Electronic newsletters

The Internet offers investors hundreds of newsletters. For your convenience, these newsletters can be sent to your e-mailbox at regular intervals. Many newsletters are free and only require that you provide your name and e-mail address. Others are fee-based and can cost between a few dollars to several hundred dollars per month.

The quality of these newsletters varies. Higher quality newsletters have educational value. Junk newsletters often promote a stock-picking methodology or recommend that you purchase a particular stock. For example, I recently received a newsletter encouraging me to buy stock in a gold mine in Bolivia. This e-mail is clearly junk e-mail, and I deleted the message immediately.

Sometimes when you visit a Web site or complete a free registration, you may not notice a prechecked box. If you do not uncheck this box, you will receive a newsletter from the Web site's sponsor after you click the submit button on the free registration form.

Daily newsletters or alerts from the Wall Street Journal (www.wsj.com) or Ziff Davis Publications (www.zdnn.com) contain breaking news. Weekly, biweekly, or monthly newsletters tend to focus on larger investor issues and are more educational. According to Newsletter Access (described in the following list), over 2,000 investor newsletters are available. The following are several useful directories that can assist you in finding the newsletters that are right for you.

✔ **Invest-O-Rama! Directory of Advisory Services on the Web** (www.investorama.com/advisory.shtml) contains reviews and lists of newsletters that provide information on stocks, options, indexes, bonds or currency picks, and timing models or trading systems.

✔ **InvestorGuide** (www.investorguide.com) provides a listing and search function for investment newsletters. You can search for newsletters by name, category, or publisher.

✔ **Newsletter Access: Investments** (www.newsletteraccess.com/subject/invest.html), shown in Figure 2-8, has an extensive searchable directory of investment newsletters. If available, information includes newsletter name, description, frequency, subscription price, organization, editor, publisher, address, e-mail, telephone, fax, and Web address.

As you can see from this section, you can get information in several *flavors* by going to different online sources. Many of these sources publish news as it develops. Trying to stay tuned to all these sources can lead to information overload, so I suggest selecting two or three sources that agree with your personality and life style. For example, if you check your e-mailbox two or three times a day, an investment newsletter with special alert editions may be for you. If you like reading all the daily news at one time, an online newspaper with a clipping service to personalize the news may be your cup of tea.

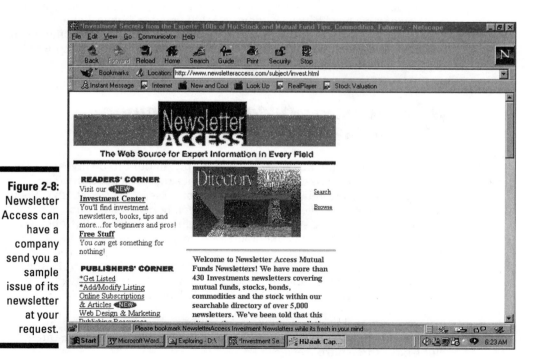

Figure 2-8: Newsletter Access can have a company send you a sample issue of its newsletter at your request.

Practicing with Your New Investment Information

In the not too distant past, only large investment firms had access to the high quality financial information that's available on the Internet. Traditional investment bankers use this financial information to pick investments that look promising and then they charge their clients substantial commissions when they buy or sell investments based on their recommendations. Now you can access the same types of information sources and make your own recommendations, which makes investing less expensive and let's you take control of your own portfolio. After all, no one is more concerned about your financial success than you.

If you look at the beginning section of this chapter, you see how much fun it can be to find out about companies, industries, the economy, and other areas that investors need to know about. However, at this time, you may not feel confident enough to start selecting your own investments. Don't despair! You can practice your new investment strategies in two ways and not risk any of your hard-earned savings. First, if you don't have a clue about how to start investing, you can join an investment club and get some one-on-one advice. Second, you can try out your strategies with one or more online investment simulations.

Join the club! Become a member of an investment club

In an investment club, members pay a monthly amount to be invested. The club makes the investments based on member recommendations. The members incur a pro-rata share of the gains or losses. In the past, investment clubs often didn't involve a lot of research. Members of many clubs purchased only safe, conservative stocks, and thus, members made small profits. Over the last five years, however, members of investment clubs have begun taking more risks, resulting in higher profits. Due to this phenomenon, the number of investment clubs is increasing at a tremendous rate. For example, the National Association of Investors Corporation (www.better-investing.org) states that their membership has tripled since 1993.

No prerequisites are necessary to join or form an investment club. So investment clubs are great for absolute beginners. Generally, investment clubs have three purposes:

- ✔ Finding out about investing
- ✔ Having fun
- ✔ Making money

You can find many investment clubs online. A good starting place is the National Association of Investors Corporation (NAIC) (`www.better-investing.org`), shown in Figure 2-9. This Web site shows how to join or start an investment club. The goal of NAIC members, and most investment clubs, is to help beginning investors become smart investors — that is, to educate investors in a disciplined approach to successful investing, portfolio management, and wealth building. The people who belong to these investment clubs often believe that finding new Web sites and investments, and meeting new people with the same interests, can be very helpful and profitable.

No cost investment simulations

Investment games allow you to invest in a virtual portfolio so that you can test your new investment strategies or try out new theories without losing any money. It's a great way to get hands-on experience with portfolio management. By playing the game, you can find out investment terms, gain confidence in your decision-making, become familiar with financial markets, see how others are faring, and have a lot of fun. Your success is measured by how many hypothetical dollars you make each month.

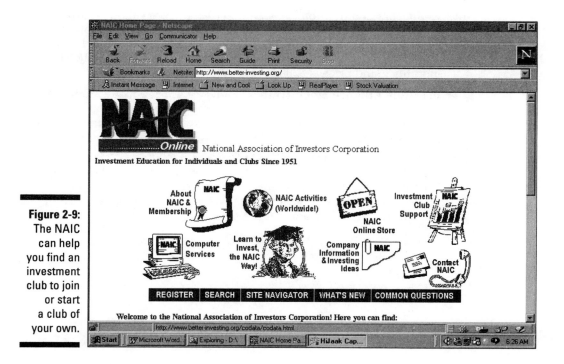

Figure 2-9: The NAIC can help you find an investment club to join or start a club of your own.

The InvestSmart Stock Market Game (hyperion.advanced.org/10326/ market_simulation) is a beginner's stock simulation game. The game is easy to play and the Web site provides helpful investor lessons and insights. You don't need any prior experience to enter the game. Complete the free registration and click Smart Stock Game. Click Get Quotes to find the latest price of your investment selection. Then decide how much of your fantasy cash you want to invest.

To purchase stock, just click on New Buy Order. To sell, click on New Sell Order. Enter the quantity and ticker symbol (the abbreviated name of a publicly owned company that is used when trading on an exchange) of your choice. The program does the rest. When you click Update, the program assigns your portfolio a rank. If your profits pile up faster and higher than other game players' profits do, you get a better ranking.

Below are examples of other stock simulation games that can help you get started with understanding the financial market and trading online.

- ✔ **Final Bell Play the Market Game** (www.sandbox.net/finalbell/ pub-doc/home.html) shows you how to take control of your financial future today. You can explore new investing strategies while you master online trading in this risk-free stock market simulation.

- ✔ **HedgeHog Competition** (www.marketplayer.com) allows participants to build their hypothetical $1 million hedge fund stock portfolio and compete with other contestants in a month-long test of their financial skills. Trading is continuous and performance is updated daily. The monthly grand prize is $200 in real cash.

- ✔ **Investors Alliance Stock Trainer Contest** (nt.freequote.com/cgi-win/contest.exe) is a monthly stock trading contest with prizes. To participate in the next contest, all you have to do is register. All participants are welcome to play for fun and practice.

- ✔ **Virtual Stock Exchange** (www.virtualstockexchange.com) is a stock simulation game that allows you to trade shares like a real brokerage account. You can test your latest profit-making strategy with stocks you are thinking about purchasing. This Web site also provides research reports, market news, and charting.

Chapter 3

Warnings about Online Frauds, Schemes, and Deceptions

● ●

In This Chapter

▶ Recognizing potential online investment scams

▶ Identifying pyramid schemes

▶ Requiring real financial disclosures

▶ Unmasking dishonest brokers by asking the right questions

▶ Knowing where to complain online if you receive an unscrupulous investment offer

▶ Evaluating the security of Internet transactions

● ●

Don't get taken for a ride on the Information Superhighway. The North American Securities Administrators Association, an association of state investment watchdogs, estimates that more than $10 billion a year is lost in investment fraud. That's about $1.1 million every hour.

In the past, swindlers used the U.S. mail and telemarketing boiler rooms to exploit unsuspecting investors. Fraudsters have now invaded cyberspace. The Federal Trade Commission database shows that in 1996 individuals reported losses due to online investment schemes ranging from $2,900 to as much as $400,000. Some organizations estimate that the average loss per investment victim is $15,000.

Investigating investments is difficult. The terms of the deal may be hard to understand, and the investment literature and salespeople may omit key facts. However, you can observe warning signs of potential scams, schemes, and deceptions. Doing so involves a little effort, homework, and investigating, but isn't that what investing is all about?

In this chapter, I provide warnings about online investment information and offers that may be too good to be true. I provide guidelines for checking out brokers and investments, and tips for identifying a pyramid scheme. I show you how to read financial disclosures to get the facts, and I explain how to complain online. I also offer a few thoughts about the online security of your personal and financial information.

Don't Believe Everything You Read

Every investor dreams of being an early stockowner in a Microsoft or Intel Corp. Dishonest brokers and stock promoters prey upon this greed and offer unsuspecting investors low-priced stocks in companies with new products or technologies (like the self-chilling soda can). Often these companies have a lot of sizzle and no steak.

Figure 3-1 shows an example of an online scam (www.ari.net/nordicalite). The Federal Trade Commission (FTC) has posted over ten *teaser* Web sites. These sites are registered with Internet search engines. Some of these teaser sites have even been singled out as *new* or *cool* sites of the week. Teaser sites purport to achieve fabulous success through some sort of business opportunity, multi-level marketing, or franchise. Users click through to the final page and discover a sober warning, "If you responded to an ad like this, you could get scammed." The warning pages provide advice on how to avoid fraudulent business opportunities and also provide links back to the FTC's Web site (www.ftc.gov), where consumers can find out more about investing in franchises or business opportunities.

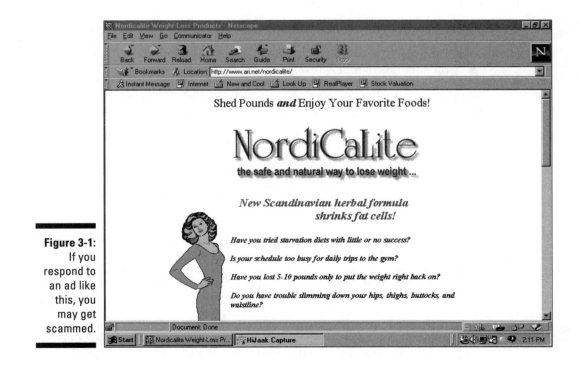

Figure 3-1:
If you respond to an ad like this, you may get scammed.

The Internet allows swindlers to inexpensively reach millions of potential victims. Currently, more than 50 million Americans are online. In contrast, *The Wall Street Journal* has a mere 2 million subscribers. One online posting designed to fleece unsuspecting investors can easily reach thousands of people. According to one regulatory agency, one of the major national online services in the U.S. had 5,600 new messages with investment topics posted to 969 different topic areas in a two-week period. The company processes about 75,000 new messages per day. (Keep in mind that these amounts are approximations due to the rapid change of the Internet and its subscribers.)

Online frauds mirror the types of frauds that are perpetrated over the phone or through the mail. Many Internet messages are about general stock-picking advice or mention other investment possibilities. However, some messages tout specific stocks, moneymaking ventures, and service providers. Investment chat rooms now have sales pitches that offer more details by private e-mail and toll-free telephone numbers.

Investment swindlers can work anywhere, from dingy telemarketing offices to expensive hotel suites to cyberspace. They may be friends of friends, and they may wear natty suits or hard hats. They may be so-called "recognized experts" or have no connection to the investment community. However, they all have one goal — to get your money into their pocket.

If an Offer Seems Too Good to Be True, It Usually Is

As the popularity of the Internet grows, millions of people flock to the new Global Village. Inevitably, individuals with criminal intent are following the crowd. They seek to deceive the innocent, the hopeful, the naive, the poor, and the greedy.

Online investor fraud often starts when you receive an e-mail message describing an appealing offer. Offers that seem too good to be true usually are. Here are a few of the warning signs to help you identify potential scams:

- **Exceptional profits:** Usually the profits are large enough to get your interest but not large enough to make you suspicious.

- **Low risk — high return:** All investments involve some risk. If a fraudster advertises "no-risk," this should be an immediate red flag that something is wrong. Don't invest if you don't know exactly what the risks are. (Remember, fraudsters don't honor money-back guarantees.)

✔ **Urgency:** Fraudsters usually offer a reason why you must invest as quickly as possible. They may tell you that delays may mean losses of big profits or that they're limiting the offer to just a few individuals. Fraudsters often play on new technological advances that create a brief market that you must get into right away. However, if you feel that the posting is valid, wait before you respond. Others won't be shy about posting their opinions.

✔ **High pressure tactics:** Fraudsters often act like they're doing you a favor by letting you get in on the investment opportunity. Don't be afraid to ask questions publicly. Post a follow-up message. If the original post is valid, the person who sent it will be happy to post a public response. (See Bonus Chapter 1 to find out how to post messages, and for more on newsgroups and mailing lists.)

Although you can find plenty of helpful investment-related postings online (after all, that's what this book is all about), the Internet, like other places, has its share of fraudsters. Figure 3-2 shows the National Association of Securities Dealers Web site at www.nasd.com. This site provides investor education about different types of investment scams, including pyramid schemes, precious metal frauds, and stock swindles. (See the section, "Determining Whether an Investment Is a Pyramid Scheme" later in this chapter to find out about pyramid schemes.)

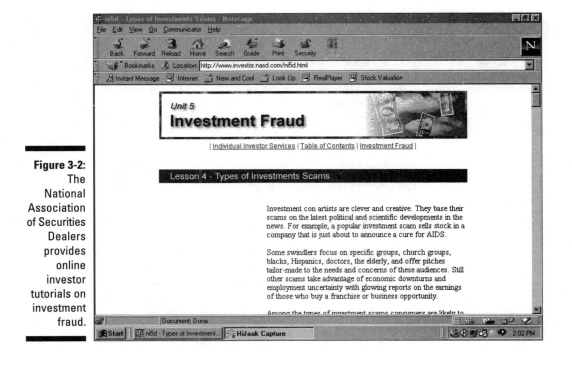

Figure 3-2:
The National Association of Securities Dealers provides online investor tutorials on investment fraud.

Checking It Out Before You Put Your Money Down

The explosion of the Internet has created new opportunities and new dangers for investors. If you're an online investment victim, the chances of getting your money back are slim. Even in cases where government agencies recover money, the consumer usually gets back less than 10 cents on the dollar. The best defense is to thoroughly investigate an online investment *before* you put your money down.

The Federal Trade Commission (FTC) inspects investment swindles and provides summaries that document recent allegations of corporate fraud and misconduct in relation to securities investors. The Alexander Law Firm sponsors a Web site (`www.defrauded.com`) that names these fraudulent organizations and provides links to the summary reports. New companies are added on a regular basis. I suggest bookmarking this page and including it as part of your investment candidate analysis. (I think of this approach as being similar to a cashier checking to see if someone's name is on the bad check list before accepting his or her check.)

Here are some suggestions about how to investigate that "once in a lifetime offer":

✔ Check with your city or state consumer protection agency; it may have information about the firm you're considering investing in. Additionally, a consumer protection agency can direct you to other organizations that may have information about the investment.

✔ Contact regulators. Organizations that you can contact include the Federal Trade Commission, the Securities and Exchange Commission, and the National Association of Securities Dealers.

✔ For the name, address, telephone number, and other contact information of your securities regulator, go to NASAA at `www.nasaa.org` and click Find Your Securities Regulator.

✔ Write or telephone law enforcement agencies. Fraud is illegal in every state in the nation. You can contact the local public prosecutor, the state attorney general, and the state securities administrator.

The Better Business Bureau Web page at `www.bbb.org` provides reliability reports on firms that can be helpful to you. You need to read reliability reports before you purchase the firm's securities. Each report indicates how long the firm has been in business, how long the Better Business Bureau has known about the company, complaint patterns (if any), and whether any government agencies — for example, the Federal Trade Commission (FTC) or the State Attorney General — have taken any enforcement actions in the last three years.

Determining Whether an Investment Is a Pyramid Scheme

Pyramid schemes, sometimes called *multilevel marketing plans,* are sure ways to lose money. One person recruits six friends; those six people recruit six more friends — and so on, in a relentless search for new recruits. If everyone cooperates, then by level 15, the scheme needs 7.6 billion participants — more than the Earth's population. See Table 3-1 for details.

Table 3-1	New Recruits Needed for a Pyramid Scheme	
Level	*New Recruits*	*Total Participants*
1	1	1
2	5	6
3	25	31
4	125	156
5	625	781
6	3,125	3,906
7	15,625	19,531
8	78,125	97,656
9	390,625	488,281
10	1,953,125	2,441,406
11	9,765,625	12,207,031
12	48,828,125	61,035,156
13	244,140,625	305,175,781
14	1,220,703,125	1,525,878,906
15	6,103,515,625	7,629,394,531

Profits from these schemes don't come from selling products or distributorships but from recruiting new participants. The endless recruiting of more participants eventually leads to an oversupply of sellers. Investors are left with garages full of products and the loss of their investment.

Three elements characterize pyramid schemes:

✔ A reliance on funds from new investors (recruits) to pay returns, commissions, or bonuses to old investors.

✔ The need for an inexhaustible supply of new recruits.

✔ The promise of earning profits without providing goods or services.

The Securities and Exchange Commission estimates that the American public has lost $400 million to fraudulent pyramid schemes. States such as New Mexico require all sales companies to register with the Attorney General so that fraudulent companies can be identified.

Figure 3-3 shows an online business opportunity at `www.ari.net/prosper`. This advertisement makes exaggerated earnings claims. The ad offers little product information but lots of glowing promises. This ad is a fake posted by the Federal Trade Commission to heighten consumer awareness of online scams. The FTC suggests using extreme caution when transmitting your address and other personal information. Your personal information could be sent to scam artists who compile "sucker" lists and use your information to take advantage of you and your money.

In September 1996, the FTC charged several defendants from Fortuna Alliance with fraud. The Fortuna Alliance induced consumers to invest $250 to $1,750 and promised $5,000 per month in "profits" as others joined the pyramid. Fortuna used its Web site to increase its credibility and to facilitate communications between the firm and its team leaders. After six months, the firm had taken $13 million from more than 25,000 investors. About half the victims live outside the U.S.

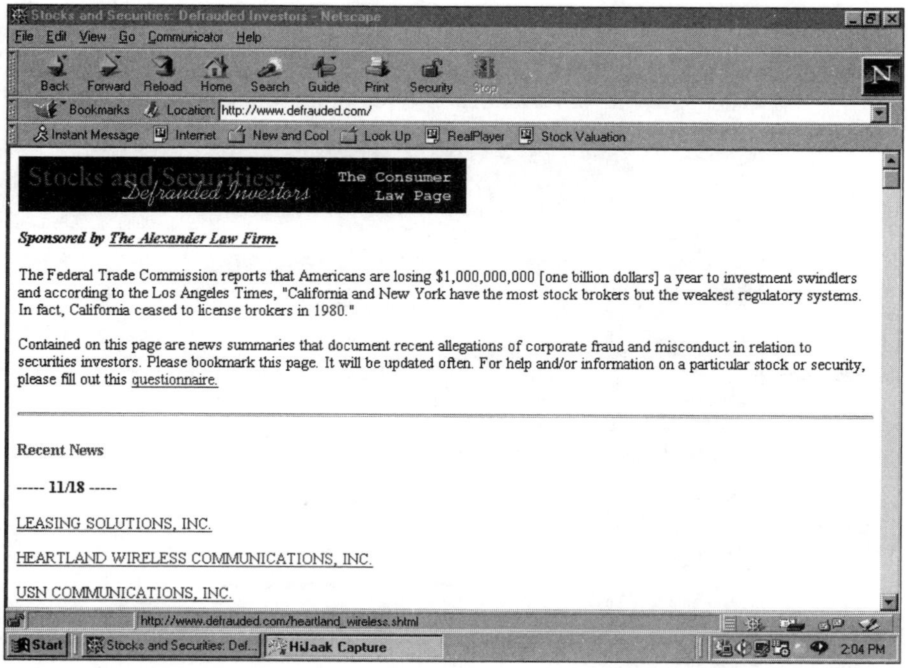

Figure 3-3:
If the Ultimate Prosperity investment seems like a great opportunity, you've been scammed.

What Real Financial Disclosures Include

If you're considering investing in a company, you may want to download and print a copy of the investment offer. If the sales literature doesn't include a prospectus with financial statements, ask for one. If you're told that the company doesn't have a prospectus, request a written financial disclosure about the company. All in all, you should have the following information:

- ✔ **Offering circular:** Sales literature that presents the investment.

- ✔ **Prospectus:** A formal written statement that discloses the terms of a public offering of a security or a mutual fund. The prospectus is required to divulge both positive and negative information to investors about the proposed offering.

- ✔ **Annual report:** A written report that includes a statement by the chief executive officer, a narrative about last year's performance, and a forecast for next year's performance. Financial statements include a balance sheet, income statement, a statement of cash flows, and retained earnings.

- ✔ **Audited financial statements:** Financial statements audited by a certified public accounting firm.

Figure 3-4 shows the Web site for the Securities and Exchange Commission (SEC) located at www.sec.gov. The SEC doesn't require companies that are seeking less than $1 million to be "registered," but it does require these firms to file a *Form D*. Form D doesn't include an audited financial statement

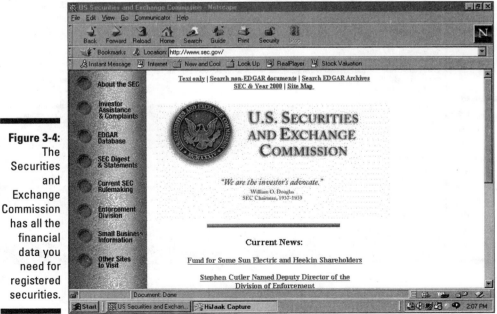

Figure 3-4:
The Securities and Exchange Commission has all the financial data you need for registered securities.

but it does state the names and addresses of the owners and promoters of the firm. Other information is limited. If a Form D isn't available, the SEC suggests that you call its Investor Education and Assistance Department at 202-942-7040.

Tell-Tale Signs of Dishonest Brokers

Dishonest brokers often ask their victims a steady stream of questions designed to derail honest investors from asking the right questions. Dishonest brokers don't want curious customers. In contrast, honest brokers encourage you to ask questions, provide you with additional educational materials, and make certain that you understand the risks involved in your investment decision. And if you decide not to spend your money, they are untroubled by your investment decision.

The National Futures Association has collected 16 questions that are turn-offs for dishonest brokers (`www.pueblo.gsa.gov/cic_text/money/swindles/swindles.txt`). In the following list, I've tailored those questions to meet the needs of online investors:

- ✔ **Where did you get my name?** The dishonest broker may say "a select list of investors," but your name was probably obtained from a Usenet newsgroup question you asked, a bulk e-mail response, or from a mailing list subscription list. Individuals who have been duped in the past may be on the "select list." They were conned before and probably can be conned again.

- ✔ **What risks are involved in the investment?** All investments except U.S. Treasury securities have some default risk. (U.S. Treasury securities are considered *risk free*. The federal government backs these securities just as it does the *legal tender* — that is, the money — in your pocket. The government isn't likely to fail, so the securities — and your money — are risk free.) Some investments have more risk than others do. A salesperson that really has a sure thing won't be on the telephone talking with you.

- ✔ **Can you send me a written explanation of the investment, so I can consider it at my leisure?** This question provides two turn-offs to dishonest brokers. First, swindlers are reluctant to put in writing anything that may become evidence in a fraud trial. Second, swindlers are impatient; they want your money right now.

- ✔ **Would you explain your investment proposal to my attorney, financial planner or investment advisor, or banker?** You know the investment is a scam if the salesperson says something like "Normally, I would be glad to, but . . ." or "Unfortunately, we don't have enough time," or "Can't you make your own decisions?"

✔ **Can you give me references and the names of your principal investors and officers?** Swindlers often change their names so you can't check their histories. Make certain that the reference list contains the names of well-known banks and reputable brokerage firms that you can easily contact. Figure 3-5 shows the Investor Protection Trust page at www. investorprotection.org, which includes links to various resources you can use to check out a broker or other financial professional.

✔ **Which exchanges are the securities traded on? Can I have copies of the prospectus, the risk disclosure statement, or the audited financial statements?** For legitimate, registered investments, these documents are normal. A legitimate investment may or may not be traded on an exchange. However, fraudulent investments never are. Exchanges have extensive rules for competitive pricing and fair dealing. Those that don't follow the rules are subject to severe sanctions.

✔ **What regulatory agency is the investment subject to?** Tell the broker that you want to check the investment's good standing with its regulatory agency before going forward. The possibility of having to talk to a representative of a regulatory agency is a real turn-off to a swindler.

✔ **How long has your company been in business, and what is your track record? Can I meet another representative of your firm?** If the broker or the investment doesn't seem to have a past, the deal may be a scam. Many swindlers have been running scams for years and aren't anxious to talk about it.

Figure 3-5:
Use the links at Investor Protection Trust to check out your broker or financial professional before you invest.

✔ **When and where can I meet you to further discuss this investment?** Legitimate brokers can tell you how much of a return investors have enjoyed in the past. Even if you do get this information in writing, keep in mind that past performance doesn't indicate future performance. However, dishonest brokers often won't take the time to meet with you, and they don't want you in their place of business. Legitimate registered brokers are happy to sit down and discuss your financial goals.

✔ **Where will my money be? What type of accounting can I expect?** Often, funds for certain investments are required to stay in separate accounts, at all times. Find out which accounting firm does the firm's auditing and what type of external audits the firm is subject to. (Make certain that the well-known accounting firm is actually the auditor.)

✔ **How much of my money will go to management fees, commissions, and similar expenses?** Legitimate investments often have restrictions on the amount of management fees the firm can charge. Getting what the firm charges in writing is important. Compare the firm's fees to charges for similar investments.

Anatomy of a potential "pump and dump" scam

On November 12, 1998 a newsgroup user called "dennismenis99" posted the same message to a dozen high-tech investment newsgroups touting AvTel Technologies (NASDAQ:AVCO), an unprofitable California network provider. The erroneous message stated that AvTel will launch high speed Internet access to about 10,000 Santa Barbara customers using ADSL (Asymmetric Digital Subscriber Lines). The message stated that this new modem-based technology provides a dedicated Internet connection that's up to 50 times faster than conventional modems and works over existing telephone lines. The result is no more waiting or busy signals.

By noon, the NASDAQ traded stock skyrocketed from $2 a share to $10 a share. By 3:30 the stock was selling at $31 a share. Around this time, short selling began. (Short sellers borrow shares of stock from a broker and sell it. When the stock price drops, they re-purchase the shares and return them to the broker. The difference in the original selling price and the new, low purchase price is the trader's profit less brokerage fees.)

At 5:40 p.m. NASDAQ halted trading. Over 3.6 million shares were traded in one day compared to an average of 3,300. AvTel's stock price increased in after-hours trading to $38 a share resulting in a 1,400 percent increase in one day. During this time, newsgroup messages were filled with misinformation about NASDAQ's actions, the company, and stock trading in general.

On November 13, 1998, AvTel admitted that, contrary to its earlier press release, it has no proprietary technology or products. Additionally, AvTel has no existing plans for national expansion. As a result of this information, when trading resumed on Monday, November 16, 1998, shares were trading at $3 per share. Over the next week, three law firms filed class action suits against the firm on behalf of the damaged November 12, 1998 AvTel share purchasers.

✔ **How can I get my money if I want to liquidate my investment?** You may discover that your investment can't be sold or that selling your investment involves substantial costs. If you're unable to get a solid answer in writing, the investment may be a scam.

✔ **If a dispute arises, how will it be resolved?** No one wants to go to court and sue. The investment should be subject to a regulatory agency's guidelines so that disputes are resolved inexpensively through arbitration, mediation, or a reparation procedure.

Is your broker dishonest or just incompetent? The Stock Detective at www.stockdetective.com/states.asp can help. This Web site provides a list of state investment watchdog agencies. It includes the name of each state's securities commission, addresses, telephone numbers, names of directors, and contact people.

Many financial information sources e-mail out to consumers analyses of small companies that are seeking additional financing. Some of these mass-mailed analyses are from companies that pay for glowing stock reports. The Stock Detective (www.stockdetective.com/list.asp), shown in Figure 3-6, provides a guide to these pseudo-research and phony financial reports.

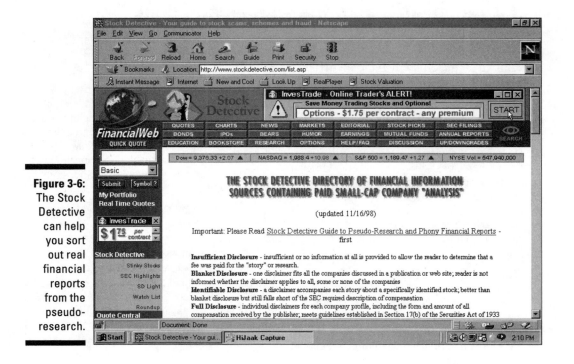

Figure 3-6:
The Stock Detective can help you sort out real financial reports from the pseudo-research.

The list includes the name of the publication, media sources (Internet, print, radio, and so on), and a disclosure rating. If the disclosure rating indicates that the publication won't disclose whether a fee was paid for the "story" or research, I suggest that you ignore the report and not waste your time with any additional research.

Where to Complain Online

The Internet provides many ways to complain about online investor fraud. Here are three good resources:

- ✔ **Better Business Bureau** (www.bbb.org) has an online complaint form and promises to follow up within two weeks of your complaint.
- ✔ **Securities and Exchange Commission** (www.sec.gov) has an excellent online complaint process.
- ✔ **National Fraud Information Center** (www.fraud.org) forwards your complaint to the appropriate organizations and includes it in their Internet fraud statistics (which may not help you get your money back but may be helpful to other online investors).

Your Bank Account Number, Security, and the Internet

Just as you take various precautions to protect your home and its contents, you must prevent online thieves from accessing your personal and financial assets via the Internet. Locked doors, alarm systems, and nosy neighbors can help you safeguard your home. Precautions on the Internet take such forms as firewalls, passwords, and encryption of important information.

Dan Farmer, an individual investor and consultant, conducted an informal (and absolutely unscientific) survey of 2,200 Internet computing systems in December 1996. The survey results indicate that approximately 66 percent of Web sites have potential security vulnerabilities (see www.trouble.org/survey). For example, in December 1996 several catalog companies incorrectly installed an Internet shopping program. Consequently, hackers were able to get the credit card numbers of the catalogs' customers.

In contrast, online banks use a distributed security system. Security is on your computer during the transmission of information and in the bank's own computer system. Online banks use several types of security systems simultaneously:

- ✔ **Encryption:** *Encryption* is a high-tech word for encoding and is used by more people than spies. It is used so that your banking information is gibberish to unauthorized individuals.

- ✔ **Passwords:** Personal passwords are necessary to access your account information.

- ✔ **Automatic sign-off protection:** When you sign off, your session terminates so that no one can continue in your absence.

- ✔ **Browser security:** Your browser isn't allowed to save any of your bank information.

- ✔ **Monitoring:** The system constantly scans for unauthorized intrusions.

At banks, the Federal Deposit Insurance Corporation (FDIC) insures your money, but online securities firms don't have similar insurance for consumers. To date, electronic theft has been slight, but as more money flows over the Internet, the need for insurance is certain to change.

Part II
Finding the Right Investments

The 5th Wave   By Rich Tennant

"Hold on— our stocks haven't plummeted. It's just a booger in the loss column."

In this part . . .

The chapters in this part of the book show you how to use the Internet to select investments that match your financial objectives. Find out how you can move from saver to investor. Discover strategies to bullet proof your investing and track your success. Find out why everyone is talking about mutual funds and how the Internet can help you select the fund that's right for you. Check out the different types of stocks and bonds and see how online stock and mutual fund screens can help you whittle down investment candidates to a manageable number.

Chapter 4
Making Your Money Work Harder

In This Chapter

▶ Using the Internet to simplify your financial planning

▶ Moving from saver to investor

▶ Setting your financial objectives and reaching them

▶ Bulletproofing your investing

*Y*ou may not have a formal investment plan, but you probably do some financial planning, even if it's only noting the bills that need to be paid on the back of your paycheck envelope. However, if you want to be a successful online investor, you need to do a little more homework to get your financial ducks in a row.

In this chapter, I show you how to make your money work as hard as you do. I explain what you need to do before you begin investing, as well as how the Internet can help you get started. I spell out how you can move from saver to investor. I illustrate how you can use an online worksheet to determine your starting point and use an online calculator to compute your personal net worth. I show you how to determine your investment objectives and figure out how much you need to earn to meet those goals. I provide guidelines for setting a ten-year goal and setting aside emergency funds. I also show you where to go online for financial planning resources, how to determine your risk-tolerance level, and how to start maximizing your personal wealth now.

Using the Internet to Simplify Financial Planning

Today, individuals find it difficult to shake off the notion that if they're not wealthy, they don't need to do any financial planning. Stock market volatility, inflation, changing interest rates, unemployment, illness, and hard times are part of life. To do no financial planning or to allow others (your spouse, employer, broker, or financial advisor) do all your planning is to flirt with disaster. Remember that no one cares more about your financial well-being than you do.

The Internet makes financial planning easier than ever before. The Web has hundreds of online worksheets, calculators, and other tools that can easily put you on the right track. This chapter shows how you can start maximizing your personal wealth by:

- ✔ **Analyzing your current financial position.** After all, you can't get to your financial finish line if you don't know your starting point. The Internet provides many online net worth worksheets and calculators to make this task easier.

- ✔ **Finding out where your cash is going each month.** Your financial well-being doesn't depend on how much you make but how much you spend. If you don't know how much you're spending, the Internet can help you gain an understanding of your spending habits and assist you in creating a budget you can live with.

- ✔ **Deciding your financial objectives.** Do you want to purchase a house in five years or retire early? The Internet can help you achieve your goal by assisting you in developing a workable plan.

- ✔ **Building your financial base so that you can start accumulating real wealth.** This approach to investing offers a diversified system that provides financial growth and protection. Discover how you can build a financial base to maximize your personal wealth.

The joys of compound interest

The most powerful investment returns are stable, compounded returns. Regardless of what's happening in the economy or stock market, you can always count on the magic of compounding. Over time, a modest but steady rate of compound interest can build into a sizable nest egg.

Table 4-1 provides examples of how much you need to save each month to reach a specific financial goal. For example, assume that you need $10,000 for your investment nest egg (retirement fund, house down-payment fund, college expenses fund, or some other large financial goal). If you save $147.05 per month for five years at a 5 percent rate of return, you'll have the money you need. The second part of Table 4-1 shows that if you put away only $139.68 a month at a 7 percent rate of return in five years you'll have $10,000. That's the magic of compounding.

Table 4-1 Monthly Savings Needed to Reach Your Financial Goal			
Dollars Needed	**Years to Achieve Goal at a 5% Rate of Return**		
	5 Years	**10 Years**	**20 Years**
$5,000	$73.52	$32.20	$12.16
$10,000	$147.05	$64.40	$24.33
$20,000	$294.09	$128.80	$48.66
$50,000	$735.23	$321.99	$121.64
$300,000	$4,411.37	$1,931.97	$729.87
Dollars Needed	**Years to Achieve Goal at a 7% Rate of Return**		
	5 Years	**10 Years**	**20 Years**
$5,000	$69.84	$28.89	$9.60
$10,000	$139.68	$57.78	$19.20
$20,000	$279.36	$115.56	$38.40
$50,000	$698.40	$288.90	$96.00
$300,000	$4,190.40	$1,733.40	$576.00

Want to be a millionaire? Go to FinanCenter at www.financenter.com. Click the Savings icon and then click the calculator titled "What will it take to become a millionaire?" Enter the required data and then click Calculate. The results show how much you need to invest today to be a millionaire in the future.

Investing versus playing the lottery

Investing in what's hot without doing the research is like buying a lottery ticket. The chances of your investment being a success have the same odds (about a million to one). Investing isn't like buying a lottery ticket. To invest wisely you need to understand an investment's liquidity (how fast you can get your money), safety (will you get all your money back?), and rate of return (how much will your money earn?). Often, investors expect too much too soon from their investments. One way to remove much of the risk and emotional turmoil of investing is to invest fixed amounts of money on a regular basis. This type of investing is called *dollar cost averaging*. For more information on dollar averaging, check out these helpful sites:

✔ **Institute of Systematic Investing Research** (`www.isir.com`) provides education and related links to help investors understand the benefits of dollar cost averaging. Check out the dollar cost averaging site of the week.

✔ **The Armchair Millionaire** (`www.armchairmillionaire.com`) features investing basics and how dollar cost averaging can help you build a strong financial plan.

✔ **The Vanguard Group** (`www.vanguard.com/educ/module4/`) provides an introduction to dollar cost averaging.

Moving Some of Your Savings to Investments

The beginning of personal wealth is the accumulation of capital that you can use for investing. This capital often begins with savings and expands into other types of more profitable investments. Savings are the beginning of your capital accumulation. Families need a regular savings program that's between 5 and 10 percent of take-home pay per month. Some people even manage to put away 15 percent. Getting into a regular rhythm with saving is important.

Additionally, individuals and families need emergency funds. Folks with fluctuating income, few job benefits, and little job security may need to have a larger emergency fund. Families with two wage earners may need a smaller emergency fund.

A general rule is to have three to six months of take-home pay in a savings account (or a near cash account similar to a market fund with check writing privileges) for emergencies. If you don't have an emergency fund, you need to increase your savings. Payroll deduction plans into a savings account or money market fund are often the most painless way to achieve the best results. On the other hand, if you've been saving a surplus, you may want to consider using these funds for investing.

Every successful investors starts with a financial plan. The plan includes clearly stating your financial objectives, saving a certain amount of money each month, and developing investment asset allocation strategies, and so on. The Internet can assist you in building your financial plan. The following are a few examples:

Ernst & Young's Prosper (www.ey.com/tax/pfc/prosper/prosper.asp)
Prosper, a personal financial planning software program (shown in Figure 4-1), includes much of Ernst & Young's knowledge and investment experience. The software assists you in conducting financial and retirement planning, planning for car and home purchases, and planning for the expenses of education, insurance, and taxes, in addition to providing a portfolio management tool. The software uses Win95. To sample Prosper, download a limited edition for free. The software costs $29.95 to own with your telephone order.

Fidelity Investments (www.fid-inv.com) provides a personal resource center, information about workplace savings plans, and shows how financial advisors can help you put it all together. The asset allocation planner demonstrates how you can develop an investment strategy to meet your financial goals.

Quicken's 99 Financial Planner (www.quicken99.com) provides more than just record-keeping. Quicken 99 Deluxe includes financial planning and monitoring. The software also includes programs for setting savings goal amounts and calculating what you need to reach your goals. Set up a budget using a budgeting spreadsheet and work with more than one budget. Strategic planning tools include planning for retirement, college expenses, a new home or refinancing your mortgage, estimating your insurance needs, and more.

Figure 4-1:
Ernst & Young's Prosper software shows how much you need to have in your retirement fund when you stop working.

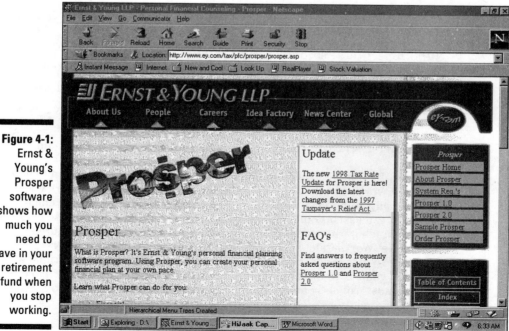

Charles Schwab (www.schwab.com) can help your financial planning with online calculators, tools, and advice. Go to the home page and click Planning and then General Investing. The next screen shows financial tools that include a primer on the principles of investing, a general goal planner (with an online savings calculator), and an asset allocation tool. If you need more help, click SchwabAnswers.

Calculating Your Current Assets Using the Internet

The first step in getting to where you want to go is figuring out where you are now. I know that calculating your net worth doesn't sound exciting, but consider this exercise the creation of a starting line for your online investment program. Later, you can compare your increased net worth to this starting line.

One of the things that makes calculating net worth difficult is organizing all your personal finance data and sorting it into the right asset classes. Finding the data you need for entries can be time consuming. You can use the following suggestions to help you organize your data for the categories used to calculate your net worth:

- **Liquid assets:** To find the value of your investments, refer to your most recent bank and brokerage statements.

- **Property assets:** For real estate assets, use your most recent property appraisal or check with a realtor who knows your neighborhood.

- **Vehicles:** Remember to deduct depreciation from the original cost.

- **Jewelry, art, and collectibles:** Use your insurer's appraised value or your best estimate.

- **Other assets:** Use your best estimate of each asset's resale value.

Many professional financial planners tell you that most people don't know their net worth and that when potential customers make a ballpark guess, they usually aren't even close. The Internet provides many online calculators that can assist you in determining your exact net worth. These calculators do much of the work for you. For example, the Altamira Resource Center Net Worth Calculator (www.altamira.com/icat/toolbox/netcalc.html) suggests that as you go through life, one of the primary financial goals is to increase your net worth. This calculator is designed to help you determine your current net worth and track the change over time.

Accumulating Something to Invest

Saving and investing are different, although savings are often the source of funds for investing. *Savings* are a set level of funds that you put aside regularly, usually at a low interest rate. You can easily access savings, and often they are insured by a financial institution.

Investment funds are the funds that you don't have earmarked for the rent, groceries, taxes, and so on. You place these funds in securities that can increase or decrease in value. They may earn interest or dividends, but you have no guarantee of increased value or future income. (Investment funds should be free of any obligations. Good examples of investment fund sources are inheritances, gifts, and disposable income.)

If you want to start investing but are having trouble making ends meet, you may be due for a financial health checkup. You can test your financial fitness by visiting the Quicken site at `www.quicken.com/saving/checkup`. Answer a series of questions covering key areas, such as investments, debt management, and retirement planning. After you complete the questionnaire, you get a summary based on your financial objectives along with a set of suggestions and remedies.

Setting — and Reaching — Your Goals

Determining how much you need to earn requires having a clear understanding of where you are and where you expect to be in the coming years. Following, I provide an example to show the factors you need to consider when setting a ten-year goal.

Suppose that you're married, both you and your spouse have relatively well-paying jobs, you own a home (with a hefty 30-year mortgage), you have $5,000 in an IRA, and you're vested in your employer's pension. You have two children; one is 6 years old, and the other is 7. You expect that both children will want to go to college.

Your financial objectives for the next ten years are pretty clear: You need to raise the cash to send your children to college and still cover your other obligations. What about the ten years after that? Do you want to retire early? How much cash will you need for a comfortable retirement? Will your investment strategies get you to your financial objectives? How much of your income should you invest?

Setting your financial objectives

Financial planning involves setting objectives. Achieving these objectives is the finish line, and to reach it, you need to set strategic and tactical goals. *Strategic* goals are long-term and tend to be general. These goals can be wishes like "I want to be a millionaire by the time I'm 50." Financial planning *tactical* goals are short-term and specific, like "I want to save $5,000 this year." Your financial plan needs to include both strategic and tactical goals. Write them down and file them. Once a year, open the file and check on your progress. If your life situation changes, update your goals.

How you achieve your financial objectives is where your investment program enters the picture. But stop and evaluate your financial situation before you start investing. You want to be certain that you're financially ready to be an investor. You don't want to pay penalties due to early withdrawals, suffer excess brokerage fees, or lose income from your Treasury securities because you needed the cash and had to sell your investments earlier than planned. Before investing, be sure that you have the following:

- ✔ **An emergency fund:** For most people, the first thing on their list should be an emergency fund, which exists to protect them from unexpected situations. Unexpected expenses can include uninsured medical costs, property losses, and unemployment. (A recent survey indicated that only 17 percent of 1,000 respondents had a sufficient emergency fund, and one out of every five respondents didn't even have an emergency fund.)

- ✔ **Adequate insurance:** You need insurance to cover disability, health, life, automobiles, and property.

- ✔ **The ability to pay the monthly bills without stretching:** For many people, the goal is to pay the monthly bills without relying on future cash sources (that year-end bonus you were promised) or credit cards. For other people, the goal is to pay their children's college tuition, take care of their parents, or help their children with the down payment for their first car or home. Some goals include taking an ocean cruise, purchasing a vacation home, making home improvements, or purchasing a new home. Whatever your goals, make certain that they don't prevent you from covering your monthly bills.

Where do you stand?

If you use a credit card to pay for everyday expenses but you don't pay off the card balance at the end of the month, you aren't ready to be an investor. You need to change your spending habits and pay off those credit cards before you begin investing.

Why you should start now

The best argument for why you should start investing is to do the math and compare the results. For example, if a 25-year-old invests about $100 a month (at a 12% return) until age 65, the investment will be worth $1 million. For someone older to make that much money it's much harder. To have a $1 million nest egg at 65, a 40-year-old needs to invest $600 a month at a 12% return for 25 years. (Assuming that all returns are reinvested and the investments escape taxes.)

Interest rates on credit-card debt are often between 16 and 21 percent. Over the last 50 years, the average annual return on stocks is 13 percent. Even if your investments beat the market, you'll still have a difficult time covering your credit-card interest expenses.

The pitfalls of paycheck-to-paycheck accounting

Your income level doesn't determine whether you'll be financially successful. Financial success means not having to stretch to pay the monthly bills, living a comfortable lifestyle, and having the resources necessary for your family and retirement.

How much you earn today leads you to ask the following questions that impact your investing decisions:

- ✔ Do you need more income now?

- ✔ How much time (in number of years) do you have to meet your financial goals?

- ✔ Do you require a stable rate of capital appreciation or are you willing to speculate?

Can you pass a Debt Repayment Test? Many lenders use a 36 percent rule. That is, if your monthly debt is greater than 36 percent of your income, lenders may not approve your loan application. For example, if your gross monthly income is $6,000, your combined expenses can't exceed $2,160 ($6,000 × 0.36 = $2,160). Individuals with higher debt-to-income ratios have a hard time qualifying for a loan and aren't likely to have any funds available for investing.

Deciding How Much Risk You Can Take

Your investment decisions need to take into consideration your attitudes about risk. The amount of risk you can tolerate often depends on your knowledge of investments, your experience, and your personality. Each person has his or her own style and needs. Knowing exactly what your risk-tolerance level is can help you select investments that offer the highest return for the investment's level of risk.

The Internet provides many personal investment profiles. Several examples follow:

- **Bank of America Investment Services** (`www.bankamerica.com/tools/sri_assetall.html`) offers a survey of 12 questions. Enter your answers and the online calculator suggests an investment allocation strategy that suits your current needs and situation.

- **Frank Russell Company** (`www.russell.com/services/individual/employee/start/lifepoints/scquize.htm`) features a Comfort Quiz to help you create an asset allocation mix that's right for you.

- **UMB Bank** (`www.umb.com/invest/retirement/investor.html`) helps you determine your investor type with ten questions. Results indicate whether you are a conservative, balanced, or aggressive investor, and which investment that your retirement plan offers suits your needs.

Establishing Your Investment Plan

Many people want to jump into investing before they know where they are and where they're going. Investing is always a risk, and you need to understand how this risk relates to your financial base.

Figure 4-2 shows a diagram of your financial base that uses information from the North Dakota State University (NDSU) Extension Service (`www.ext.nodak.edu/extpubs`). The first (bottom) level is your budget, setting up a savings plan for an emergency fund, acquiring insurance, and developing a home ownership plan. The second level is developing a savings plan that meets your short-, intermediate-, and long-term financial goals. The third level is having six months of take-home pay ready for emergencies. The fourth level is keeping your contributions to your individual retirement plan on track.

Stocks, Bonds, Real Estate, Collectibles, and Other Investments			
Mutual Funds			
Qualified Retirement Plan			
Half-a-Year's Income in Low Risk Investments			
Systematic Savings Plan to meet short term goals, intermediate, and long-range goals			
Budget	Emergency fund	Insurance	Home mortgage

Figure 4-2:
Diagram of an investor's financial base.

Source: North Dakota Statue University, NDSU Extension Service (www.ext.nodak.edu/extpubs/yf/fammagmt/he258.htm)

Figure 4-2 shows how successful investors use a "financial pyramid." Regardless of your financial history, your current net worth, or how large your paycheck is, the pyramid crumbles if any of the foundation is missing.

Don't let this happen to you. For some individuals it takes years to establish a sturdy foundation. For others it means simply reallocating assets. After your financial foundation is set in place, you'll be ready to invest in mutual funds and then in stocks, bonds, real estate, and collectibles.

Determining How Much You Can Invest

Deciding how much you can invest isn't based on guesswork. It requires some analysis and setting up a budget. A budget is a blueprint that guides you through the process of paying bills, purchasing needed items, putting money into savings, and knowing how much you can invest. Where you can often run into problems is not budgeting for predictable but occasional expenses. Occasional expenses can include car repairs, annual life insurance premiums, tuition, and so on.

Gaining a good understanding of how much money you can expect to earn and understanding where your cash goes are the first steps to determining how much you can invest. Make a budget using pen and paper, Internet tools, or personal financial software like Money 99 (microsoft.com/money) or Quicken 99 (www.intuit.com/quicken99) to track your finances. Because the pen and paper method is too time consuming, and personal software programs can be costly and difficult to learn, I recommend using Internet tools. The Internet offers many online budgeting resources that are free, easy-to-use, and quick.

Using the Internet to control your finances

Whatever your personal situation dictates, you can find investments that are tailor-made for your requirements. Determining how much money to invest (or whether you have any money to invest) is a big step in the right direction.

The hundreds of existing online calculators can make setting up a budget almost painless. Using the following online calculators can help you determine your *net cash flow,* which is the amount of money that comes into your household each year and the amount of money you spend:

✔ **Understanding and Controlling Your Finances** (`www.bygpub.com/finance/CashFlowCalc.htm`) provides an online calculator that shows your income and expenses and determines whether you're living within your means.

✔ **FinanCenter** (`www.financenter.com`) offers a "How Much Am I Spending?" calculator that you can access by clicking on the Budget icon. This calculator shows your income, how much you're spending, and the amount available for investment. The online calculator even derives the future value of your investments if invested for ten years. With this feature, you know exactly what the benefits are of changing your spending habits.

The shortfall problem

A *surplus* means that you have excess funds — that is, money that may be available for investment. A *shortfall* means that you're living beyond your means and may need some assistance with debt management. If you spend more than you make, you may need to make some lifestyle changes. Following, I list two examples of Internet sources that can help you with the shortfall problem:

✔ **Dollar 4 Dollar** (`www.dollar4dollar.com`) provides worksheets, checklists, and other helpful guides to help you analyze your financial situation. This software also features money saving tips, financial strategies, and in-depth planning advice each week, and more.

✔ **Ohio State University Extension** (`www.ag.ohio-state.edu/%7eohioline/home/money`) offers a tutorial for managing your money. The tutorial includes six lessons: Where do I begin?, Where does your money go?, Stop spending leaks, Developing a spending plan, How much credit can you afford?, and Keeping records in order.

Investing in Securities That Meet Your Goals

Investors often receive hot tips from neighbors, e-mail messages, and message boards or chat rooms. However, studies indicate that chasing these investments, even if the investments are top performers, rarely produces the returns investors expect. Keep in mind that each security purchase is part of your investment plan, which is tied to your long-term goals. Specifically, how you choose to invest your capital (in mutual funds, stocks, bonds, Treasury securities, money market funds, and other types of investments) depends on the following:

- ✔ Your required rate of return
- ✔ How much risk you can tolerate
- ✔ How long you can invest your capital
- ✔ Your personal tax liability
- ✔ Your need for quick access to your cash

The Internet provides many sources that can assist you in developing your investment approach. For example, Legg Mason, a brokerage firm at www.leggmason.com/invest/strategy.htm, can help you develop your investment strategy with its online questionnaire. Just answer the questions and read the suggestions.

Checking Out What the Experts Are Doing

After factoring all the elements of this chapter into your investment plan, you may want to find out which stocks are creating the biggest buzz on the Internet and find out what the experts are doing. Keep in mind that you can follow investment candidates for years cost-free. Following, I list some of the best Internet investment starting points:

- ✔ **Investorguide** (www.investorguide.com) offers links to thousands of investor-related sites. This well-organized guide includes site reviews, summaries, and an extensive section on initial public offerings (IPOs).

- ✔ **Morningstar** (www.morningstar.net) specializes in mutual funds. This Chicago-based independent rating company site includes information about stocks and mutual funds, easy-to-use screening tools, and research sources.

✓ **The Syndicate** (www.moneypages.com/syndicate) offers informative articles on investor topics, more than 2,000 links to related investor sites, and information on brokers, bonds, and more.

✓ **Wall Street Research Net** (www.wsrn.com) focuses on stock market research. The site offers more than 65,000 links to company information, the economy, market news, investor reports, quotes, mutual fund indexes, and more.

✓ **Zacks Investment Research** (www.zacks.com) specializes in free and fee-based investment research. Get company reports, broker recommendations, analysts' forecasts, earnings announcements, and more.

Tracking and Measuring Your Success

After selecting, analyzing, and purchasing securities, your work still isn't done. Managing your investment portfolio can help you squeeze every bit of profit from your investments and realize your financial goals. You need to find information on changing market conditions, study analytical techniques, and update your financial plan regularly. The Internet provides many portfolio-management tools that include all these features. (See Chapter 16 for more details about online portfolio tracking.)

If you want to calculate your returns or expected returns with pencil and paper, its relatively easy, assuming that no additional purchases or redemptions were made during the period you're calculating (other than the reinvestment of dividends, interest payments, or capital gains distributions). To calculate your return, start with the ending balance and subtract the beginning balance. Divide this number by the beginning balance and then multiply by 100 to determine a percentage. This percentage is your return. The formulas is as follows:

Total Return =
[(Ending Balance − Beginning Balance) / Beginning Balance] × 100

Suppose that you invest $10,000 in stocks on January 1, 1999 and on December 31, 1999 your account has a value of $12,174:

1. **Start with the ending balance and deduct the beginning balance.**

   $12,174 − $10,000 = $2,174

2. **Divided the result by the beginning balance:**

   $2,174 / $10,000 = 0.21740

Setting realistic expectations

When you start your investment program, don't expect to become a millionaire overnight. History has shown that the market has many ups and downs. However, when looking at the long term (five years or more), investors have been rewarded for their patience. Additionally, riskier investments held over the long term provide higher rewards than low-risk investments. As you can see from the following statistics, less risk equals less return. For example, from 1970 to 1996, $1 invested in Treasury bills grew to $6.22. For bonds, $1 invested from 1970 to 1996 increased to $11.07, and $1 invested in stocks for the same period grew to $22.62.

---

3. Multiply the result by 100:

   $0.2174 \times 100 = 21.74\%$

   Your return is **21.74%**.

A return of 21.74% in one year (by anyone's standard) is pretty good. This rate means that for each dollar invested, you earned $0.22. To determine whether this rate of return "beat the market," you need to compare it to the appropriate benchmark. See Chapter 7 for more information on where to find benchmarks and indices online.

Bulletproof Investing

This chapter details the beginnings of the investment process, and if you glanced through, you can see that selecting securities isn't the first thing investors do. Choosing investments is just one of many elements in the process. To bulletproof your investing, you need to complete the many tasks detailed in this chapter. The following is a checklist that summarizes this chapter and outlines how you can bulletproof your investment plan:

✔ **Determine where you stand.** Gain a good understanding of what your financial commitments are for now and the future. Make certain you have an emergency fund and a savings plan.

✔ **Clearly state your financial goals.** How much do you need? When do you need it? How much risk can you tolerate? If you lost the principal of an investment, could you mentally recover and invest again?

✔ **Determine the appropriate allocation of your personal assets for your age (young adult, middle aged, retiree, and so on).** Develop a regular investing program and stick to it regardless of market volatility.

✔ **Select the investments that meet your financial goals and risk tolerance level.** How much time do you have (in years) to invest? Should you be an active trader and invest often during the day or a passive investor with a buy-and-hold policy? (See Chapter 15 for details on answering such questions.)

✔ **Analyze your investment candidates.** Before you call your online broker, make certain that you can tell a child in two minutes or less why you want to own a particular investment. Determine how long you plan to hold the security, and decide at what price you will sell (and take your profits or cut your losses).

✔ **Select an online broker that suits your needs.** Avoid mutual fund *loads* and high fees. Use automatic investment plans, dividend reinvestment programs, investment clubs, and other programs to reduce brokerage commissions. (See Chapter 6 for more information.)

✔ **Monitor your portfolio and reevaluate your goals on a regular basis.** Rank the performance of your investments and make the appropriate changes. You can expect that changes in general market conditions, new products that are introduced, and new technology will change how established businesses operate. Use this information to gain an understanding of when to hold and when to fold.

For more information about the investment process and bulletproofing your portfolio, check out Investor Home at (www.investorhome.com).

Chapter 5

What's So Great about Mutual Funds?

* *

In This Chapter

▶ Understanding why mutual funds are so wonderful

▶ Finding mutual fund resources on the Internet

▶ Buying mutual funds online

▶ Selling a mutual fund

▶ Starting a mutual fund account with as little as $25

▶ Finding online investment clubs

* *

*W*ant to participate in spectacular stock market profits but you're scared of the risks? Want to start investing but you don't have $1,000 to $2,500 for an initial minimum balance? Don't want to pay high brokerage commissions and fees? Well, a *mutual fund* (a managed investment company that is ready to purchase shares and constantly offers new shares to the public) may be for you. When you buy shares in a mutual fund, you are really buying shares of an investment company. The investment company's assets are stocks, bonds, certificates of deposit, and so on.

Mutual fund mania is rampant. Everyone is talking about mutual funds. Mutual funds are rapidly becoming the most popular way for Americans to invest — which is remarkable, considering that before the 1920s mutual funds didn't even exist. In the 1940s, only 68 funds existed, with $400 million in assets. Today, more than 7,000 mutual funds exist, with assets of $2.8 trillion. About 25 percent of all U.S. households are invested in mutual funds. In the nation, individuals are collectively investing about $20 billion per month.

In this chapter, I explain how you use the Internet to select mutual funds, and I list the latest Internet tools and resources. I also provide step-by-step instructions for opening a mutual fund account online, and I show you how to use the Internet to start a mutual fund account for as little as $25. I also explain how you can join an online investment club.

Mutual Fund Mania

Mutual funds offer a good solution for individuals who don't have the time and the technical knowledge to track individual stocks. Mutual funds are a convenient way of investing in stocks, bonds, cash, gold, and so on. In a mutual fund, professional managers pool the money of small investors. The goal of the investment company is to make more money for the small investors. In return for handling the investments, a fee is paid to the investment manager of a mutual fund for supervising the investment portfolio and administering the fund. Management fees are normally calculated as a percentage of the total assets of the fund.

Often, the portfolio manager and technical analysts invest in a collection of about 35 securities. However, any one fund can include anywhere from 20 to 200 securities. The portfolio manager expects these investments to earn interest from bonds, dividends from stocks, capital gains from buying and selling stocks at opportune times, and any other spin-off profits that can increase the value of the mutual fund. The mutual fund doesn't pay any taxes because all the profits are distributed as dividends and capital gains to the small investors (the shareholders).

The shareholder pays the management fee, registration fees, expenses for annual meetings, custodial bank and transfer agent fees, interest and taxes, brokerage commissions, marketing costs, and sometimes expenses related to the distribution of fund materials (prospectus, annual statement, and so on). These fees and expenses are usually deducted from the dividends paid to shareholders.

Visit Mutual Funds Interactive at www.fundsinteractive.com/newbie.html for more information about mutual funds. This Web site offers tutorials for beginners interested in mutual fund investing. For example, Figure 5-1 shows "Funds 101 — Mutual Funds for the New Investor." Also, check out *Investing For Dummies* by Eric Tyson, MBA (published by IDG Books Worldwide, Inc.).

Mutual funds are a good investment choice because funds offer individual investors several benefits that they don't ordinarily receive:

 ✔ **Diversification:** Mutual funds add securities to a portfolio so that the portfolio's unique risk is lowered. In other words, mutual funds allow you to spread your risk by purchasing several types of investments in one fund. For 75 percent of the fund, no single security can be greater than 5 percent of the fund's total assets. However, 25 percent of the fund's total assets can be in any one issue.

 Before you purchase a fund, read the prospectus and see how the assets are allocated. Well-diversified funds provide lots of investor protection. If one stock loses half its value in one day, the effect on the entire fund is small. On the other hand, if one stock skyrockets, you won't be able to buy that yacht you want.

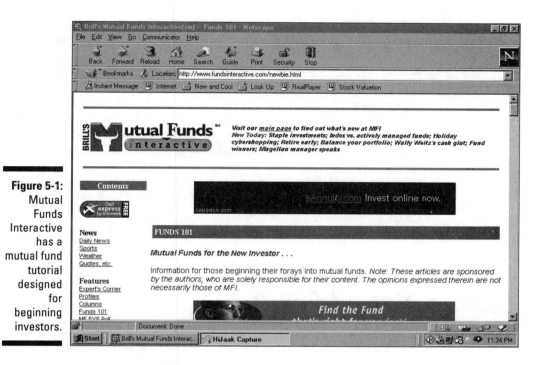

Figure 5-1:
Mutual
Funds
Interactive
has a
mutual fund
tutorial
designed
for
beginning
investors.

✔ **No broker required:** If you're confident about your investment choices, you're likely to purchase no-load mutual funds directly from the mutual fund company, instead of paying a *load* (a broker's commission). For more information about no-load funds, see Chapter 6.

✔ **No investor homework:** The mutual fund does the tracking and record keeping for you.

✔ **Professional management:** The professional managers, employed by the fund, search for fast-growing investments on your behalf. To have these professionals working for you full-time provides you with competitive advantages over other investors.

Finding Mutual Fund Information on the Internet

The Internet provides many mutual fund supersites that are timely, interesting, and best of all, useful. Here are a few examples of these all-purpose sites:

✔ **Mutual Funds Interactive (**www.fundsinteractive.com/profiles.html**)** has fund manager profiles and strategies for using funds to meet your investment goals.

- ✔ **Mutual Funds INVESTOR'S CENTER (**www.mfea.com**)** provides a news center, information about the new tax rules, links to mutual funds, and a research center that allows you to track from a list of more than 1,000 funds.

- ✔ **CBS MarketWatch — Super Star Funds (**cbs.marketwatch.com/news/ newsroom.htx**)** provides articles, news, market data, fund research, links to fund sites, mutual fund tutorials for new investors, market data, portfolios, and a stock chat room.

- ✔ **Mutual Fund Magazine (**www.mfmag.com**)** requires your free registration, but the site is worth registering for. This online magazine has a wide variety of features, departments, screens, reports, online calculators, and tools to assist you in making your mutual fund selections.

- ✔ **Charles Schwab & Co., Inc. (**www.schwab.com**)** provides the mutual funds marketplace with a comprehensive list of mutual funds with Morningstar Ratings.

Buying Mutual Funds

Mutual funds can give you a much better return than savings accounts, money market deposit accounts, or certificates of deposit. However, the Federal Deposit Insurance Corporation (FDIC) doesn't insure mutual funds. The FDIC doesn't even insure the mutual funds sold by your bank. Even mutual fund portfolios consisting only of guaranteed U.S. government bonds contain some element of risk. On the other hand, returns from stock mutual funds average about 12 percent a year, whereas savings accounts may earn only 4 percent. Although your savings account pays 4 percent year after year, your mutual fund may be up 35 percent this year and down 10 percent the next.

Over the years, the stock market has outperformed any other investment. Unlike a mutual fund, however, individual investors frequently can't purchase a large number of different securities to diversify their investment risk. Buying shares in a mutual fund solves this problem. When you invest in a mutual fund, the diversity of the portfolio reduces the risk of losing your total investment. Selecting the right fund may be difficult, but you can find plenty of online help.

Assume that you have $1,000 to invest in a mutual fund. With your investment, you're purchasing a share of the total assets in the fund. If the share price of the fund is $10 per share, you can purchase 100 shares. The price of each share is the Net Asset Value (NAV). The fund manager calculates the NAV of the mutual fund by adding up the value of the securities in the fund and dividing by the number of outstanding shares.

The NAV increases and decreases as the market fluctuates. The Securities and Exchange Commission (SEC) requires that the NAV of each mutual fund is calculated and published for investors at the end of each business day. Here are a few examples of online quote servers that provide mutual fund NAV information:

✔ **Briefing.com** (www.briefing.com) provides a free introductory service that includes market commentaries, mutual fund and stock quotes, charts, portfolio tracking, sector ratings, and an economic calendar. They have two levels of premium service. The first level, called Stock Analysis, is $6.95 per month (with a free trial) and includes stocks on the move, technical stock analysis, earnings calendar, splits calendar, stock ratings, upgrade and downgrade reports, company reports, and more. The highest level of service, called Professional, is $25 per month (with a free trial) and includes stock analysis, constant bond analysis (real-time commentary covering releases, events, and flows affecting the Treasury market), economic analysis, 15-minute bond quotes, FX analysis, yield curves, federal policy analysis, calendars, and more.

✔ **CNNfn** (www.cnnfn.com) is affiliated with Cable News Network (CNN) and provides links to financial sites, investment articles, market information, and online research sources. Market information shows the current level, amount of change, and time of the last update for the Dow Jones Industrial Averages, NASDAQ composite, S&P 500, Russell 2000, NYSE Composite, Dow Transports, Dow Utilities, Amex Composite, and S&P Futures. For mutual fund data, click on Stock Quotes. Enter the ticker symbol for your mutual fund or stock. CNNfn provides charts and company snapshots of selected firms. For mutual funds, CNNfn provides the latest performance data from Lipper Analytical.

✔ **Data Broadcasting Online** (www.dbc.com) retrieves up to seven ticker symbols at one time. Stock quotes include last price, change, currency, percent change, opening price, day low, day high, previous day's closing price, and volume. For mutual fund and stock quotes, markets, and portfolio information, you need to go to separate financial market menus. For access to premium data and real-time quotes, the firm charges $29.95 per month.

✔ **PC Quote** (www.pcquote.com) offers five levels of service that range from $75 per month to $300 per month or $750 per year to $3,000 per year for real-time quotes, charts, and more. (See the Web site for details.) Free services include ticker symbol lookup, current mutual fund and stock prices, fundamental data, Market Guide company snapshots, Zacks Investment Research broker recommendations, annual earnings and earning estimates, current company news, charts of a company's stock price history and volume, and market indexes. Overall, you can search for stocks, bonds, futures, options, mutual funds, and indexes. You can also maintain up to five portfolios with 20 ticker symbols in each portfolio.

Understanding the real cost of sales fees

If you purchase a load fund, it costs the same amount whether you purchase it through a broker or directly from the mutual fund company. However, you really don't need to pay a "load" to get a great mutual fund. One of the advantages of no-load mutual funds is that you can purchase them directly from the mutual fund company and skip paying a sales commission. In the past, if you purchased a no-load fund through a broker, you were charged a brokerage fee. Now, many discount brokerages and large mutual fund companies offer no-load funds (and even some load funds) with no transaction fees. (Brokers receive a portion of the fund's annual expenses instead.) For more information about one-stop shopping for your mutual funds, check out:

- ✔ **Charles Schwab & Co., Inc.** (www.schwab.com), Schwab's Mutual Fund OneSource service, includes over 850 no-load mutual fund families, all available without transaction fees. For online information about a fund, just click on any family to see the no-load, no-transaction fees Mutual Fund OneSource@Reg funds profile report.

- ✔ **T Rowe Price** (www.troweprice.com) offers Mutual Fund Gateway, with more than 1,000 mutual funds from more than 80 fund families. These funds are available to customers who use the company's Asset Management Account feature. You pay no transaction fees for no-load funds and pay the load-only fees for loaded funds. Certain load funds also include a $35 transaction fee.

- ✔ **Waterhouse Securities** (www.webbroker.com) has over 7,400 mutual funds with no transaction fees for no-load funds, a combination of no-load and low-load funds with transaction fees, and loaded funds with transaction fees.

Purchasing several mutual funds from one firm can help you with your investment tracking. However, closed-end funds are usually traded through a broker (as are stocks), though some closed-end funds have dividend reinvestment plans. (For more information on dividend reinvestment plans, see Chapter 14.)

If you have to pay a sales charge for purchasing your mutual fund, deduct this amount from your return for the year. For example, if you pay a 5-percent sales charge for your $1,000 investment in mutual funds, the amount invested in the funds is $950. If the fund increases by 10 percent in one year, you have a $1,045 investment. Your true yield is $95, or 9.5 percent ($95 ÷ $1,000) — not the full 10 percent.

On the other hand, if you purchase a no-load mutual fund, your yield is 10 percent because you don't pay the sales fee. Your original $1,000 investment in mutual funds is now worth $1,100, which is $55 more than the fund with the sales fee.

A better way to buy mutual funds

I suggest that you visit the Charles Schwab site (www.schwab.com) for the details on a revolutionary way to purchase mutual funds. You can purchase several mutual funds in the same fund family and thus save time and effort because you don't have to call several mutual fund companies to open accounts and make your purchases.

If you are unhappy with one of the mutual funds, you can swap it with another mutual fund in the same family at no cost, subject to certain restrictions. At the end of the month, you receive only one statement that covers all your funds.

Schwab also provides you with one statement for your taxes. This statement makes calculating the tax you owe on your profits easier than usual.

Here are a few examples of firms that can sell you a mutual fund without a sales charge (or load):

- ✔ **Invesco** (www.invesco.com) provides plenty of information about its no-load funds. If you're a beginning investor, you'll appreciate the useful advice at this site. The site includes online prospectuses, charts to compare rates of return, and a list of the firm's financial services.

- ✔ **Janus** (www.janus.com) has a family of no-load funds. The site provides account access, brief overviews of fund performance, application forms, investor chats, and articles. If you want a prospectus, just ask for one at this Web site; Janus mails one to you.

- ✔ **Vanguard** (www.vanguard.com), one of the largest mutual fund families, has around 90 funds that don't charge sales fees. The Vanguard Web site includes brief fund descriptions, downloadable prospectuses, and an education center. This site offers an online library, online calculators, a portfolio planner, a listing of their upcoming events (such as end-of-the-year returns), and investment articles.

Opening a mutual fund account

Before you invest in a mutual fund, read the fund's prospectus so that you understand exactly what you're investing in. Next, fill out the online account application form for the mutual fund company. SEC regulations require your signature to open an account. Figure 5-2 shows the application form for Lipper Funds, Inc., at www.lipper.com/howto.htm. This site indicates all the necessary steps for opening an account.

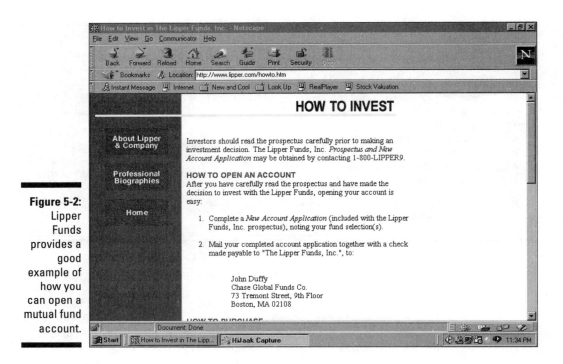

Figure 5-2:
Lipper
Funds
provides a
good
example of
how you
can open a
mutual fund
account.

For specific details about opening an account, contact the fund company or broker. In general, you need to complete the following steps:

1. **Indicate your fund selections.**

2. **Mark what type of account you want: individual, joint, or trust.**

3. **Include your social security number.**

4. **Mark whether you want check-writing privileges.**

5. **Indicate whether you want direct or automatic deposits (when you sell or if you receive a dividend) from a checking account or a paper check.**

6. **Mail your completed account application form and your check, made payable to the mutual fund.**

Selling Your Mutual Funds

The prospectus of a mutual fund details how you can sell your funds. Liquidating your shares may take a little time, so don't wait until the last minute to sell. Generally, the selling process works like this:

1. **Call your fund company or your broker.**
2. **Direct the representative to sell your shares.**

   You get that day's closing price, provided that you call before 4:00 EST.

If you are holding the certificate shares of a mutual fund, the selling process involves additional steps:

1. **Write a letter to the fund's agent requesting redemption of your fund shares at their market value at the time your request is received.**
2. **Enclose the certificates you hold.**

   If a custodial bank holds your shares, this step isn't necessary.
3. **Sign the letter and the certificates.**
4. **Have your signature guaranteed by your local bank or broker-dealer who is a member of the New York Stock Exchange (NYSE) or the National Association of Securities Dealers (NASD).**
5. **Insure the mailing for the full market value of the securities on the date they're sent.**

   Federal law requires redemption within seven days of when the fund's agent receives your request.

Starting Your Mutual Fund Account with as Little as $25

You don't need a great deal of money to buy a mutual fund. Before you start reading prospectuses, find out which mutual funds have automatic investment plans (AIPs). A mutual fund with an automatic investment plan often allows you to invest as little as $25 per month, after you meet the minimum investment.

The Internet provides information about which mutual funds offer AIPs. Here are a few examples of online mutual funds with automatic investment plans:

✔ **TD's Green Line Family of No-Load Mutual Funds (**`www.tdbank.ca`**)** has a pre-authorized purchase plan of more than 30 funds to choose from. Invest quarterly, monthly, weekly, or even on your payday. Minimum initial and subsequent investments can be as low as $25. You can change your investment amount, frequency of purchase, and choice of funds at any time.

✔ **Strong Automatic Investment Plan** (`www.strong-funds.com/strong/ LearningCenter/started.htm`), shown in Figure 5-3, has an automatic investment plan for 36 of its no-load funds. The program allows you to invest at predetermined intervals for as low as $50. No charges are required to establish or maintain this service.

✔ **Vanguard Fund Express** (`www.vanguard.com/catalog/service/ 5_3_1_2.html`) is a plan that allows monthly, bimonthly, quarterly, semiannual, and annual automatic payment to be transferred to your Vanguard account. The maximum amount is $100,000, and the minimum amount is $25.

✔ **T. Rowe Price** (`www.troweprice.com`) has over 20 no-load funds in its automatic investment plan that allow monthly, bimonthly, quarterly, semiannual, and annual automatic payments. Minimum payments can be as little as $25.

After you select several mutual funds with AIPs, ask for the funds' prospectuses and application forms. You can request the forms online, by telephone, or by mail. Fill out the section marked automatic investments and complete the form. You are authorizing the mutual fund company to make regular electronic withdrawals from your checking account. Many funds let you decide how much you want to invest. For example, you may decide to invest $50 per month or $25 every payday. If you reinvest your fund's cash distribution, you'll enjoy the benefits of compounding and your capital gains can add up quickly.

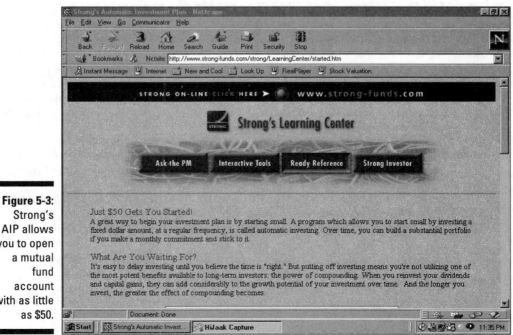

Figure 5-3:
Strong's AIP allows you to open a mutual fund account with as little as $50.

Chapter 6

The Keys to Successful Internet Mutual Fund Investing

● ●

In This Chapter

▶ Understanding mutual fund types, fees, and risks

▶ Locating and reading online prospectuses and other information

▶ Using online screening tools to find mutual funds that meet your requirements

● ●

*T*his chapter provides you with all the basic online tools for identifying mutual fund candidates. I present some general information about mutual fund investment, including types of funds, fees, and potential risks. I offer suggestions about where to find mutual fund facts and figures online. I also describe five online screening tools that can help you choose the mutual fund that best meets your needs. These mutual fund screens vary from simple to more advanced. By the way, the best online mutual fund screen is the one that includes the investment criteria you feel are important.

Mutual Fund Basics

With more than 9,000 funds to choose from, selecting a mutual fund has become a complex process — meaning that online screening tools are more important than ever before. When you select your investment criteria, you need to consider several factors:

✔ How long do you plan to own the mutual fund?

✔ How much risk to your principal can you tolerate?

✔ Which mutual fund category meets your personal financial objectives?

The funds you select will be based on the answers to these questions. If you need your money in a year, and can't afford much risk, because, for example, you plan to use the money to purchase a house, you want to consider a safe, short-term bond fund. On the other hand, if this money is your retirement fund that you don't plan to tap for ten years, and you can stomach some ups and downs, you should consider a growth stock fund.

Before you start screening mutual fund candidates, you need to understand some general information: the types of funds you can choose, the fees that mutual fund companies charge, the types of risk associated with mutual funds, and how to read a prospectus.

Discovering the differences between open-end and closed-end mutual funds

An *open-end mutual fund* has an unlimited number of shares. You can buy these shares either through the mutual fund company or your broker. The Securities and Exchange Commission requires that each mutual fund company calculate the NAV of each fund every day at the close of business.

A *closed-end mutual fund* is a hybrid: part mutual fund and part stock. A closed-end mutual fund is a publicly traded investment company with a limited number of shares. It doesn't stand ready to redeem its own shares from shareholders, and rarely issues new shares beyond its initial offering. That's why it's a "closed fund." You can only buy or sell these shares through a broker on the major stock exchanges. The value of these shares isn't calculated by using the NAV methodology. Instead, shares are valued by using a method similar to bonds and are traded at either a discount or a premium. Market prices of publicly traded closed-end mutual fund shares are published daily.

Closed fund types include closed-end stock funds (investments in common and preferred stocks), closed-end bond funds (investments in a range of bonds), closed-end convertible bond funds (have portfolios of bonds that can be converted to common stocks), closed-end single country funds (that specialize in stocks from one country or geographical region), and so on.

Minimizing fees

Loads are the fees with which mutual fund companies compensate the broker who sold you the fund. About half of all stock and bond funds have loads; money market funds normally don't have loads. Loads and other fees are important because they are deducted from your investment returns.

Loading it on

A *front-end load* is the most common type of fee that mutual fund companies charge. Investors pay this fee when they purchase shares in the mutual fund. No additional fees are charged for redeeming or selling your mutual fund shares. By law, front-end loads can't be greater than 8.5 percent. Loads average 5 percent for stock funds and 4 percent for bond funds.

The less common *back-end load* fee is charged when you sell or redeem the shares. Back-end fees are usually based on time, starting at 5 percent during the first year and declining a percentage point a year — by year five, no fees are charged. However, back-end load funds often have Rule 12b-1 fees, which are usually the amounts charged to investors for promoting the mutual fund. Fees range from 0.25 percent to 0.30 percent but can be as high as 1.25 percent. Rule 12b-1 fees are included in the funds expense ratio.

Rule 12b-1 marketing fees increase manager fees and aren't related to maximizing shareholder wealth. As an investor, you need to be on the lookout for these expenses when you read the prospectus.

Generally, funds with back-end fees are more expensive than funds with front-end fees due to the high Rule 12b-1 fees. However, if you are willing to hold your investment for five years or more (which really, you ought to, if you're investing in stocks), you pay no load (back-end loads usually disappear after five years).

Excluding the maximum fee for front-end loads of 8.5 percent, mutual funds can't charge more than 7.25 percent for the life of the investment. Overall, load fees vary from 4.0 percent to 8.5 percent of the NAV for the shares purchased.

What does all this fee information mean? If you purchase 300 shares at $10 per share with an 8-percent front-end fee, you're purchasing only $2,760 worth of shares. The other $240 goes to compensate the broker who sold you the fund. In other words, your investment needs to increase by $240 just to break even.

Taking it off

Some funds have no loads, which means that they have no front-end or back-end fees. These no-load funds generally don't have a sales force, so you have to contact the Investment Company to make a purchase. Nevertheless, no-load funds do charge service fees, proving that there's no such thing as a free lunch. Mutual fund companies charge annual fees for their management services, deducting these amounts before calculating the NAV.

Annual fees for the fund managers are about 0.50 percent of the fund's net assets. Other service fees include legal and auditing fees, the cost of preparing and distributing annual reports and proxy statements, director's fees, and transaction expenses. When added to the management fee, a fund's total yearly expenses can range from 0.75 to 1.25 percent of fund assets.

Experienced mutual fund investors typically avoid funds with expense ratios greater than 1.25 percent.

Some mutual fund companies may have low up-front fees but charge high rates for managing fund operations. The prospectus details whether the mutual fund charges these fees.

For more information on operating expenses and other fees, see *Investing For Dummies* by Eric Tyson, MBA (published by IDG Books Worldwide, Inc.).

Understanding Mutual Fund Risks

Mutual funds provide statements about their objectives and risk posture (which is briefly explained in qualitative terms in the prospectus). Rather than provide precise information to help you evaluate the riskiness of a mutual fund, however, these statements typically offer vague, general explanations of a fund's approach to risk. For more precise, statistical evaluations of a fund's risks, you can turn to independent mutual fund rating services such as Morningstar (www.morningstar.net).

Morningstar and other independent rating services calculate such statistics as the standard deviation of a fund's return. I don't want to turn this chapter into an introductory statistics course, but I can tell you that standard deviation helps you judge how volatile, or risky, a fund is. This statistic shows you how much a fund has deviated from its average return over a period of time. Figure 6-1 shows Morningstar's standard deviation calculation for a mutual fund, which you can find at www.morningstar.net/FundQT/RR_Risk/RPMGX.msfhtml.

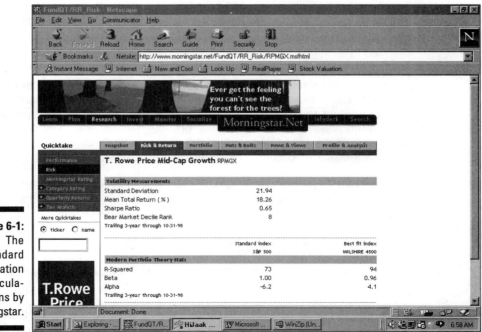

Figure 6-1: The standard deviation calculations by Morningstar.

Standard deviation offers a clear indicator of a fund's consistency over time. A fund's standard deviation is a simple measure of the fund's highest and lowest returns over a specific time period. Just remember this point: The higher the standard deviation, the higher the fund's risk.

For example, if the 3-year return on a fund is 33 percent, that statistic may mean that the fund earned 11 percent in the first year, 11 percent in the second year, and 11 percent in the third year. On the other hand, the fund may have earned 28 percent in the first year, 5 percent in the second year, and 0 percent in the third year. If your financial plan requires an 11 percent annual return, this fund is not for you!

A Fund for You, a Fund for Me

You can choose from a wide variety of mutual fund categories. As a matter of fact, so many types of funds are available that you're almost guaranteed to find a fund that is an excellent fit for your personal financial objectives. You can summarize the funds into nine groups:

- **Aggressive growth funds:** Aggressive growth funds tend to be investments in small, young companies and may involve the use of options and futures to reap greater profits. Aggressive growth funds primarily seek increases in capital gains. If the stock market is hot, these funds often provide the biggest return of all mutual funds, mostly due to the capital gains of the stocks in the fund. They typically drop the most, when the market is cold. Their volatility makes them a poor choice for the short-term investor.

- **Bond funds:** Investment grade bond funds usually have less risk than funds with stocks, but they are not risk free. These types of bond funds are usually good investment choices for short-, medium-, and long-term investors who desire low risk. Investment grade bond funds focus on current income. For more information on bonds, see Chapter 9.

- **Growth and income funds:** Funds in the growth and income category target a steady return with capital growth potential. They often invest in companies that are growing, as well as in companies that are paying high or increasing dividends. Growth and income funds are more diverse than are growth funds — they may include bonds — and are less risky, which means that these funds reap fewer rewards if the stock market soars, and lose less if the stock market drops.

- **Growth funds:** Growth funds are similar to aggressive growth funds but have less risk. They may invest in larger, well-established firms with a long track record of earnings that may continue to grow faster than average. These funds also seek stocks with capital gain potential. In addition to stocks, these funds generally include bonds and cash equivalents. Growth funds are best for investors with medium- to long-term objectives.

✔ **International funds:** International funds include a mix of stocks and bonds from other nations or governments. These funds are subject to several types of risks that domestic mutual funds don't experience, such as political risk and exchange rate risk (losing money because of changes in the currency exchange rate).

✔ **Money market funds:** Money market funds provide less return and less risk than other types of mutual funds and are good investments for short-term investors. The principal advantage of these funds is their safety. Also, if you ever need to get to your money fast, money market funds may be the type of fund for you.

✔ **Balanced Funds:** Balanced Funds are a mix of stocks, bonds, and treasury bills, and possibly some foreign assets. Each fund has a different strategy for determining their asset allocation mix.

✔ **Dividend Fund:** Dividend Funds are investments in common and preferred stocks offered by corporations that generate a high, steady stream of dividend income. In Canada, the dividends are usually eligible for the dividend tax credit, thereby increasing the after-tax yield to the unitholder. This makes dividend funds attractive to Canadian investors who prefer to pay the lower tax rates on dividend income than the higher tax rates on interest income.

✔ **Equity Funds:** Equity Funds have higher risk than money market or bond funds, but they also can offer the highest returns. A stock fund's Net Asset Value (NAV) can rise and fall quickly over the short term, but historically stocks have performed better over the long term than other types of investments. Not all equity (stock) funds are the same. For example, some equity funds specialize in growth or technology stocks.

Table 6-1 provides a brief overview of the time period and risk tolerance level of the major mutual fund categories. Please note the difference in risk level between money market funds (that are not insured by the Federal Deposit Insurance Corporation) and Money Market Deposit Accounts that are insured.

Table 6-1	Choosing the Right Type of Mutual Fund	
Investment Time Period	*Risk-Tolerance Level*	*Category of Mutual Fund*
Less than 2 years	Minimum risk to principal	Money market fund (not a money market deposit account, or MMDA)
	Some risk to principal	Bond fund (short to intermediate bond fund)
Between 2 and 4 years	Minimum risk to principal	Money market fund (not an MMDA)
	Some risk to principal	Bond fund (short to intermediate term)

Investment Time Period	Risk-Tolerance Level	Category of Mutual Fund
	Moderate risk to principal	Bond fund (intermediate to long-term)
Between 4 and 6 years	Minimum risk to principal	Money market fund (not an MMDA)
	Some risk to principal	Bond fund (short to intermediate)
	Moderate risk to principal	Growth and income funds
	Excessive risk to principal	Growth funds and international funds

Setting realistic expectations for your investment choices is important. The Internet provides many information sources about the average rates of return for different categories of mutual funds. You can find out how the fund category you select stacks up against other categories of funds at BusinessWeek Online (www.businessweek.com/1998/05/b3563018.htm).

Finding Facts and Figures Online

This list of online information services can assist you in finding the right mutual fund:

- ✔ **MoneyNet (**www.moneynet.com/content/MONEYNET/ResSummary/Summary.asp**)**, shown in Figure 6-2, provides research and summaries of mutual funds. Enter either the ticker symbol or the name of the fund for a fund summary.

- ✔ **Mutual Funds Interactive (The Mutual Funds Homepage)** (www.fundsinteractive.com/index.shtml) offers tutorials for beginning mutual fund investors, interviews, descriptions of fund strategies with top mutual fund managers, analyses of the mutual funds market, and links to mutual fund home pages.

- ✔ **The Wall Street Journal (**interactive.wsj.com**)** provides information on mutual funds as part of its Money & Investing section. This free information includes news and features, statistics on the top performers in various fund categories, mutual fund profiles, scorecards, and closed-end fund prices.

- ✔ **Standard & Poor's Micropal (**www.micropal.com**)** provides fund information and monitoring for over 38,000 funds across the globe on a daily, weekly, and monthly basis. Additionally, Micropal supplies summaries on the funds it monitors.

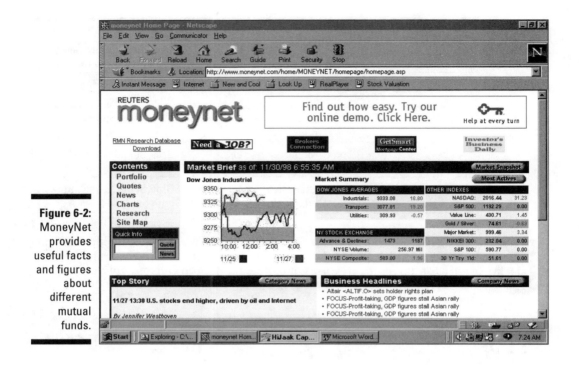

Figure 6-2:
MoneyNet
provides
useful facts
and figures
about
different
mutual
funds.

✔ **The Street.com** (www.thestreet.com) provides fund profiles and scorecards at www.thestreet.com/MutualFundProfiles/ funds.asp, as shown in Figure 6-3. You can search Lipper Analytical's top performers for the week. Additionally, you can search funds by asset size, category, fund symbol, or fund name.

Locating and Reading the Prospectus

Fast EDGAR Mutual Funds Reporting is located at edgar.stern.nyu.edu/ mutual.html. This Web site, shown in Figure 6-4, provides prospectuses for more than 7,000 mutual funds. If you know the name of the fund you're interested in, you can investigate the fund's activities at this site. Target your search by determining the range of dates you want, which filing forms (quarterly, annually, and so on) you want to read, and the name of the specific fund.

If you don't know the exact name of the fund you want, refer to Morningstar at www.morningstar.net. Morningstar provides a mutual fund search engine. Just enter what you know of the mutual fund's name. The search engine's results provide you with several mutual funds that have similar names. It is likely that the mutual fund you are seeking is one of the funds listed.

Figure 6-3:
The Street.com provides mutual fund profiles, scorecards, and the capability to search for mutual fund reports and statistics.

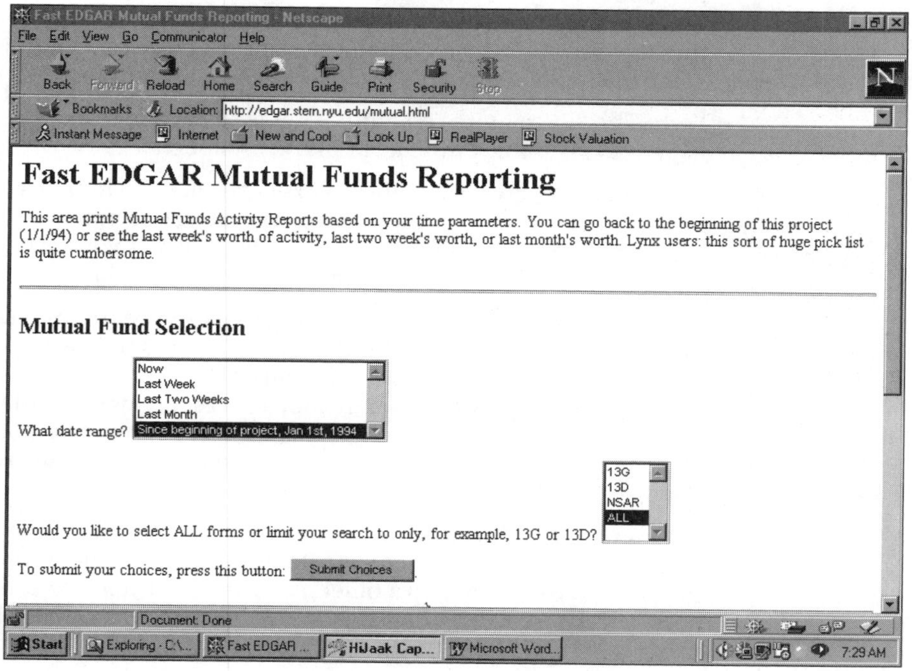

Figure 6-4:
Get the prospectus for the mutual fund you're investigating online from Fast EDGAR.

After you find the prospectus you want, download it to your computer so that you can read it at your leisure. Here's how you download a prospectus that you have accessed via the EDGAR for Mutual Funds Web site:

1. **With the prospectus displayed in your Web browser, choose File⇨Save.**

   Your browser displays the Save As dialog box.

2. **Enter a file name for the prospectus and select the directory in which you want to save the file.**

3. **Click on Save.**

   Your browser saves the prospectus on your computer. If you have a dial-up connection to the Internet, you can disconnect from your ISP.

4. **Minimize your Internet browser.**

5. **Open your word-processing program.**

6. **Open the prospectus file.**

   You can now read the prospectus at your leisure offline.

When you read the prospectus you have downloaded, look for the following information:

- ✔ **Investment objectives:** The first paragraph of the prospectus describes the fund's investment objectives and lists the types of securities the fund invests in. If the fund doesn't meet your investment objectives, you can stop reading and start evaluating another fund.

- ✔ **Fees:** The SEC requires all mutual funds to list all fees, costs, and expenses in a table at the front of the prospectus.

- ✔ **Additional expenses:** Additional expenses may be for extra services, such as printed shareholder materials, toll-free telephone numbers with 24-hour service, accumulation plans that reinvest your distributions (shareholder profits), and related support and guidance.

- ✔ **Performance:** Year-to-year data for the last ten years (or less if the fund isn't that old) in condensed financial statements indicates the fund's performance. Statistics track the fund's NAV, shareholder distributions, and expenses. For funds that include stocks, dividends and price information also may be included. Many funds provide graphs that show how a $1,000 investment in the fund increased or decreased over a ten-year period.

- ✔ **Statement of additional information:** This section of the prospectus covers fund details and complex items such as the biographies of the fund's directors, the fund's objectives, and contracts for professional services. These reports are free to the fund's shareholders that request them.

The SEC requires the prospectus to indicate what fees the fund charges for a $1,000 investment with a 5-percent return redeemed at the end of one year, three years, five years, and ten years. Keep in mind that both load and no-load funds have management fees and operating expenses that are charged to the fund.

How to Screen Mutual Funds Online

The Internet provides a variety of mutual fund screening tools that sort more than 9,000 mutual funds by criteria that you select. For example, you may want one type of fund for your children's education — something long-term because you don't need the money for 10 to 20 years — and a different fund for your retirement to help you reduce your current tax liabilities. With these online screening tools, you can evaluate several funds that meet your financial needs.

Most of the stock-screening sites on the Internet are free. These database searches are an inexpensive way to isolate mutual funds that meet your special criteria. Some databases list funds incorrectly or have outdated information. However, they are useful for pruning a large list of candidates to a manageable short list.

Some mutual fund screening programs — for example, Quicken's Mutual Fund Finder (www.quicken.com/investments/mutualfunds/finder/) and MSN Investor (investor.msn.com) — are for beginners to use. Others, such as ResearchMag (www.researchmag.com), require some practice. Some mutual fund screens allow you to download the data to your spreadsheet so that you can do additional analysis.

Each screening site uses different criteria to sort mutual funds. You have to decide which criteria you care about and then use the site that offers the criteria you want. Any way you look at it, the selection of the right mutual fund is still up to you.

Here's an overview of the features of five mutual fund screens that are best for beginning online investors:

✔ **Investor Square** (www.investorsquare.com), shown in Figure 6-5, has a mutual fund screen called Mutual Fund Explorer (at the home page, click on Power Screen). This screen is one of the best mutual fund screens available for beginning investors. The free service screens, ranks, and profiles more than 9,500 mutual funds using up to 100 different variables. The program is designed to help you find the best 25 performers by category, detailed objective, or specific category (like short-term or long-term bond fund). Just highlight the category and click on Submit.

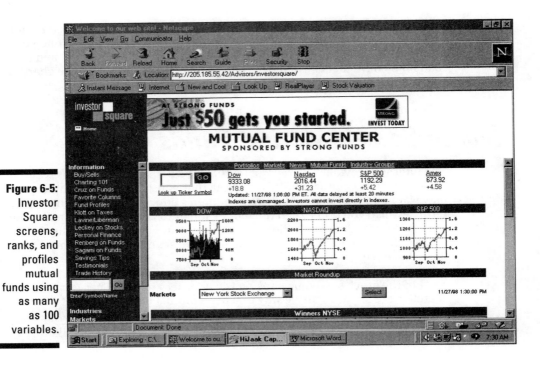

Figure 6-5:
Investor
Square
screens,
ranks, and
profiles
mutual
funds using
as many
as 100
variables.

✔ **Microsoft Investor** (investor.msn.com) charges $9.95 per month for a full package of features that include mutual fund and stock screens. A 30-day free trial period is available. To access the mutual fund screen just click on Finder, then Funds. Shown in Figure 6-6, the mutual fund finder screen has eleven pre-built screens that may include the criteria that you feel are the most important when selecting a mutual fund. Examples of the pre-built screens include: (1) Safety first funds, (2) Do-it-yourself funds — this screen lets you experiment with your own pain threshold, (3) Foreign stock funds, (4) High yield bond funds, (5) Hot, no-load funds, (6) Large blend funds, (7) NAIC equity screen, (8) NAIC fixed income screen, (9) Small cap growth funds, (10) Specialty technology funds, and (11) Top rated funds. You can also design your own mutual fund screens.

✔ **Morningstar** (www.morningstar.net) offers a free, independent service that evaluates more than 6,800 mutual funds. At Morningstar's home page, click on Mutual Fund Screen to access the Morning Star Mutual Fund Screen. One drawback of the program is that you can't copy screen results to a spreadsheet.

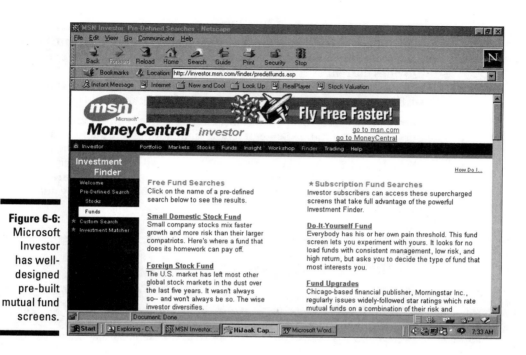

Figure 6-6:
Microsoft Investor has well-designed pre-built mutual fund screens.

✔ **Quicken.com** (www.quicken.com) provides its mutual fund screen free of charge. At the Quicken.com home page, click on Mutual Fund Finder to access the pre-built mutual fund screens. Easy Step Search has additional variables and is geared for more experienced investors. Full Search has 20 variables on one page and numerous advanced options. You can move freely between different searches to sample each screen.

✔ **Quote.com Mutual Fund Screening** (www.quote.com/screening) is cost-free with your free registration. This mutual fund screen has a unique twist: Two of the criteria ask about performance in a bear or a bull market. Click on Help for descriptions of the headings and fields used in the screening tool.

The following three mutual funds screens are great for more experienced investors:

✔ **ResearchMag** (www.researchmag.com) is a free service that is definitely for the experienced investor. However, after you get familiar with its 40 research variables, the service is easy to use. ResearchMag requires your free registration. To access the screen from ReseachMag's home page, click on Mutual Fund Screens. To save time and to avoid making the same mistake over and over, be sure to keep a list of what works and what doesn't. The program searches more than 3,500 equity mutual funds. You can copy screen results to a spreadsheet.

✔ **Smart Money Interactive** (www.smartmoney.com) has a do-it-yourself mutual fund finder that searches a database of over 6,000 mutual funds. You can screen for dozens of factors. For additional help, the screen provides current averages for factors like EPS, ROE, and so on. To analyze your selections, click on Analyze First 15 Funds. This function sorts your best candidates so that you can compare your results.

✔ **Thomson Investors Network** (www.thomsoninvest.net) charges $9.95 per month for a full package of features, including mutual fund and stock screens. Guests and members need to log in before using the Mutual Fund Screen. Click on Research. Next, click on Mutual Fund Screen and select the characteristics of the mutual fund you are seeking. Click on Submit to enter your choices. You can't copy search results to a spreadsheet program.

Socially conscious mutual funds

How about a new mutual fund category — socially conscious mutual funds? Check out this socially conscious mutual fund screen at Co-op America (www.coopamerica.org/mfsc.htm). This screen shows when the mutual fund started, minimum initial investment amount, minimum initial investment amount for an IRA, and telephone number. Funds are screened for awareness of: (1) the environment, (2) labor and employment, (3) products and services, (4) defense and weapons, (5) alcohol, tobacco, and gambling, and (6) human rights and equality.

Chapter 7

The Basics of Stocks and Rates of Return

The focus of this chapter is stock selection. The savvy online investor prospects all possible stock candidates, looking for companies that are exceptional in some way and positioned to perform well in the future.

In this chapter, I discuss using the Internet to decide which types of securities are right for you. I also show you how to keep current with online news services, read a stock table, and find the ticker symbols of securities online, so that you can make wise investment decisions.

Taking Stock of You . . .

Most people spend the bulk of their income on no-frills necessities such as housing, food, transportation, and education. People who don't invest often believe that they can't afford to do so. Investing today usually means giving up some immediate pleasure, such as a European vacation, taking the family to see a play, or going to that great new restaurant. However, even a small amount of money invested each month can make a big impact on your long-term financial security. For example, you can start a mutual fund automatic investment program with as little as $25 (see Chapter 5 for details).

Investing can help you stay ahead of inflation and assist you in accumulating real personal wealth with the power of compounding. Successful investing has several key factors, some of which must be in place before you invest your first dollar:

✔ **Know yourself.** How much risk to your savings can you tolerate and still sleep at night? How much experience, technical knowledge, and time do you have for making investment decisions?

✔ **Know your goals and the time you have to accomplish those goals.** Understand exactly what's needed to achieve your financial objectives.

✔ **Decide how you want to allocate your assets into the three main classes: stocks, bonds, and cash.** You decide how much you want to invest in each class based on how much risk you can tolerate, your required rate of return, and the investment time period.

✔ **Select specific investment candidates in the three asset classes.** Bear in mind the importance of compounding and the impact of taxes and fees on your returns.

✔ **Determine how much risk you can take and other investment criteria for selecting the right investments.** For example, how much risk can you take? How long can you invest your cash? What is your required rate of return? (For more help in determining your personal investment criteria, see Chapter 8.)

✔ **Keep current with changes in the economy and other factors that affect your investments.** Strive to make proactive rather than reactive investment decisions. You can keep current by using the online news services listed in this chapter and in this book's Internet Directory. I offer additional how-to information in Chapter 12.

✔ **Decide how you plan to define success for your investment selections.** Monitor your investments and keep good financial records.

You can find many asset allocation worksheets on the Internet. Check out the worksheet from Community Financial Planning Services, Inc. (`www.comfin.com/assetq.html`). This free, easy-to-use worksheet can immediately assist you in matching your risk tolerance levels to your financial goals. However, this is a commercial site, so be forewarned that ComFin will try to sell you something.

Understanding Stocks

When you buy shares of a company, you purchase part ownership in that company. As a shareholder, you also expect to receive *capital appreciation* on your investment — that is, the difference between your purchase price and the market price of your shares. If the company prospers, your shares of stock increase in value. If company performance declines, the market value of your shares also decreases.

As a shareholder, you're entitled to periodic cash dividends. (The board of directors decides whether dividends are paid.) The amount of cash dividends paid per year can vary, but they're generally predictable.

Some successful firms like Berkshire Hathaway and Microsoft do not pay dividends. These companies usually plow dividend payout funds back into the company to finance its expansion. This increases the value of the company and price of shares stockholders own. In other words, if all goes as planned, the stockholders get "capital appreciation" instead of a dividend check. Some investors in high tax brackets prefer this approach. They don't have to pay taxes on capital appreciation until they sell the stock. With dividends, investors have to pay the tax man right away.

The *annual return* is the percentage difference of the stock price at the beginning of the year from the stock price at the end of the year and any dividends paid. The price at which you can buy or sell a share of common stock can change radically. As a matter of fact, stock prices are so volatile that accurately predicting annual returns is impossible. (If we had this gift, we would all be rich!)

Common stock returns can vary — for example, from a depressing –43.34 percent in 1931 to a thrilling 53.99 percent in 1933. However, investments in the stock market have consistently outperformed any other type of investment. Total stock returns over the last 50 years have averaged 13 percent, meaning that a stock investment of $500 in 1947 would be worth $1,729,670 today.

For answers to questions like "What is stock?" "Why does a company issue stock?" "Why do investors pay good money for little pieces of paper called stock certificates?" "What do investors look for?" "What about ratings and what about dividends?", see Investor FAQ (Frequently Asked Questions) at invest-faq.com/articles/stock-a-basics.html.

Types of Stock

Just like other investments, several types of stocks are available to try. Each stock type has characteristics, benefits, and drawbacks that you should be aware of before you invest. The following is a quick summary to help you gain an understanding of these financial instruments.

Common stocks

When we think about investing, we tend to think primarily of common stocks. After all, it's difficult not to be bombarded daily with stock market news and commentary. Additionally, American history is filled with stories about how the Vanderbilts, Rockefellers, Carnegies, and other turn-of-the-century entrepreneurs made their fortunes on Wall Street with common stocks.

Both new and old companies sell common stock to raise capital to fund operations and expand their businesses. Common stocks represent shares of ownership in a corporation. Shareholders have a right to dividends and can vote on mergers, acquisitions, and other major issues affecting the corporation. Additionally, shareholders have a voice in the election of the board of directors. Dividends are paid at the discretion of the board of directors. The liabilities of being a shareholder are limited. Shareholders can't lose any more than the amount of their investments.

Preferred stocks

Preferred stocks are also equity stocks in a corporation. However, preferred stockholders cannot cast their votes on issues regarding company management. For this trade-off, the stockholder gets another benefit: a fixed dividend. Preferred stock is sold at par value (face value). The par value of preferred stocks is usually $25, $35, or $100. The company assigns a fixed dividend. Preferred stocks (sometimes called hybrids, because they include the features of both stocks and bonds) compete with bonds and other interest-bearing financial instruments, which means that the amount of the dividend is affected by the current interest rate at the time that the preferred stock is issued. Higher dividends tend to be issued when interest rates are high. Lower dividends are issued when interest rates are low. Preferred stockholders are paid their dividends regularly and the stock has no maturity date.

Stock rights and warrants

Stock rights are derivative financial instruments that are similar to stock options. Stock rights allow current shareholders to purchase stock ahead of the public and directly from the company with no commissions or fees, and usually at a discount of 5 to 10 percent. The life of a stock right is generally only 30 days. During this time, the investors can exercise their rights, purchase shares at a discount, and sell them for a quick profit. If investors don't want to purchase the shares outright, they can sell the stock rights for a profit. After the expiration date, stock rights have no value, so stock right investors need to be quick.

Warrants are a way to gain control of a large amount of stock without having to purchase it outright. Warrants are options to purchase a pre-set amount of stock at a pre-set price, during a specified time period (5 years, 10 years, 20 years, or perpetually). At the time the warrant is issued, the price is fixed above the market price. Warrants have no voting rights or claims on corporate assets. When the warrant expires, it has no trading value. Warrants only have value if the stock is trading at a price that is above the amount stated on the warrant. Often, warrants are sold with bonds, as part of an initial public offering, or as part of a merger or acquisition.

For more information about the topics covered in this section, go to Investment FAQ at (www.invest-faq.com/articles/index.html). Click on an article's subject (investor basics, preferred stocks, and so on) to jump directly to the subject matter.)

Picking the Right Stock for the Right Goal

Selecting your own stocks can be hard work. The exciting thing is that the Internet has much of the information you need, and most of this information is free. With the power of your computer, you can utilize Internet data to gain real insight. As you start to determine which stocks you're interested in, you should be aware of the different types of stocks. Stocks have distinct characteristics, and as general economic conditions change, they behave in special ways.

Write a short list of your financial goals and then investigate how different types of stock relate to those objectives. Different stocks have different rates of return — some are better for young, aggressive investors; others are better for retirees or for people in high tax brackets. Here are a few examples of the different types of stocks:

- **Blue-chip stocks:** Usually the most prestigious stocks on Wall Street. They're high-quality stocks that have a long history of earnings and dividend payments. These stocks are often good long-term investments.

- **Cyclical stocks:** Stocks of companies whose fortunes rise when business conditions are good. When business conditions deteriorate, their earnings and stock prices decline. These companies are likely to be manufacturers of automobiles, steel, cement, and machine tools.

- **Seasonal stocks:** Similar to cyclical stocks; their fortunes change with the seasons. Good examples of seasonal companies are retail corporations whose sales and profits increase at Christmastime.

✔ **Defensive stocks:** Tend to be stable and relatively safe in declining markets. Defensive stocks are from companies that provide necessary services, such as electricity and gas, which everyone needs regardless of the economic climate. Companies in this category also provide essentials such as drugs and food, so their sales remain stable when the economy is depressed. (Note: Defensive stocks are *not* related to the military.)

✔ **Growth stocks:** Growth companies are positioned for future growth and capital appreciation. However, their market price can change rapidly. Rather than pay dividends, growth companies typically spend their profits on research and development to fuel future growth. These stocks are good for aggressive, long-term investors who are willing to bet on the future. If you're in a high tax bracket, these stocks may be for you; low dividends mean fewer taxes. However, if expected earnings don't match analyst predictions, expect a big decline in stock price.

✔ **Income stocks:** Purchased for their regular, high dividends. Income stocks usually pay bigger dividends than their peers do. Income stocks are attractive to retirees who may depend on their dividends for monthly expenses. Income stocks are often utilities companies and similar firms that pay higher dividends than comparable companies. These companies are often slow to expand because they spend most of their cash on dividend payouts. During times of declining interest rates, bonds are better investments.

✔ **International stocks:** Investors in these stocks often believe that U.S. domestic stocks are overpriced. These investors are seeking bargains overseas. However, international stocks include some risks that U.S. stocks don't have, such as trading in another currency, operating in a different economy, being subject to a different government, and using accounting standards that do not follow U.S. generally accepted accounting principles. Additionally, public information may have to be translated, which causes delays and sometimes miscommunication. All these elements add cost and risk to foreign stocks.

✔ **Speculative stocks and initial public offerings:** Speculative stocks are easy to identify because they have price/earnings (P/E) ratios that are between 50 and 100 when other stocks have multiples of 15 to 20. A second type of speculative stock is an initial public offering (IPO). This type of stock often has no track record. A good example of speculative stock is Netscape; its stock price is high and revenues are small.

✔ **Value stocks:** Some Wall Street analysts consider these stocks to be bargains. These stocks have sound financial statements and increases in earnings but are priced less than stocks of similar companies in the same industry.

You can find additional information about stock sectors at Briefing.com (www.briefing.com/Schwab/sectors.htm), shown in Figure 7-1. Each stock sector has a descriptive narrative, rating, and review date.

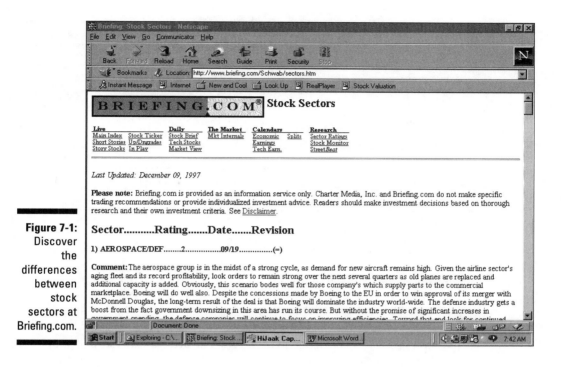

Figure 7-1:
Discover
the
differences
between
stock
sectors at
Briefing.com.

How to Read a Stock Chart or Table

Most newspapers and many Internet sites, such as The Wall Street Journal Interactive Edition (www.wsj.com) and Barron's (www.barrons.com), have a listing of the day's stock activities. Table 7-1 shows the information you find in a typical listing from The Wall Street Journal Interactive Edition. (The values in the table are hypothetical.) The stock detailed is Compaq (CPQ). Compaq designs, develops, manufactures, and markets a wide range of computing products, including desktop and portable computers.

Table 7-1	Reading the Stock Pages at The Wall Street Journal Interactive Edition
Entry	*Value*
Date	November 16, 1999
Last	66 $^7/_{16}$
Change	+3 $^7/_8$
Volume	14,122,200
Time	4:21 p.m. EST

(continued)

Table 7-1 _(continued)_

Entry	Value
Exchange	NYSE
Day Open	64 $^7/_8$
Day High	67 $^3/_{16}$
Day Low	64 $^1/_8$
Close	62 $^9/_{16}$
Change	+ $^5/_{16}$ (Previous day)
Volume	9,323,900 (Previous day)
52-Week High	79 $^9/_{16}$
52-Week Low	28 $^{13}/_{32}$

Here's how to interpret all this information about Compaq's stock:

- ✔ **Last: 66 $^7/_{16}$.** The dollar amount of the last price for the Compaq stock. (All stock prices are customarily shown in fractions instead of decimals.)

- ✔ **Change: +3 $^7/_8$.** The change in the current price to the day's closing price. This change compares the current price to the previous day's closing price. It is the amount of today's gain or loss.

- ✔ **Volume: 14,122,220.** The volume or number of shares traded that day.

- ✔ **Time: 4:21 p.m. EST.** The time of the price quote. Some Internet quote services provide real-time quotes; others may be delayed as much as 20 minutes.

- ✔ **Exchange: NYSE.** The exchange that the stock is traded on. Compaq is traded on the New York Stock Exchange (NYSE).

- ✔ **Day Open: 64 $^7/_8$.** The price of the stock at the beginning of the day.

- ✔ **Day High: 67 $^3/_{16}$.** The highest stock price of the day.

- ✔ **Day Low: 64 $^1/_8$.** The lowest stock price of the day.

- ✔ **Close: 62 $^9/_{16}$.** The closing price from the previous day. The market closes on Saturday and Sunday, so the previous day for Monday, November 16, 1999 is Friday, November 13, 1999.

- ✔ **Change: + $^5/_{16}$.** The change from the closing price of the previous day. This change compares yesterday's price at this time to yesterday's closing price.

- ✔ **Volume 9,323,900.** The number of shares traded as of this time, on the previous day.

- ✔ **52-Week High: 79 $^9/_{16}$.** The highest stock price in the last year.

- ✔ **52-Week Low: 28 $^{13}/_{32}$.** The lowest stock price in the last year.

The Wall Street Journal Interactive Edition is continually updated. For more about how this financial newspaper is structured, see `interactive.wsj.com/edition/resources/documents/help.htm`. (This page is for subscribers, but you can see samples of the information they offer.)

Finding Ticker Symbols and Stock Prices Online

A ticker symbol is the letter code representing the company's name in the listing for a publicly traded security. For example, if you want to find the current price for a share of Compaq's stock (as I do in the preceding section of this chapter), look for the company's ticker symbol — CPQ. Ticker symbols for companies traded on the NYSE have between one and three letters, stocks traded on NASDAQ have four or five letters.

Many commercial organizations provide ticker symbols and quotes on the Internet. Figure 7-2 shows one such company, called PC Quote. PC Quote (`www.pcquote.com`) is an excellent quote service that has a link to a symbol lookup page and other features that make it a good place to start researching stock prices. For example, you can type in the partial name of a company, and the PC Quote program automatically finds the ticker symbol.

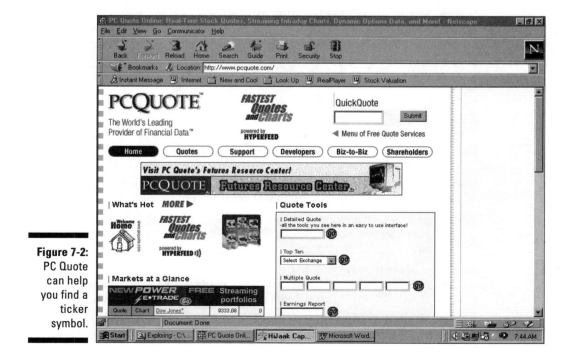

Figure 7-2: PC Quote can help you find a ticker symbol.

PC Quote offers five levels of service that range from $75 per month to $300 per month or $750 per year to $3,000 per year for real-time quotes, charts, and more. Free services include ticker symbol lookup, current stock prices and fundamental data, Market Guide company snapshot, Zack's Investment Research broker recommendations, annual earnings and earning estimates, current company news, charts of the company's stock price history and volume, and market indexes. You can search for stocks, bonds, futures, options, mutual funds, and indexes. You can also maintain as many as five portfolios of 20 ticker symbols each.

If the PC Quote program can't find the company's ticker symbol based on the partial name you enter, it suggests several candidates, including the ticker symbol, company name, and stock exchange. You can scroll through the companies until you find the one you want. Click on the company's name, and the program fetches the latest stock prices. (The free service is delayed 20 minutes. For subscribers, quotes are real-time.)

One of the advantages of PC Quote is that it can look up five ticker symbols at a time; just leave a space between each company's name or ticker symbol as you enter them. Many other quote services can accommodate only one ticker symbol or company name at a time.

PC Quote provides links to charts, news, earnings information, fundamental analysis data, and Securities and Exchange Commission (SEC) filings that detail the company's financial position. Stock price data includes the amount of the last sale, time of the last sale, net change, percent change, highest sale of the day, name of the exchange, previous closing price, opening price, and volume. PC Quote also shows the following information:

- **52 week high:** The highest stock price in the last year.
- **52 week low:** The lowest stock price in the last year.
- **Annual dividend:** Cash payments made to stockholders by the corporation.
- **Dividend yield:** The current annualized dividend paid on a share of common stock, expressed as a percentage of the current market price of the company's common stock.
- **Earnings per share (EPS):** The company's earnings for the last 12 months divided by the number of common shares outstanding.
- **Beta:** The relationship between the investment's returns and the market's average returns, expressed as a number with one decimal point.
- **Price/earnings ratio:** The price the market places on the firm's earnings. For example, if a firm has earnings per share of $2 and a stock price of $50, its price/earnings ratio is 25 ($50 ÷ $2).
- **Amount of shares outstanding:** The total number of shares the firm has issued to common stockholders.

In addition to PC Quote, two other online quote services are:

- **Data Broadcasting Online (**www.dbc.com**),** shown in Figure 7-3, retrieves as many as seven ticker symbols at one time. Quotes include last price, change, currency, percent change, opening price, day low, day high, previous day's closing price, and volume. The ticker symbol lookup requires you to click on the title of where the stock is traded (for example, North America) and then click on the first letter in the company's name. Next, you have to scroll through a list of all stocks beginning with that letter. DBC offers real-time quotes in three different packages. For access to wireless real-time quotes, it's $49 per month. Signal Online offers a real-time quotes service for active trading in stocks, futures, and options for $150 per month. StockEdge Online provides real-time continuous equity quotes via the Internet for $79 per month.

- **Briefing.com (**www.briefing.com**)** provides a free introductory service that includes market comments, quotes, charts, portfolio tracking, sector ratings, and an economic calendar. Briefing.com has two levels of premium service. The first level, called Stock Analysis, is $6.95 per month (with a free trial) and includes stocks on the move, technical stock analysis, earnings calendar, splits calendar, stock ratings, upgrade/downgrade reports, and company reports. The highest level of service, called Professional, is $25 per month (with a free trial) and includes many advanced investor services.

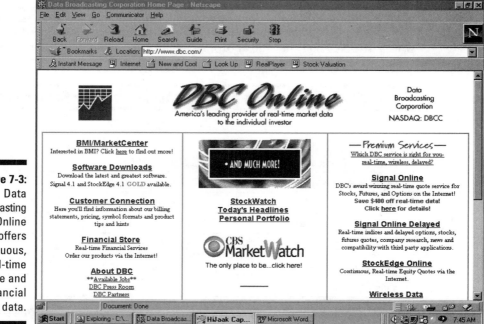

Figure 7-3:
Data Broadcasting Online offers continuous, real-time quote and financial data.

What Does the S&P 500 Have to Do with Anything?

You can measure how good or bad an investment is by comparing it to a market index. For example, the Standard & Poor's (S&P) 500 tracks a broad group of large capitalization stocks that are traded on the New York Stock Exchange and NASDAQ/AMEX. You can see the S&P Web site at www.stockinfo.standardpoor.com.

Each stock in the S&P 500 index is weighted by the relative market value of its outstanding shares. Overall, the index represents the performance obtained in the stock market for large capitalization stocks. (I define the term *large capitalization stocks,* or *large cap stocks,* later in this section.) This index provides performance information so that you can compare the stocks in your portfolio to "the market." If your returns are better than the market, you're doing well. If your returns are lower than the market, you need to re-evaluate your stock selections.

When you compare the performance of your stock to a market index, you can determine whether the stock outperformed the market, maintained the market rate, or underperformed. As Table 7-2 shows, however, not all market indexes are alike. For example, the Dow Jones Industrial Average is the most well-known index, but it includes only 30 large, mature, consumer-oriented companies. The Wilshire 5000 is the most comprehensive index of common stock prices regularly published in the U.S. and may be the best indicator of overall market performance. As you can see in Table 7-2, the S&P 500 tracks the performance of large capitalization stocks. In other words, the S&P 500 isn't the appropriate index for evaluating the performance of your small capitalization stock.

Table 7-2	Comparing Apples to Apples with the Right Index
Index	**Type of Security**
Dow Jones Industrial Average	Large capitalization stocks
Financial Times World	World stocks
Lehman Bros. Corporate Bonds	Corporate bonds
Lehman Bros. Government Bonds	U.S. Treasury bonds
Morgan Stanley EAFE	International stocks
Russell 2000	Small capitalization stocks
S&P 500	Large capitalization stocks
Wilshire 5000	Entire market

Source: Jim Jubak, *The Worth Guide to Electronic Investing* (1996, Harper Business, New York, NY).

Table 7-3 helps to explain why the S&P 500 may not be the appropriate index to compare to your small capitalization stock. *Capitalization* (or *cap*) is the total number of shares outstanding multiplied by the current stock price of those shares. For example, a firm with 1 million common shares outstanding at $55 per share has capitalization of $55 million, which makes the company a small cap firm. Table 7-3 shows a quick estimate of how the capitalization of different companies sorts out.

Table 7-3	Defining the Capitalization of Companies
Category	*Capitalization*
Micro Cap	Less than $50 million
Small Cap	$50 million to $500 million
Mid Cap	$500 million to $5 billion
Large Cap	More than $5 billion

According to Standard & Poor's, small capitalization stocks have outperformed large capitalization stocks over time. Over certain short-term periods, however, this may not hold true. From 1983 to 1990, small capitalization stocks, as a group, underperformed larger capitalization firms. From 1991 to 1993, both small and mid capitalization firms have outperformed large capitalization companies. During times of market volatility, small capitalization stocks tend to fall faster and harder than their bigger brethren. For example, between June 12 and August 23, 1996, NASDAQ was down 7.48 %. During the same time period, the MicroCap 50 was down 24.52 %.

Valuing Stocks

Stocks are more difficult to value than bonds. Bonds have a limited life and a stated payment rate. Common stocks don't have a limited life or an upper dollar limit on cash payments. This uncertainty makes stocks harder to value than bonds. Many ways exist to value common stock. Overall, the value of a stock is the present value of all its future dividends. However, common stockholders aren't promised a certain dividend each year. The dividend is based on the profitability of the company and the board of directors' decision to pay dividends to stockholders.

The second source of return for a stock is the increased market price of the stock. If the company decides not to pay dividends and reinvests profits in the firm, the company's future profits and dividends should grow. This additional value should be reflected in a stock price increase in the future.

Fundamental analysis seeks to determine the intrinsic value of securities based on underlying economic factors. It is the most widely accepted method for determining a stock's true value, which you can then compare to current prices to estimate current levels of mispricing. Fundamental analysts usually forecast future sales growth, expenses, and earnings.

If you are averse to math, then the Value Point Analysis Financial Forum at www.eduvest.com can help. The Value Point Analysis Financial Forum, shown in Figure 7-4, includes a community of investors who share information about their stock picks and analyses using the Web site's valuation model. To use the model, at the homepage click on Value Point Analysis Model. Just enter the 13 factors used by the Model into the fundamental analysis model. For additional insight, you can post your results and get feedback from others. All this at a price you can't beat — it's free.

To determine the intrinsic value (and what some people feel is the real value) of a stock, the Value Point Analysis Model uses 13 factors. (I define and discuss these factors in Chapter 11. Overall, the Value Point Analysis Model, which was designed in 1979, is used to evaluate a stock's worth in terms of its fundamental economic underpinnings and the general money market. The factors used are as follows:

1. **Corporate Name, Ticker Symbol, and Exchange that the stock is traded on.** This information is used to identify the specific stock you are analyzing.

2. **Number of the corporation's shares outstanding (in millions).** This number represents how many other common shareholders will be paid dividends.

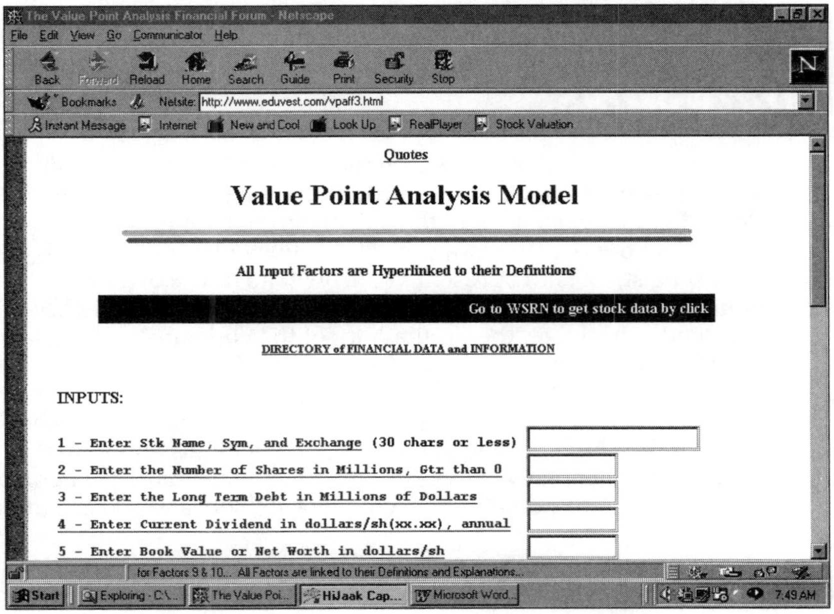

Figure 7-4:
Value Point
Analysis
calculates
the fair
value of a
stock so
that you
don't have
to do the
math.

3. **Long term debt (in millions).** Long term debt is the amount of any loans or bonds outstanding that mature in one year or more. Debts with terms of one to four years are considered short- or mid-term liabilities.

4. **Current dividend payout ($ per share).** This number is the annualized amount of this year's dividend. For example, imagine that we are in the middle of the second quarter. The first quarter dividend is $0.25. The company pays dividends each quarter. The annualized current dividend is $1.00. (In other words, 4 × $0.25 = $1.00).

5. **Book value or net worth ($ per share).** Many company reports have calculated this number for you. This value is often listed at the bottom of the balance sheet. The formula to calculate net worth is total assets less total liabilities. For example, total assets ($100 million) less total liabilities ($75 million) equals a net worth of $25 million. Net worth divided by the number of outstanding shares equals the book value per share.

6. **Projected earnings ($ per share).** Many company reports include expert forecasts of expected earnings. For example, if earnings for one year are $1.00 and next year the earnings are $1.10, the growth rate is 10%.

You can use experts' earnings forecasts or the amount you believe is correct for your analyses. Remember that each quarter you may see "earnings surprises," and individual investors have often outsmarted the so-called experts.

7. **Projected average growth in earnings (percent).** Without revenue (sales), you have no profits (earnings), and corporate earnings are what make stocks valuable. At the beginning of each company's annual report is a letter from the CEO. In this letter, the CEO usually states what he or she expects sales to be for the next year. You may or may not agree with this statement. Enter the percentage amount that, in your judgment and based on your research, is correct.

8. **Current earnings ($ per share).** Current earnings are often called Earnings Per Share and are calculated for you at the bottom of the income statement. In case you have to do your own math, take net after-tax income and divide it by the number of outstanding shares of common stock. For example, $1.5 million net after-tax income divided by 1 million shares is $1.50 per share.

9. **Current sales price ($ per share).** Check with an online quote server for the current sales price of a share of stock.

10. **Number of years the earning growth rate is expected to be sustained (1, 1.5, 2.0 years, etc.).** Some companies have variable growth rates and others have a steady increase that can go on for ten years or more. You need to decide whether the company will sustain its growth rate and for how long. This decision is a judgment call that investors have to make.

11. **Current yield of AAA Bonds (percent).** Luckily, the Value Point Model fills this number in for you.

12. **Projected change of AAA Bonds (percent, 100 basis points = 1%).** The Value Point Analysis Model enters a default amount here. If you agree with the amount, don't change it.

Valuation model input and results

No investor wants to pay more for a stock than it is worth. The following mini-table illustrates the input data and results for an online stock valuation using the Value Point Analysis Model, which can help you determine a stock's fair value. An example of user input and results looks like this:

Description	*Model Input*
1. Stock Name, Ticker Symbol, and Exchange	Example Corporation, EXCC, NYSE
2. The number of shares in millions, greater than 0	1010.00
3. The long term debt in millions of dollars	28200.00
4. Current dividend in $/sh (xx.xx), annual	8.00
5. Book value or net worth in dollars/sh	20.12
6. Projected earnings in $/sh, annual	8.80
7. Projected average growth in earnings (%)	5.00
8. Projected average growth in sales (%)	5.00
9. Current yield of AAA bonds, greater than 0	6.55
10. Projected change of AAA bonds(%)	0.00
11. Current earnings in $/sh, annual amount	8.17
12. Current price in $/sh, greater than 0	138.00
13. Number of years the earnings growth rate is expected to be sustained (for example, 1, 1.5, 2, and so on)	1.00

Description	Stock Evaluation Results
NAME SYM EXCH	Example name, Example symbol, NYSE
VALUE POINT ($/sh)	133.55
PROJECTED EARNINGS ($/sh)	8.80
PROJECTED P/E	15.18
VALUE POINT /CURRENT PRICE	0.97
CURRENT P/E	16.89
CURRENT YIELD (%)	5.80
CURRENT PRICE. ($/sh)	138.00
RELATIVE RISK FACTOR	0.90

This table indicates that the Value Point determined fair value for the stock is $133.55. Additionally, the model forecasts earnings of $8.80 and a projected P/E ratio of 15.18. The Value Point price is 0.97 of the stock's current price. The stock's current P/E ratio is 16.89. The current yield is 5.80 percent and the current price is $138. The model assigns a relative risk factor of 0.90 to its estimate of the stock's fair value.

In summary, this chart indicates that the stock's intrinsic value is $133.55. The stock is currently selling for $138.00. This amount is greater than $133.55, which indicates that the stock is overpriced. If I were you, I wouldn't even think about buying this expensive stock. However, if you already own the stock, it might be a good time to sell.

You can visit the following Web sites for more about fundamental analysis and valuing stocks:

- ✔ **J & E Research, Inc.** (www.jeresearch.com) is a group of PhDs and MBAs who specialize in financial modeling, research, and analysis. Try their Stock Analysis program. It uses an Excel spreadsheet that can assist you in completing the fundamental analysis of any stock.

- ✔ **Simtel** (http://ftp.urz.uni-heidelberg.de/ftp/pub/ simtel_win95/finance/) offers many downloadable financial management programs that can help value stocks and other securities.

Double-checking your Internet valuations

Working with a pen and pencil is okay, but using a spreadsheet program (Excel, Lotus 1-2-3, and so on) is quicker and better. I suggest that you create the table and enter the formulas shown below into your spreadsheet program. Let your computer do the math for you. Your table will look similar to Table 7-4, shown later in this chapter.

To use this fair value model, create a table with seven rows and five columns. The first column is a description; the next columns are for different stock factors in the next four years.

1. In the first row, first column, type **Current Sales Price.** In the next column, enter the current sales price. The next three cells leave blank.

2. In the second row, first column, type **Dividends (A).** In the next cell, enter the current dividend. In the following three cells, enter the projected dividends for the next year, the second year, and the third year.

3. In the third row, first column, type **Earnings (B).** In the next cell, enter the current earnings. In each of the next three cells, enter earnings forecasts for each of the next three years.

4. In the forth row, first column, type **Payout % (C) (A/B = C).** In the next cell, type **N/A** (not applicable). In the following cell (using the ex-ample), divide the next year's projected dividends (A) by the projected earnings (B) to create the payout percentage (C). The example uses $6.50 / $11.50 = .56 = 56%.

5. In the fifth row, first column, type **Earnings Growth.** In the next cell, type **N/A** (not applicable). In the following cell, enter the percentage of earnings growth from one year to the next. The example uses $11.50 (projected earnings) divided by $10.00 (current earning) equals 1.15, which is a growth rate of 15% over last year.

6. In the sixth row, first column, type **Investors Required Rate of Return.** You determine this amount. It is your personal level of return. The example uses 15% for all four years, but your requirements may be different.

7. In the seventh row, first column, type **Projected Growth Rate of Dividends and Earnings.** This is the estimate of how fast the company is growing. The example uses 10% for all four years.

Using the example shown in Table 7-4, just "plug and chug." That is, just "plug" the numbers used in the example into your spreadsheet program and let it do the work for you. Multiply the formula's Price/Earnings Ratio times the Current Dividend. The result is the stock's Fair Value. In our example the Fair Value is $110.00.

Summing it up, the formula's results are used to compare the fair market value to the current price of a stock. The example has a Fair Value of $110 and the stock's Current Sales Price is $109. If the current stock price is less than the fair market value, then the stock is undervalued and possibly a bargain. The stock in the example is selling for $1 less than the Fair Value and might be a good purchase. (If the current stock price is greater than the fair market value, then the stock is overvalued, which means it's too expensive and not a good buy.)

The type of valuation shown in the formula (and all financial valuation models used in this chapter) should be used with caution. Your good judgement is required for any successful investment. Paying the right price is only one aspect of good investing. For more information on how pick winners, see Chapter 13.

Table 7-4 shows how you can use some of the Value Point Analysis factors in a second model to determine the fair value of a stock. The financial experts have figured out the math, so all you need to do is "plug and chug."

Table 7-4	Calculating the Fair Market Value of a Stock			
Description	**1998**	**Projected 1999**	**Projected 2000**	**Projected 2001**
(1) Current sales price	$109.00	N/A	N/A	N/A
(2) Dividends (A)	6.00	6.50	7.26	7.99
(3) Earnings (B)	10.00	11.50	12.65	13.92
(4) Payout % (A/B = C)	N/A	56%*	60%	60%
(5) Earnings Growth	N/A	15%**	10%	10%
(6) Investors Required Rate of Return	15%	15%	15%	15%
(7) Projected Growth Rate of Dividends and Earnings	10%	10% 10%	10%	

*$6.50/$11.50 = .56 = 56% Percentage of dividends paid from earnings
**($11.50/$10.00=1.15 = 15% Increase in earnings over the previous year

The Formula:

Price/Earnings Ratio = [.56(1 + .15) /(1 + .15)] + [.60 (1 + .56) (1 + .10) / (1+.15) (1+.15)] + {.60 (1 + .56)(1 +.10) (1 + .10)/ (.15-.10)[(1 +.15) (1 + .15)]}

Price/Earnings Ratio = .644/1.15 + 1.030 / 1.322 + 1.1326 / .066

Price Earnings Ratio = .56 + .78 + 17.16 = 18.5

Fair Value = 18.5 (Price/Earnings Ratio) X $6.00 (Current Dividend) = $110.00

Source: Investments, 4th Edition, by William F. Sharpe and Gordon J. Alexander (1990)
Prentice Hall, Inglewood Cliffs, NJ.

Chapter 8

Internet Stock Screening

• •

• •

Stock screening boils down to finding the answer to one fundamental question: Which stock (among all stocks) should I buy right now? Of course, finding the answer to this question requires asking many more specific questions about stocks — questions that are difficult to answer without the help of computerized databases.

This chapter shows how you can use the Internet and PC-based stock screening tools to whittle down the universe of stocks to a manageable few candidates. You can then analyze your short list of stocks for gems that may bring you above-average returns. This chapter also tells you where to find daily or weekly results of prebuilt stock screens.

Finding the Best Stock Electronically

Screening is a process that permits investors to discover and distill information within a larger set of information. The Internet provides many screening tools that help you prospect stock issues. The goal of stock screens is to point out which stocks are worth your research and analysis time.

Some people believe that using a stock screen is like panning for gold. You use your computer to screen ("pan") for investment "nuggets" from a long list of possibilities. The online investor sets the objectives of any single screen. Different people get different results because no two people have exactly the same selection criteria or investment philosophy.

Overall, the benefit of stock screens is that they let you generate your own ideas — ideas that generate profits based on your investor savvy. Stock-screening programs allow you to go beyond finding good stock investments and assist you in finding the very best stocks.

To identify investment candidates, the stock screen uses your preset criteria, such as *growth* (stocks that are expanding faster than the market or their peers); *value* (stocks that have strong financial statements but are selling at prices below their peers); or *income* (stocks that provide higher than average dividends).

Depending upon the criteria you select, you may have to run several itera-tions of the stock screen. For example, your first screen may result in several hundred possibilities. Because you can't investigate and analyze so many candidates, you have to run a second screen of these results. This fine-tuning should lead to a manageable list of investment candidates that you can research and analyze — perhaps between 10 and 20 candidates. It is likely that you can quickly pare this number down by using common sense and your investor savvy.

Choosing the criteria for your first stock screen

Typically, you build a stock screen by accessing an online stock-screening tool and filling out an online form. I offer examples of the variables used in these forms later in this chapter, in the section "Important ratios for screen-ing stocks." The first stock screen that you develop may include quantifiable variables that you believe are the most important — for example:

- **Earnings growth:** The percentage of change between current earnings and earnings for the last quarter or last year.

- **Recent earnings surprises:** The difference between predicted and actual earnings.

- **Price/earnings (P/E) ratio:** The current price of the stock divided by the earnings per share — that is, net income divided by the total number of common shares outstanding. For example, value stocks have P/E ratios below 10 or 12, and growth stocks have P/Es above 20.

- **Dividends:** The annual cash dividend paid by the company.

- **Market capitalization:** The number of outstanding shares multiplied by the current stock price of those shares. Market capitalization is some-times abbreviated to *cap*. This value is a measurement of the company's size. Firms with high market capitalization are called "large cap" and companies with a low market capitalization are called "small cap."

Fine-tuning your stock screen

After you select your initial screening criteria, you click on Submit, Sort, or a similar command. A list of stock candidates appears. Often this list includes several hundred stocks. This number is still too large to research, so you should narrow this list by selecting more variables.

You may have some special knowledge about the industry you work in. You may have used certain products over the years and can use your knowledge to your advantage. However, keep in mind that a good product doesn't necessarily mean a good company. You may want to filter out companies that you just don't understand. You may also want to filter out companies about which you lack information. Without at least some basic information, you can't perform a complete analysis.

Using your stock screen results

After you complete your second stock screen and sort the data, you should have a list of about 10 to 20 companies. Start a file for each firm and begin to gather data for your analysis. At this point, you may discover that some companies aren't worth additional research — a finding that further reduces your short list. For example, the company may have filed for bankruptcy, or it may be targeted for federal investigation. Maybe the company recently paid a large fine for shady dealings, or the executive management was recently indicted for fraud, misconduct, or some other crime.

Check out the stock screen at Daily Stocks (www.dailystocks.net). After you reach the Daily Stocks home page, click either Advance Stock Screen or Basic Stock Screen. The basic stock screens are prebuilt. The advanced stock screens allow you to enter the industry and criteria that you feel are important. You can then query the database for fundamental and historical stock information by using your own investment criteria.

Important ratios for screening stocks

Every industry has its own language, and the financial industry is no exception. In the following sections, I define the key terms that the finance industry uses for stock-screening variables.

Figure 8-1 shows Hoover's StockScreener (www.stockscreener.com), which uses up to 20 variables and sorts the results alphabetically. Hoover's StockScreener screens more than 7,800 publicly traded companies, including major foreign companies and most NASDAQ small cap stocks. (For more information about small cap stocks, see Chapter 7.) Each stock screen's

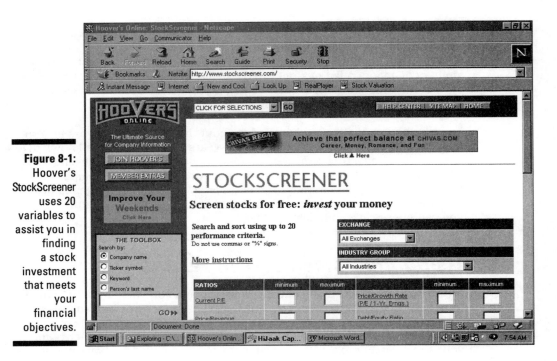

Figure 8-1:
Hoover's
StockScreener
uses 20
variables to
assist you in
finding
a stock
investment
that meets
your
financial
objectives.

results are hyperlinked to a Hoover's *company capsule* (a snapshot of the company), as well as the company's home page, stock quotes and charts, SEC filings, and investment news.

Beta

Beta is the measurement of market risk. The beta is the relationship between investment returns and market returns. Risk-free Treasury securities have a beta of 0.0. If the beta is negative, the company is inversely correlated to the market — that is, if the market goes up, the company's stock tends to go down. If a stock's volatility is equal to the market, the beta is 1.0. In this case, if the stock market increases 10 percent, the stock price increases 10 percent. Betas greater than 1.0 indicate that the company is more volatile than the market. For example, if the stock is 50 percent more volatile than the market, the beta is 1.5.

Book value

Book value is the original cost, less depreciation of the company's assets, less the outstanding liabilities. (*Depreciation* is the means by which an asset's value is expensed over its useful life for federal income tax purposes.)

Cash flow to share price

The ratio of *cash flow to share price* is the company's net income plus depreciation (expenses not paid in cash) divided by the number of shares outstanding. For companies that are building their infrastructure (such as cable companies or new cellular companies) and, therefore, don't yet have earnings, this ratio may be a better measure of their value than earnings per share (EPS).

Current ratio

Current ratio is current assets divided by current liabilities. A current ratio of 1.00 or greater means that the company can pay all current obligations without using future earnings.

Debt to equity ratio

To determine the *debt to equity ratio,* divide the company's total amount of long-term debt by the total amount of equity. (*Equity* is defined as the residual claim, by stockholders of company assets after creditors and preferred stockholders have been paid.) This ratio measures the percentage of debt the company is carrying. Many firms average a debt level of 50 percent. Debt to equity ratios greater than 50 percent may indicate trouble. That is, if sales decline, the firm may not be able to pay the interest payments due on its debt.

Dividends

Dividends are paid quarterly out of retained earnings. However, some high-growth companies reinvest earnings and don't pay dividends.

Dividend yield

Dividend yield is the amount of the dividend divided by the most current stock price. You can use dividends as a valuation indicator by comparing them to the company's own historical dividend yield. If a stock is selling at a historically low yield, it may be overvalued. Companies that don't pay a dividend have a dividend yield of zero.

Earnings per share (EPS)

Earnings are one of the stock's most important features. After all, the price you pay for a stock is based on the future earnings of the company. The consistency and growth of a company's past earnings indicate the likelihood of stock price appreciation and future dividends. *Earnings per share* is often referred to as EPS.

Market capitalization

Market capitalization is calculated by multiplying the number of outstanding shares times the current stock price of those shares. Market capitalization is sometimes called *market value.*

P/E ratio

You calculate the *price/earnings ratio* by dividing the price of the stock by the current earnings per share. A low P/E ratio indicates that the company may be undervalued. A high P/E ratio indicates that the company may be overvalued.

Price-to-book value

Price-to-book value is tangible assets less liabilities, and the price-to-book value is the current price of the stock divided by the book value. If the current stock price is below the price-to-book value, the stock may be a real bargain. On the other hand, impending unprofitability may be the reason.

Return on equity (ROE)

Return on equity (ROE) is usually equity earnings as a proportion of net worth. You divide the most recent year's net income by shareholders equity (*shareholders equity* is assets minus liabilities) to calculate ROE.

Shares outstanding

The term *shares outstanding* refers to the total number of shares for a company's stock. To determine the firm's outstanding shares, you need the most recent data. The shares outstanding can be calculated by taking issued shares on the balance sheet and subtracting treasury stock. *Treasury stock* is stock issued but not outstanding by virtue of being held (after it is repurchased) by the firm.

Watching Out for Investment Risks

No one invests in securities to lose money. However, each security has its own fine print. The Securities and Exchange Commission (www.sec.gov) has put together a list of some things to watch for:

- ✔ The higher the return, the greater the risk. You may lose some or all of your investment.

- ✔ Some investments can't be easily sold or converted to cash. For example, you may have a hard time selling a municipal bond before it matures.

- ✔ If you want to sell an investment quickly, you may have to pay some penalties or transaction charges.

- ✔ Investments in new companies or companies that don't have a long history may involve greater risk.

- ✔ Securities, like mutual funds, are not Federal Deposit Insurance Corporation (FDIC) insured.

✔ The securities you own may change due to corporate reorganizations, mergers, or third-party actions. You may be asked to sell your current shares, or you may be offered new shares due to this activity. Make certain that you understand the complexities of this investment decision before you act.

✔ Past performance of a security is no guarantee of future performance.

Using Online Stock Screens

Web-based stock screens can require between 2 and 30 variables. Their computerized stock databases can include anywhere from 1,100 stocks to more than 9,000 stocks. Additionally, some computerized stock databases are updated daily, weekly, or monthly. The best stock screen is the one that includes your personal investment criteria. A few examples follow:

✔ **Market Guide's NetScreen** (www.marketguide.com) allows you to screen for stocks by using any of 20 variables. To access the stock screen, go to the home page and click Screening. This stock screen features comparisons of variables, user-defined variables, comparison of variables to a constant, use of a variable more than once, and use of operators (greater than, less than, equals, and so on). The database is updated weekly. The stock screen was started in September 1997. Your screening results are limited to no more than 200 companies at a time.

✔ **IQ Net Basic Stock Scan** (www.iqc.com/scan) uses less than 12 variables to screen stocks. Stock data is updated daily, about 2 $\frac{1}{2}$ hours after the close of the U.S. markets. You can use this Web site for free. The company also has a more advanced product called IQ Chart Profit Tools. This online tool provides real time technical charts, a technical stock scan, and IQC zone indicators. The monthly subscription fee is $24.95, with a free two-week trial.

✔ **MSN Investor** (investor.msn.com) shows how to use 12 prebuilt stock screens, how to set up and maintain the screens, customize displays, import or export data, compare stock screens, and create sample searches. The Investment Finder stock screen searches 8,000 companies to locate securities that meet your specific criteria. The program uses dozens of variable combinations. The monthly subscription fee is $9.95, with a free one-month trial.

✔ **ResearchMag** (www.researchmag.com) requires you to register (for free) before you begin. The stock screen has 12 basic variables that screen more than 9,000 stocks. The service is free of charge, but you need to subscribe to use the advanced stock screen. Subscriptions are based on the number of reports you use per year. Rates start at $55 for 25 of any combination of three reports.

Using Stock Screening Software

PC-based stock screens use their own stock screening software and databases. The advantage of these programs over Web-based stock screens is that they use hundreds of variables to screen stocks. I describe a few examples in this section.

Investor's Prospector (www.better-investing.org/computer/ software.html) is a product of the National Association of Investors Corporation (NAIC). The NAIC (www.naic.com) has negotiated an agreement with Standard & Poors to provide stock selection data for more than 3,500 stocks traded on the New York Stock Exchange, the American Stock Exchange, and NASDAQ. The NAIC software imports data directly from the S&P database. Each company has its own datafile. This special datafile has 5 to 10 years of fundamental data, S&P Analyst estimates for 5-year EPS growth, and current year EPS. Datafiles are updated quarterly. Annual subscriptions start at $179 for NAIC computer group members, $209 for NAIC members, and $244 for nonmembers.

Equis International — MetaStock (www.equis.com) is a technical analysis software product that includes a stock search engine, real-time charting, and an analysis tool. The program is compatible with Microsoft Office 97, which means that you can download data to an Excel spreadsheet or embed charts in Word programs. You set the rules to identify trends and highlight important ratios. Click on a stock price, and the program links your Internet browser to a free Web site that provides the current stock prices. When you purchase the software, you receive a CD-ROM with a historical database of more than 2,100 different U.S. securities, Canadian stocks, mutual funds, futures, and indexes. The price of MetaStock 6.5 for Windows is $349.

Figure 8-2 shows the home page of MetaStock software. The makers of MetaStock use their software program to make stock recommendations. For example, they show the top five stocks that had the biggest gains (more than $5 a share) over the last week. Gains are measured on a percentage basis. For example, a $20 stock that increases in price to $25 has a $5 gain or a 25 percent gain.

American Association of Individual Investors (www.aaii.org) has a downloadable library of stock software and screens for members. Its Stock Investor program and database provides fundamental data for 7,000 stocks and includes a screening engine with more than 350 variables for each company, covering eight quarters of quarterly data. Data includes earnings estimates for 4,000 companies and information about business sectors and industries. Annual subscriptions are $99 for members and $150 for nonmembers.

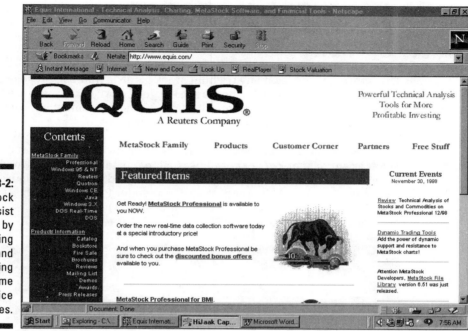

Figure 8-2:
MetaStock
can assist
you by
screening
stocks and
providing
real-time
price
analyses.

Telescan's Pro Search Module (www.telescan.com**)** allows you to target
your best investment opportunities with its stock-screening program. Select
from 207 variables to isolate stocks that have the highest performance
based on your investment goals. The program includes the Analyzer Module, which performs in-depth technical and fundamental analysis using data
from Telescan's 20-year historical database. The program, which sells for
$395, also includes Quotelink, a data downloader, and Optimizer programs.

Telescan provides many screen results of the Telescan Prospector online.
This Web page shows the results of various Telescan stock searches. The
company computes more than 25 million search combinations every week
to find the searches that have worked the best or worst over the last 12
months. The latest searches are available every Monday. The firm displays
the best 25 stocks for categories that include NASDAQ stocks, NYSE stocks,
AMEX stocks, micro cap stocks, small cap stocks, medium cap stocks, large
cap stocks, all stocks, and industry groups.

Using Those Terrific Prebuilt Stock Screens

The Internet provides many prebuilt stock screens that use preselected criteria. Some of these screens may make your work easier because they already include the investment criteria that you feel is most important. In the following paragraphs, I describe a few examples.

Quicken.com — Popular Stock Searches (www.quicken.excite.com/ investments/stocks/search/) uses a large database that's owned by an independent financial information company called Disclosure. Figure 8-3 shows the Quicken.com prebuilt stock screen for Popular Searches (at the Search entry page, just click on Popular Searches).

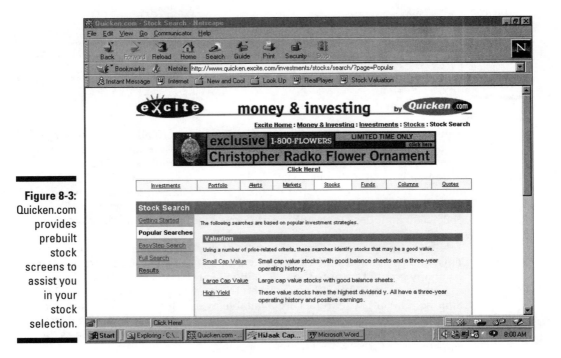

Figure 8-3: Quicken.com provides prebuilt stock screens to assist you in your stock selection.

Quicken's Stock Evaluator compares your search results and explains the benefits and limitations of using each variable as a stock selection criterion. The prebuilt stock screens are divided into three categories:

- ✔ **Popular Searches:** Uses preset criteria that match the most popular investing strategies.

- ✔ **EasyStep Search:** Walks you through six steps that use important variables one step at a time. Each step provides definitions about the variable and shows why the variable is important in your stock search.

- ✔ **Full Search:** Uses 33 variables on one page and many advanced search options.

MarketPlayer (www.marketplayer.com) requires your free registration. After you register, click Screening. MarketPlayer provides instructions, sample screens, and an advanced stock screening engine. Instructions for using the engine are easy to understand, but you should allow some time for getting used to the program. MarketPlayer, shown in Figure 8-4, features simple and industry stock screens that you may find useful. With over 100 screening ratios, MarketPlayer offers a unique screening environment for the serious investor. (If you're an experienced online investor, the prebuilt sample screens may provide some ideas about how you can improve your own screens.)

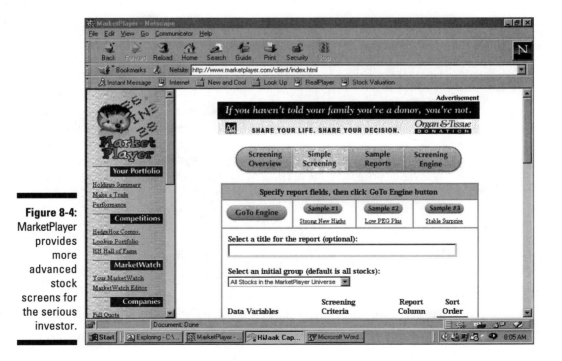

Figure 8-4:
MarketPlayer
provides
more
advanced
stock
screens for
the serious
investor.

The Motley Fool (www.fool.com) offers a weekly discussion of its stock screens. Motley Fool screens for companies that missed or beat analysts' consensus estimates by 9 percent or more. Stocks are listed alphabetically as well as by descending percentages.

Determining Your Own Investment Criteria for Stock Screens

This section outlines several ways to set up stock screens that may be beneficial for your information mining. I offer a few examples of ways that you can build stock screens to discover specific categories of stocks. I've chosen the categories of growth stocks, income stocks, and value stocks for these examples.

Screening for growth stocks

Growth stocks are expanding at rates faster than their counterparts. They have different degrees of risk and are a way of betting on the future. Your stock screen for growth stocks may consider the following criteria:

- **Basic growth:** Any stock that has earnings growth of 15 percent or more in one year.

- **Long-term growth:** Any stocks that grew 15 percent or more in one year over the past five years. (Companies must have historical EPS records of over five years.)

- **Earnings for growth:** Stocks that have a price-to-earnings ratio that is equal to or less than the growth rate of the stock plus its dividend yield.

- **Aggressive growth companies with low P/E ratios:** Stocks with annual earnings growth of more than 24 percent and P/E ratios of less than 15. (P/E ratios of less than 15 are preferable, but rare in the current market.)

Screening for income stocks

Income stocks tend to be stodgy, boring, slow-growth companies that are steady income producers. You may want to include dividend yield in your stock screen for income stocks. For example, you may screen for any stocks with a dividend yield that's at least equal to the S&P 500 and never falls below 4 percent. (This criterion rules out growth stocks that don't pay dividends.)

Screening for value stocks

Value stocks are companies that have strong financial statements and good earnings but are traded at stock prices that are less than their industry peers. Some criteria that you may want to include in your stock screen for value stocks include the following:

- **Book value:** Stocks for which the book value of the company is less than 80 percent of the average S&P 500 stock.

- **Debt-equity ratio:** Stocks for companies with a debt/equity ratio of 50 percent or less.

- **Price-earnings ratio:** Stocks for which the average of the company's five-year earnings is not less than 70 percent of the average P/E ratio of the S&P 500. Don't include stocks with a P/E ratio greater than 12. (A low P/E ratio may indicate that the stock is selling at a bargain price.)

- **Underpriced stocks:** Three criteria exist for this stock screen:
    - Small cap stocks with *quick ratios* (current assets less inventory divided by current liabilities) greater than 1.0 and return on assets (ROA) greater than 0.0
    - A price to earnings ratio (P/E ratio) that is half of that industry's average
    - A price-to-book value ratio of 80 percent or less, and a price-to-sales ratio of 33 percent or less

Screening for Investment Bargains

Investors are always searching for a *competitive edge* that will allow them to *beat the market*. (Beating the market is usually defined as selecting stocks that outperform, that is, provide greater returns, than the S&P 500 Index.) The following are several stock screen variables that you may want to factor in to your stock selection strategy. However, keep your risk tolerance level. After all, you want to sleep at night.

Stocks selling at below book value

Some stock screens allow you to sort for stocks that have a current selling price that is below book value. *Book value* is defined as the depreciated value of a company's assets (original cost less accumulated depreciation) less the outstanding liabilities.

Purchasing stocks selling at below book value may be a bargain hunter's dream but will require additional research on your part. A company's total assets are often the accounting values of assets purchased over time; in other words, the historical price of an asset less depreciation. For example, the firm may have fully depreciated a 20-year-old building. The sales value of the building may be in the millions, but the listed value listed on the balance sheet may be zero. (This difference causes the book value to be understated.) Or the building may have environmental problems (due to improper disposal of industrial wastes, for example) that will cost the owners millions to clean up. In this case, the book value is overstated.

The prudent investor determines why a company is selling at below book value before he or she purchases the stock. Check out these good online sources for this type of data: Companies Online (www.companiesonline.com) and the company's annual, quarterly, and other miscellaneous reports filed with the Securities and Exchange Commission (www.sec.gov).

Try different approaches to your research. For example, you may be able to discover some interesting facts about the company if it was a failed merger or acquisition candidate. If a large corporation or an investment bank didn't want to buy the company, you may want to follow their lead.

Securities selling below liquidation value

Your bargain hunting may guide you to screening for stocks that are selling below their liquidation value. *Liquidation value* of a company is defined as the dollar sum that could be realized if an asset were sold independently of the going concern. (Assets are listed in company annual reports. Good Internet sources for these reports include Disclosure at www.disclosure.com and CompanyLink at www.companylink.com.) For example, say that no market demand exists for the company's hula-hoops or buggy-whips, and the company discontinues that product line. The machinery used to manufacture this product still bears value. The appraised value of the manufacturing equipment is determined as a separate collection. The values of the firm's ongoing or discontinued operations are not factored into this price.

Stocks selling at below liquidation value may be valuable, but you should consider the priority of claims if the company is forced into bankruptcy. Claims against company assets are paid in the following order: (1) secured creditors, (2) expenses incurred for administration and bankruptcy costs, (3) expenses incurred after filing bankruptcy, (4) salaries and commissions (not to exceed a set amount) that were earned within three months of filing bankruptcy, (5) federal, state, and local taxes, (6) unsecured creditors, (7) preferred stock, and (8) finally you, the common stockholder.

Stocks with low P/E ratios

The price/earnings (P/E) ratio is the current price of a stock divided by the earning for one share of stock and is the value that the investment community places on $1 of the company's earnings. For example, if the current price of the stock is $60 and the earning per share (for the last 12 months) is $3, then the P/E ratio is 20 ($60/$3). *Note:* In Wall Street Speak, the earnings per share (EPS) for the last 12 months when used in the preceding formula is often called the *trailing P/E ratio.* You are likely to see the trailing P/E ratio listed as a variable in the online stock screens.

P/E ratios vary by industry, so unless you find out the industry average, you can't determine whether a stock has a low P/E ratio . Luckily, Hoovers (www.hoovers.com) Company Capsules and Zack's Company Reports (www.zacks.com) provide this information for free. When analyzing a P/E ratio you want to look at the trend of the company's P/E ratio over the last five to seven years. Companies that the investment community expects to grow will have higher P/E ratios that others in the same industry.

Bargain hunters may want to set the variables in their stock screens for low P/E ratios because a company with a P/E ratio of 20 is a more expensive stock than one with a P/E ratio of 10. However, companies with low P/E ratios may be *cheap* for good reason. For example, one way to analyze the P/E ratio is to compare it to the company's growth rate. The company's P/E ratio and growth rate should be equal. (**Remember:** The stock price is the present value of all the future earnings.) Therefore, if the P/E ratio is low, the company may be plagued by slow growth.

What a low P/E ratio is or what it indicates may be difficult to determine. For example, the company may have a low P/E ratio because investors are bailing out, which can drive the stock price down and make the stock appear inexpensive. Say that a $60 stock drops to $30 per share. The P/E ratio will be reduced to 10 ($30/$3). The stock is now half-priced, but it may not be a good purchase if the company is headed towards bankruptcy or has a major problem.

Companies reporting deficits

You may want to set up your stock screen to determine which companies in a certain cyclical industry are reporting deficits (losses). Cyclical stocks are dependent on external environmental factors, such as the national economy, housing sales, and consumer confidence. You can check out these good online sources of industry information: Lexis-Nexis (www.lexis-nexis.com) and US STAT (www.stat-usa.gov). Cyclical stocks have peaks and valleys (low points) in their revenues, profits, and stock prices. These peaks and valleys can mean that some cyclical companies with strong foundations may be experiencing flat earnings or deficits due to their business cycles.

Be certain that you understand the company's business operations. High fliers can crash and burn. For example, you may want to avoid companies that have no earnings and stock prices based on planned new products, corporate restructuring, or strategic partnering.

The trick with cyclical stocks is to purchase the stock when it's in a valley in the cycle and sell when it's near the peak. A good indicator that the upward part of the cycle may be about to begin is when the P/E ratio is high and the EPS (earnings per share) is low. Other external environmental factors may indicate that the stock is approaching its peak. For example, a sudden drop in housing starts might indicate that your shares in a furniture company are near their peak and it's time to sell.

Prospective turnaround candidates

Using stock screen variables to locate companies that are laggards in sales, earnings, and profits is one way to locate turnaround candidates. The value of investing in turnarounds is that the stock may increase two or three times as the company becomes successful. (A rare few companies will increase ten times. The 40 times increase for Chrysler may be the biggest increase on record.)

Early stage companies often have ups and downs, but mature companies that have problems frequently don't get a second chance to improve their fundamentals. These fallen angels often have problems with inconsistent product quality, respond slowly to changing market conditions, have high operating costs, low employee involvement, poor customer service, and inadequate methods of allocating resources. Often, management is negative, risk-adverse, and bureaucratic. All these factors prevent the company from becoming competitive. The result is that analysts and investors are waiting for a turnaround that never appears.

The preceding situation highlights how timing is everything when investing in troubled companies. The company has to survive long enough to get well. For troubled companies, a larger, more mature company that owns real estate and has cash on hand is superior to a small company with limited resources and rented office space. After all, the company needs to be solvent in order to make a comeback.

Don't be fooled by quick profits when the company starts slashing budgets and implementing a recovery plan. These short-term gains will likely disappear as customers become wary of doing business with the troubled company. The comeback road is bumpy. Many companies get off to false starts and then stumble. Some pick themselves up again.

Chapter 9

Going with Bonds: Which Type Is Best for You?

In This Chapter

▶ Understanding the basics of bonds

▶ Finding online information about the four general types of bonds

*B*onds are similar to stocks because you make money in two ways. The first way is *capital appreciation;* the bond increases in value if interest rates decline, which means that you can sell the bond at a *premium.* That is, you can sell the bond for more money than you paid for it. (By the way, the profit you make is called *capital gains.*) The second way to make money is the periodic interest payment that you receive during the bond term.

Bonds are often called *fixed income investments.* They represent debts or IOUs from the issuer. The amount of the loan is the *principal;* the compensation given to the investor is called *interest payments.* In this chapter, I show you how the Internet provides information about Treasury, federal agency, municipal, and corporate bond auctions and offerings, historical and current yield rates, education, tax information, and more.

Bonds can be virtually risk-free and guaranteed by the U.S. government, or they can be speculative, high-flyers that can crash and go into default. You may decide that these investments aren't for you, but if you own a mutual fund, you may already be invested in the bond market.

Generic Features of Bonds

Bonds are simply defined as long-term promissory notes from an issuer. Issuers tend to be large corporations, like the federal government and its agencies, and state and local governments. Bonds are contracts that state the interest payment (coupon rate) to be paid to the investor, the *par value* (principal or face value of the bond), and when the par value will be repaid to the investor. Overall, bonds provide the investor with security and a fixed income under a legal contract.

Bondholders want to minimize the business, market, and political risks of investing. From the date of issue the bond's rate of interest payments (the coupon rate) and maturity date don't change. The price of the bond (the par or face value of the bond when it's issued) can vary during the bond term depending on changes in interest rates. Generally, if interest rates increase, the bond's value falls. On other hand, if interest rates decline, then the value of the bond increases.

A different type of bond contract is a *variable rate note* or *floating-rate note*. A few corporate bonds have floating rates. The coupon rate is fixed for a short period of time and then varies with a specific short-term rate (such as a Treasury bill). With floating rate notes, the investor's interest payments go up and down rather than the price of the bond.

Corporate and municipal bonds are usually purchased through a broker. Treasury securities (bills, notes, and bonds) can be purchased without a broker directly from the government.

The most popular bonds are often long-term debt that matures in ten or more years. A bond is a commitment by a public or private entity to pay the bondholder certain interest payments at specific times and the *principal* (the original investment) at the end of a specified time period.

Bonds have clearly stated terms and maturity dates. These terms can be as short as 13 weeks or as long as 30 years. Sometimes you can't recover your investment until the bond matures. If you have to sell the bond before it matures, you may have a difficult time finding a buyer. The broker's commission takes some of your return, and you lose the sizable return you were going to receive on your original investment. Bonds have their own terminology that you need to understand:

- ✔ **Par value:** Refers to the face value of the bond and the amount returned to the bondholder at maturity. Most corporate bonds have a par value of $1,000, many federal, state, and local bonds have par values of $5,000 or $10,000.

- ✔ **Coupon interest rate:** Indicates what percentage of the par value of the bond is paid out annually in the form of interest.

- ✔ **Maturity:** Indicates the length of time until the bond issuer returns the face value to the bondholder and terminates the bond.

- ✔ **Current yield:** Refers to the ratio of the annual interest payment to the bond's current selling price. For example, assume that the bond has an 11 percent coupon rate, a par value of $1,000, and a market value of $700. It has a current yield of 15.71 percent ([$0.11 \times \$1,000] \div \$700$).

> ✔ **Yield to maturity:** Indicates how much you would pay today for the future benefits of the bond. Yield to maturity is the investor's required rate of return used as the discount rate to arrive at the current value of a bond. (The current value of a bond is determined by the present value of future interest payments and the repayment of the principal at maturity.)

Special benefits and exposures

As evidence that there are no guarantees with bonds, the 1994 bond market experienced worldwide losses of around $1.5 trillion. (Among other things, this was attributed to the Peso Crisis in Mexico.) Since that time, the market has radically changed. It's no longer the sleepy market it was before derivatives and similar financial instruments were introduced (see Bonus Chapter 3 for more information). However, if you know what you are doing, bonds can provide a fixed cash flow over time. A fixed cash flow from bonds is important if you are planning a comfortable retirement.

The benefit of a fixed cash flow isn't cost free. Bond returns are usually lower than other investments because of the risk and return tradeoff. (High risk brings high returns and low risk brings low returns.) Bonds are contracts for a certain amount of interest payments along with repayments of the principal at the end of a specified period. The investor can make financial plans based on these contracts. Stocks have no guarantees (or limits) on dividend payments and the sales price. A stock's dividends and value can skyrocket or plummet.

Table 9-1 shows the historical risk and return tradeoffs of different types of bonds compared to different types of stocks over the last 50, 20, 10 and 5 years. For instance, a comparison of the annualized returns of stocks to corporate bonds for the last five years indicates that investing in stocks would have delivered twice the returns of bonds (a return of 20.2 percent versus a return of 9.2 percent). And stock investments provided three times the return of treasury securities (a return of 20.2 percent versus a return of 6.4 percent).

Table 9-1   Historical Returns for Different Types of Investments

| | Annualized returns for periods ended 12/31/97 | | | |
	50 Years (%)	20 Years (%)	10 Years (%)	5 Years (%)
Small company stocks	14.9	17.7	16.5	19.4
Large company stocks	13.1	16.7	18.1	20.2
Corporate bonds	6.1	10.3	10.9	9.2

(continued)

Table 9-1 *(continued)*

| | Annualized returns for periods ended 12/31/97 | | | |
	50 Years (%)	20 Years (%)	10 Years (%)	5 Years (%)
3-5 year treasury bonds	6.0	9.5	8.3	6.4
Treasury bills	5.0	7.3	5.4	4.6
U.S. inflation	3.9	4.9	3.4	2.6

Source: T. Rowe Price (www.troweprice.com/retirement/historical.html)

For more information about investing in bonds see:

- ✔ **Consumer Guide to Investing** (`afs.financialsecurity.org/guide/ investing/bonds.html`) Investment Bonds 101 discusses the characteristics of bonds and what rate of returns the investor can expect.

- ✔ **Corporate Bonds** (`www.vanguard.com/educ/module1/m1_3_2.html`) at the Vanguard Learning Center provides consumer information about the ABCs of Bonds, different types of bonds, quality ratings, the risks and rewards of bonds, and bond mutual funds.

Using the Internet to find new bond offerings

New bond issues generally provide a slightly better yield than comparable issues of existing bonds offered on the secondary market. That's because bond issuers are anxious to get the new bonds sold. Following, I list online sources for information about new bond offerings:

- ✔ **The Bond Buyer** (`www.bondbuyer.com`) covers the municipal bond market in minute detail. The online publication provides daily municipal bond news, analysis, and commentary. Five bureaus and 30 reporters cover the bond market geographically and topically. This online edition of The Bond Buyer covers new municipal bond offerings, city and state officials involved in issuing debt, underwriters and underwriting, brokerages, bond lawyers, and more. The subscription-based service has a free 30-day trial and the subscription rate is $1,550 per year. (A printed version of The Bond Buyer is also available.)

- ✔ **Fidelity Brokerage Services** (`www.fidelity.com`) at the home page click Site Map. Next, at Through an Advisor, click Products and Education. Then click on the type of bond that interests you. This section of the Fidelity Web site also includes new and daily offerings of Treasury securities and municipal bonds.

- ✔ **Municipal Trading Association** (`www.munitrading.com`) provides documents, news, developments, and financial information to the high yield bond trader. This site also features pages where municipal bond traders can publish new issues information, inventory offerings, and general information about their companies. Just click New Issues to see what members are offering.

✔ **Salomon Smith Barney Municipal New Issues Calendar** (www.smithbarney.com/prod_svc/bonds/munical.html), shown in Figure 9-1, provides a free listing of new municipal free issues and bond issues that Smith Barney is involved in or intends to bid on its own, or as part of a syndicate. (A syndicate is a group of investment bankers that jointly share in the underwriting, distribution, selling, and management of a new issue). The bonds listed at the Web site are updated weekly but are subject to prior sale (and may not be available).

Finding bond indexes and historical data online

Bond indexes are designed to represent either the average yield to maturity or the average price on a portfolio of bonds that have certain similar characteristics. Historical data can also provide bond performance insights. The Internet offers several sources for these averages and historical data. Here are a few examples:

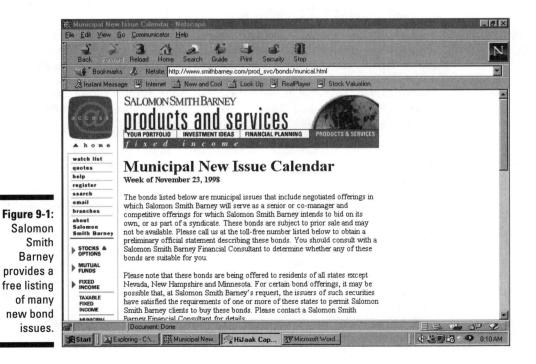

Figure 9-1: Salomon Smith Barney provides a free listing of many new bond issues.

✔ **Moody's Investor Services** (www.moodys.com) provides long-term corporate bond yield averages based on bonds with maturities of 20 years and above. Corporate bond averages are sorted into average corporate, average industrial and average public utility groups, and by bond ratings.

✔ **Bondsonline** (www.bondsonline.com/bcgraphs.htm) provides charts and historical data that compare various bond market sectors and stock market indexes — for example, a comparison of the 30-year Treasury bonds, 10-year Treasury notes, and the Dow Jones Industrial Average. This site also offers a comparison of tax-free municipal yields as a percentage of U.S. Treasury yields.

✔ **Federal Reserve Bank of St. Louis** (www.stls.frb.org) lists the monthly interest rate for each type of Treasury security. Files for specific Treasuries (for example, the one-year Treasury bill rate — auction average) and a downloadable zipped file that contains all the Interest Rate Series (historical archives of interest rate data) are available.

Risks and stability

Moody's Investor Services (www.moodys.com), Standard & Poor's Corporation (www.standardpoor.com), Fitch Investor Services, L.P. (www.fitch.com), and Duff & Phelps Credit Rating Company (DCR) (www.dcr.com) are the best-known and most prominent credit-rating agencies. These companies assess the risk of bonds by studying all the bond's information and then assign the bond a rank that reflects the issuer's ability to meet the promised principal and interest payments. This rating may change during the life of the bond, and a change in the rating can dramatically change the value of the bond. All the credit rating companies rate bonds in descending alphabetical order from A to C, but each company uses a somewhat different letter scheme.

Figure 9-2 shows a comparison of the leading bond rating agency's alpha-numeric grading systems. See Equity Analytics at www.e-analytics.com/bonds/bond19.htm.

Ratings are not absolute measures of quality. Each rating takes into consideration factors such as the issuer's past earnings record and future earnings expectations, the financial condition of the issuer, the nature of the issuer's business, the backing for a particular issue, and the rating agencies appraisals of the issuer's management.

The rating agencies warn investors that a bond's rating isn't a "buy" recommendation. However, due to the risk-reward ratio, bonds with higher ratings offer lower yields; bonds with lower ratings, which represent a riskier investment, offer higher yields.

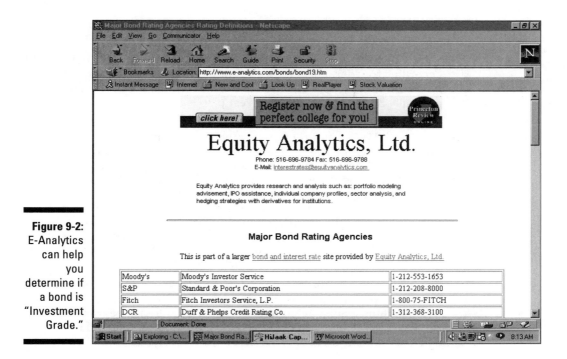

Figure 9-2:
E-Analytics
can help
you
determine if
a bond is
"Investment
Grade."

How Small Investors Can Make Money with Fixed Income Investments and Bonds

Banks and savings and loan associations have developed new ways of keeping customer assets in their financial institutions. They offer a variety of investment plans that provide higher returns than traditional fixed rate savings accounts. For example, many savings and loan associations allow their customers to invest in commercial paper (uninsured promissory notes to large business entities) instead of certificates of deposit (an insured type of time deposit). The following shows four types of fixed income and bond investments that are targeted for small investors seeking greater returns:

✔ **Fixed Rate Certificates:** In the past, federal regulations required a minimum deposit amount of $1,000 with maturities of at least four years for fixed rate certificates of deposit (CDs). Financial institutions now set their own minimum amounts (which often range between $100 and $500) for time periods ranging from three months, six months, one year, two years, and five years.

Banks impose hefty penalties for early withdrawals. These fees can wipe out any gains you may have made.

✔ **Small Saver Certificates:** Deposits do not require any minimum amount according to federal banking laws, but many banks have established a minimum requirement of deposits of $100 to $500. Maturities are generally 30 months and the interest paid is slightly below the 30-month treasury yield. Expect high penalties for early withdrawals.

✔ **Six-Month Money Market Certificates:** These certificates are for investors with more cash (there is a $10,000 minimum) than time. Yields are higher than short-term money market certificates. The interest rate paid is generally slightly higher than the six-month Treasury bill rate. Like the savers certificate, the interest rate ceiling of six-month money market certificates is a floating interest rate until you purchase the certificate. After you purchase the certificate, the rate is locked until the certificate matures. When the certificate matures, you are free to reinvest (rollover) your investment. If the current treasury security rate is higher, you'll make more money.

✔ **Short-Term Bond Funds:** Purchasing short-term, no-load bond funds is one way investors can earn higher-than-passbook returns and still have lots of liquidity. Some bond funds even have limited check-writing privileges. (Writing a check is certainly more convenient and inexpensive than placing a sell order.)

With short-term bond funds, small investors tend to pay more for bonds than professional bond fund managers (who keenly watch every movement of the bond market). Bond funds come in two flavors: tax-free and taxable. If you are in a high-income bracket, tax-free bonds may be to your advantage. However, all of these benefits aren't cost-free. Investors will incur an annual fund management fee that averages 0.2 percent. (That is, $200 for every $100,000 invested in the fund).

Investors can enjoy the type of liquidity that bond funds offer and not pay management fees by purchasing Treasury securities directly from the government (see "The Four Basic Types of Bonds" next in this chapter for details). If you want to buy directly from the government but avoid doing the paperwork yourself, brokerages like Schwab can complete your transaction for about $50.

The Internet provides more information about fixed investments for small investors. You can discover online what the benchmark rates are and which financial institutions have the best deals. The following are a few examples:

✔ **Bank Rate Monitor (**www.bankrate.com**)** shows the average rates for money market accounts and certificates of deposits. Discover who has the best deals by checking the annual percentage yield for savings money market accounts, certificates of deposit, and treasury securities in your state. You may find that your current bank has a better money market rate than other banks in your area.

✔ **IBC's Money Fund Selector** (www.ibcdata.com/basics.htm) provides information about what a money fund is, the difference between taxable and tax-free money funds, a discussion about how safe money funds are, and how to read a money fund prospectus.

✔ **Money-rates.com** (www.money-rates.com), shown in Figure 9-3, has market updates; information about the economy; consumer interest rates; and investment rates for money market funds, certificates of deposit, Treasury securities, and special bank offerings.

The Four Basic Types of Bonds

Many organizations issue bonds, but the following types of organizations issue most bonds:

✔ The federal government (Treasury securities)

✔ Federal government agencies

✔ State and local government agencies (municipal bonds)

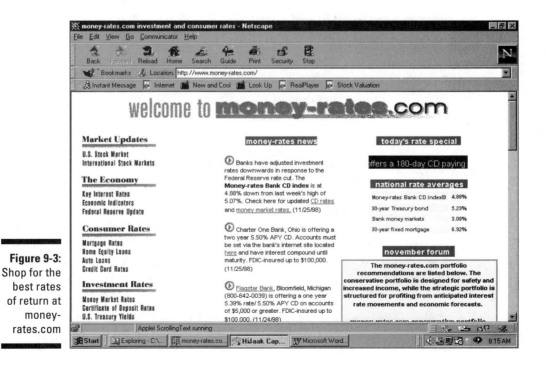

Figure 9-3: Shop for the best rates of return at money-rates.com

Uncle Sam's bonds: Treasury securities

Treasury securities are U.S. government securities called Treasury bills, notes, and bonds. These securities are a major source of government funds and a key investment for many consumers. The U.S. government is highly unlikely to default on its Treasury securities, but if it does, your dollar is also probably worthless, so your investment is, essentially, risk-free.

The disadvantage of the risk-free rate of Treasury securities is that it's generally considered the bottom of the yield pile — the lowest yield you can get. As the level of risk gets greater, the reward also increases. You can expect a better yield (but more risk) from corporate bonds with similar maturities.

You can purchase Treasury securities without a broker, directly from the government, in a program called Treasury Direct. Check out www.publicdebt.treas.gov/sec/sectrdir.htm for more information about Treasury Direct and instructions on how to open an account.

The Treasury Direct program allows investors to participate in regularly scheduled auctions. The minimum investments are $10,000 for bills, $5,000 for notes maturing in less than five years, and $1,000 for securities that mature in five or more years. Your interest payments are paid into your Treasury Direct account, as is a security's par value at maturity.

See the Bureau of Public Debt's Web page at www.publicdebt.treas.gov/of/ofannce.htm for more information about Treasury auction dates.

Treasury bills are sold for less than their face value. The discount represents the interest the investor earns. Interest income on Treasuries is usually exempt from state and local taxes but is subject to federal taxes.

Internet information on Treasury securities

For more information on U.S. Treasury securities, see the following Web sites:

- ✔ **Kirlin: About Investments** (www.kirlin.com/aboutinv/ust.html) provides a good overview of Treasury securities. This tutorial includes information on safety and availability.
- ✔ **Media Logic** (www.mlinet.com/mle/ec_1000.htm) provides links to Treasury security auction results, Treasury quotes, government bond indexes, historical treasury yield information, and more.

Figure 9-4 shows a market forecast by the Financial Forecast Center (www.neatideas.com). Forecasts are based on data from the last ten years and a forecasting methodology. You may find this information useful for spotting market trends.

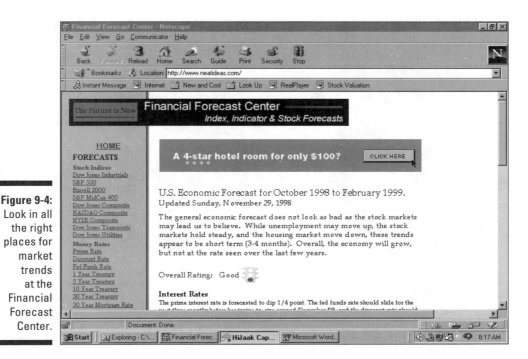

Figure 9-4:
Look in all
the right
places for
market
trends
at the
Financial
Forecast
Center.

Savings bonds: The easiest way to save

Series EE savings bonds are easy to buy. You can purchase them at any
bank. In addition, some employers have savings bonds automatic investment programs. The employee has a certain amount of money deducted
from his or her paycheck, and that money is used to purchase savings
bonds. For some people, this kind of investment program is the easiest and
only way they can save money.

The full faith and credit of the United States back U.S. savings bonds. The
Series EE savings bonds that you buy today earn market-based rates for 30
years. However, you can cash in the bonds at any time after six months from
the purchase date.

Income from U.S. savings bonds is exempt from state and local income tax.
You can also defer paying federal income tax on the interest until you cash
in the bond or until it stops earning interest in 30 years. If you use savings
bonds for educational purposes, they may provide you with additional tax
savings.

Figure 9-5 shows the Web site for the Bureau of Public Debt at
`www.publicdebt.treas.gov/sav/sav.htm`. This site provides information
about the different types of savings bonds and notes that are available.

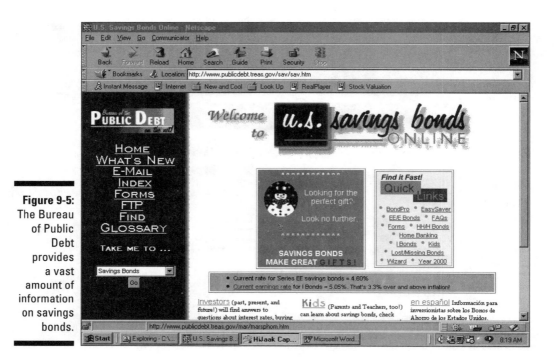

Figure 9-5:
The Bureau
of Public
Debt
provides
a vast
amount of
information
on savings
bonds.

Federal government agency bonds

Agency bonds are similar to Treasury bonds but have marginally higher risk and higher returns. They can be sold at $1,000 to $25,000 and sometimes more. Federal agencies issue bonds to support housing (either with direct loans or the purchase of existing mortgages); export and import activities with loans, credit guarantees, and insurance; the postal service; and the activities of the Tennessee Valley Authority.

Not all government agency bonds are equal. The full faith and credit of the U.S. government guarantees many issues. Although government agency bonds aren't a direct obligation of the U.S. government, they offer little, if any, credit risk. However, some bonds (for example, those of the Tennessee Valley Authority) do not have this guarantee.

The Internet provides additional information on specific types of government agency bonds. The following are two examples:

✔ **Fannie Mae** (www.fanniemae.com/financilinfo.index.html) provides investors with background information about the bonds they issue. In the Search In box, select Investor. In the Search For box, type in Bonds and then click Search. A list of hyperlinked topics appears. Check out bond topics that interest you.

✔ **Ginnie Mae** (www.ginniemae.com) is a government agency that specializes in non-conforming home loans. Consequently, this agency is always issuing to fund its activities. For investor information click Guides.

The beauty of tax-free municipal bonds

Towns, cities, and regional and local agencies issue municipal bonds. Municipal bonds usually have lower interest rates than comparably rated corporate bonds and Treasury securities. The minimum amount required for investment in municipal bonds is $5,000, and municipal bonds are sometimes issued at a discount. This discount compensates investors for the additional risk that these bonds may have due to the financial difficulties of some local governments.

The most important feature of municipal bonds is their tax-exempt feature. In subsequent judgments based on the 1819 *McCullough v. Maryland* ruling, the federal government and state and local governments don't possess the power to tax each other. Consequently, municipal bonds can't be subject to federal tax. Additionally, income from state and local municipal bonds can't be taxed if purchased within the geographic area. For example, Virginia residents don't pay state taxes on Virginia bonds. However, residents of California are subject to state income taxes on their Virginia bonds. This tax-exempt feature makes municipal bonds very attractive to investors in high tax brackets. You treat capital gains on such bonds as normal income.

Three primary types of municipal bonds exist. Each bond type has special features:

✔ **General obligation bonds** are backed by the full faith and credit of the issuing agency. For municipal bonds, full faith and credit also means the taxing power of the issuing municipality.

✔ **Revenue bonds** are backed by the funds from a designated tax or the revenues from a specific project, authority, or agency. These bonds are not backed by the full faith and credit (or the taxing power) of the issuing agency. In other words, revenue bonds are only as good (and as creditworthy) as the ventures they support.

✔ **Industrial development bonds (IDBs)** are used to finance the purchase or construction of industrial facilities that are to be leased to businesses. Leasing fees of the facilities are used to meet construction expenses and the repayment requirements of the bonds. Often these bonds provide inexpensive financing to firms choosing to locate in the geographical area of the issuer. Examples of IDBs are bonds for the construction of piers and wharves.

Municipalities can also issue short-term securities called tax-exempt commercial paper and variable-rate demand obligations.

The following brokerages provide a variety of bond information such as frequently updated offerings for individual investors, informative articles, and starter kits. The offerings shown at these Web sites are used for information purposes only. The securities listed by these firms are subject to changes in price and availability.

- **Bank of America** (www.bankamerica.com/muni/munical.html) is now a coast-to-coast operation thanks to its acquisition of NationsBank. The financial institution provides a daily listing of tax-exempt municipal notes and bonds for individual investors.

- **First Miami Securities** (www.firstmiami.com/yields.htm) is a financial institution that provides tables and charts of investment grade municipal bond yields, among other things.

- **Lebenthal & Company** (www.lebenthal.com), shown in Figure 9-6, will send you a "Bond Kit" that is designed for first time municipal bond purchasers. The Bond Kit covers general obligation and revenue bonds, bond insurance, coupons, taxes, how to sell your bonds, and more.

- **Seafirst Bank** (www.bondsonline.com/seafirst.htm) provides information about investing in bonds.

- **Stone & Youngberg** (www.styo.com) offer weekly listings of mortgage-backed securities, corporate bonds, and municipal bonds. At the homepage, click Weekly Market Update for the listing.

- **TaxFreeBond.com** (www.taxfreebond.com) is an online brokerage that specializes in tax-free bonds. Member services include e-mail newsletters and daily updated bond offerings from several hundred trading desks. Research tools include a primer on municipal bonds, a taxable equivalent yield calculator to help put tax-free yields into perspective, ratings definitions from Standard & Poors and Moody's, and research from BT Alex. Brown. The minimum amount necessary to open an account is $10,000.

Floating with corporate bonds

Corporate bonds are a major source of corporate borrowing. When corporations make corporate bonds, they "float a bond issue." Such bond issues take the form of either debentures (which are unsecured corporate bonds backed by the general credit of the corporation) or asset-backed bonds (which are backed by specific corporate assets like property or equipment). Income from these bonds is taxable. However, top-rated corporate bonds are often almost risk-free and have a higher return than Treasury securities. Corporate bonds are generally considered safer than stocks because of two factors:

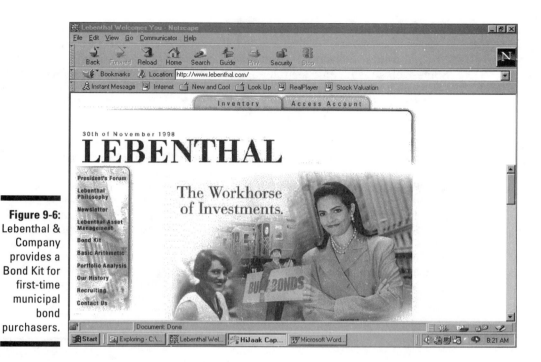

Figure 9-6:
Lebenthal &
Company
provides a
Bond Kit for
first-time
municipal
bond
purchasers.

✓ **The bonds state exactly how much the corporation will pay the bondholder.** Shareholders are entitled to cash dividends, but payment and the amount of the dividend is at the discretion of the corporation.

✓ **Bondholders are creditors.** They receive payment before the corporation can distribute any cash dividends to shareholders, which means that bondholders have greater protection in getting at least some return on their investment. (In bankruptcy, bondholders are paid from corporate assets before common stockholders.)

Some risk of default always exists. In the 1980s, many companies used junk bonds to finance highly leveraged takeovers of rival companies. Their bonds were rated noninvestment grade and speculative by the bond-rating agencies. Due to the additional risk, these bonds paid above-average interest rates. For some bondholders, these bonds were a windfall. For bondholders who invested in the corporate bonds of companies that failed, their bonds went into default and became worthless junk.

Some professional money managers are required by law to purchase investment-grade securities so that they can't purchase junk bonds. These organizations generally limit their corporate bond purchases to issues rated B or higher by Moody's Investors.

Using the Internet to select bonds

The Internet provides many online tools to help you make bond selections. Some Web sites include search engines that sort through thousands of bond offerings while looking for bonds that meet your criteria. These services are free but often accompanied by a sales pitch. The Internet provides many tools and resources for analyzing bonds. The following lists some popular bond sites:

✔ **Bondtrac** (`www.bondtrac.com`) is a security dealer bond tracking software company. Use of this Web site requires your free registration. Bondtrac, shown in Figure 9-7, provides a partial list of its services to demonstrate the use of its data and the functionality of its software. The free services don't show offer, concession, price, yield, or dealer information; these types of data are considered restricted information for licensed security brokers. With your free registration, you can look up corporate bonds, as well as municipal bonds and U.S. government agency bonds by using a variety of search criteria. Your screen results include information about bond amount, minimum purchase amount, rating, symbol, description, coupon, and maturity date.

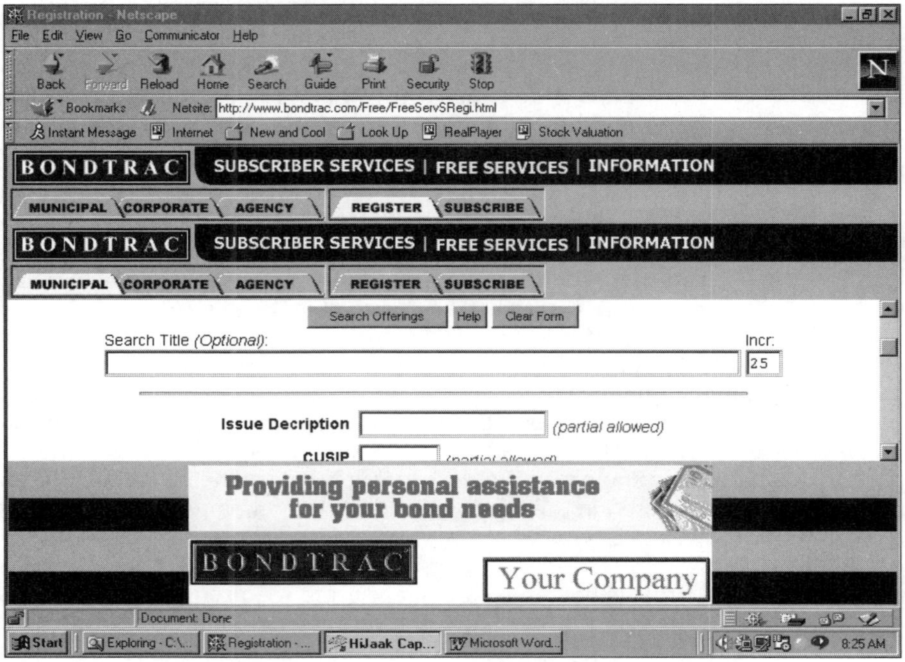

Figure 9-7: Bondtrac allows you to use your own investment criteria to sort municipal, corporate, and U.S. government bond investment candidates

- **First Chicago NBD Online Brokerage** (www.fcnis.com) is an electronic brokerage that provides free real-time quotes and financial news. Online tools include a search engine for municipal, corporate, CMO, zero-coupon, and treasury bonds. Each bond type has a query definition page where you can define the search, a query result page that lists the bonds that match your search, and a bond detail page where you can get more information about a bond that interests you.

- **The Standard & Poor's Blue List** (www.bluelist.com/bltsdemo.dem) shows current municipal and corporate bond offerings. This Web site has a static demo scan of their "Blue List Offerings" available to individual investors. The demo scans a maximum of 14 items and is designed to demonstrate the company's software. You can search the database for state issuers, maturity dates, lot size of the issue, coupon, and CUSIP.

CUSIP is a numbering system endorsed by major segments of the financial community. See the CUSIP service bureau operated by Standard & Poor's for the American Bankers Association at www.cusip.com for more information about cusip numbering.

Two Alternate Types of Bonds

These relatively new types of bonds may be of interest to online investors:

- **Zero coupon bonds:** Zero coupon bonds offer no interest payments but are put on the market at prices substantially below their face values. The return to the investor is the difference between the investor's cost and the face value received at the end of the life of the bond. If you don't rely on interest payment income, zero coupon bonds may be the way to go for your non-taxable retirement plan (such as an individual retirement account, Keogh plan, or other non-taxable pension fund). The Internal Revenue Service taxes zero coupon bonds as if investors received regular interest payments. This tax is based on amortizing the built-in gain over the life of the bond. In other words, for taxable accounts, investors have to pay taxes on income they haven't received, but for non-taxable accounts, they're a great investment choice.

Some brokerages offer *treasury strips*. Large companies purchase 30-year treasury securities and clip the interest bearing coupons. The brokers then sell these treasury coupons like zero coupon bonds. You purchase the treasury strip at a discount (say $4,300) and redeem the coupon at face value ($5,000). Treasury strips are like zero coupon bonds because no interest is paid during the maturity term.

✔ **Eurobonds:** Investments in foreign securities typically involve many government restrictions. Eurobonds are bonds offered outside the country of the borrower and usually outside the country in whose currency the securities are denominated. For example, a Eurobond may be issued by an American corporation, denominated in German deutsche marks, and sold in Japan and Switzerland.

For additional information about Eurobonds, see the following sites:

- **Bradynet CyberExchange (**`www.bradynet.com`**)** provides bond prices, analysis, research, ratings, news, information about new issues, forums, and more. Enter Eurobonds in the Search engine on the homepage and select Search Bradynet. You get a page that includes a demonstration program that searches for specific Eurobond issues.

- **Petercam Eurobonds (**`www.petercam.be`**)** provides valuation techniques for Eurobonds, benchmarks, and information about Eurobond primary and secondary markets. At the homepage, click on Eurobond Desk.

J.P. Morgan & Company, Inc. (`www.jpmorgan.com`) provides a government bond index that is a widely used benchmark for assessing and quantifying risk across international fixed-income bond markets. If you're looking for benchmarks, go to the J.P. Morgan homepage and click on Index.

The indexes measure the total, principal, and interest returns in each market and can be reported in 19 currencies. You can compare Eurobonds to the index to provide a realistic measure of market performance.

The Investing Online For Dummies, 2nd Edition, Internet Directory

In this directory . . .

Throughout the pages of *Investing Online For Dummies,* 2nd Edition, I describe dozens of Internet resources that can assist you in your wealth-building efforts. In this part of the book, I provide you with a listing of the sites you are most likely to use for analyzing investment candidates, selecting the right financial assets for your objectives, monitoring your portfolio, and buying and selling your investments online.

The Investing Online For Dummies, 2nd Edition, Internet Directory

In This Directory

▶ Discovering the best-rated Internet investment sites available and navigate your path to profitability

▶ Gaining easy access to great online services, from online trading and stock quote services to electronic brokerages and investment education

▶ Constructing a successful portfolio with online information about all types of investments

The Internet has a wide variety of resources for online investors, and this directory provides a sampling of some of the latest and greatest online investing sites available at this time. I don't claim that this guide is comprehensive. With the constant growth and change that characterizes the Internet, it is almost impossible for anyone to create a directory that lives up to such a claim.

The Internet is a constantly changing resource. Some sites listed in this directory (and elsewhere in this book) may have changed or gone away due to mergers with larger sites. Some Web sites just vanish for no reason. If a site has moved, you may find a link to the new location. If not, try a search engine (like AltaVista or Infoseek) to locate the resource you need.

About Those Micons

To give you as much information as possible, this directory uses these *micons*, small graphics that point out some of the special features of a Web site:

$ This site charges an access fee. I use this micon if most of the site's content — or the most important content — is available only to paying subscribers.

D-4

You need a special piece of software — a *plug-in,* such as Shockwave or Real Audio — to get the most out of this site.

This site features shopping opportunities.

This site has software that you can download.

An increasing number of sites on the Internet require your free registration.

The site has interactive message boards that you can use for communicating with other online investors.

This micon identifies sites that offer chat rooms where you interact with other visitors or an investment expert. Participating in chat rooms (and sometimes, message boards) often requires registering at the site.

Analyst Evaluations

Finding out what the experts are saying about your investment selection is often useful. Here are a few of my favorite sources for analysts' evaluations.

S&P Advisor Insight

www.advisorinsight.com/

$

For the pros: More of a professional resource than S&P Personal Wealth, this site enables you to buy full S&P research reports. You can also find market commentaries and some information on foreign-owned public companies.

S&P Personal Wealth

www.personalwealth.com

$

Reports for the individual investor: To get a quote on a public company's shares, just enter its ticker symbol and click Go. If you subscribe, you can get advice from S&P's analysts. Plus, the welcome page has free news and market status information.

Zacks Investment Research

www.zacks.com

$

Compilations of experts' knowledge: Zacks reports on what hundreds of expert analysts around the world are saying about stocks you can invest in.

Some of these reports are free; others require you to pay a fee. All of them are top-quality reports.

Basics of Investing

If you're looking for good investor starting places, try the Web sites I list in this section.

Invest-O-Rama

www.investorama.com

Lots of good stuff: Put together by Douglas Gerlach, Invest-O-Rama is a collection of links to online sources, such as electronic brokers, mutual funds, financial reports, and related investor sources.

InvestorGuide

www.investorguide.com

Start here: InvestorGuide features newsletters, articles, stock analyses, and links to thousands of investment sites. Plus, the site features loads of educational materials that can help you figure out what you want to do with your money, and why. Much of this educational information is goal-oriented, so it contains information about saving for college, in addition to investments in general.

Other Stuff to Check Out

www.financialweb.com
www.pawws.com
www.quicken.com/investments
www.wsdinc.com

Bonds

Bonds (sometimes called fixed income investments) can be short-term or long-term, high-risk (like junk bonds) or low-risk (like Treasury bonds). If you own mutual fund shares, you may already be a bond investor. Check out the following sites for bond-related information.

The Bond Market

www.bondcan.com

"Eh"-rated debt: The Bond Market is the best online resource for those investing in Canadian bonds. It lists all the news about the Bank of Canada, dispatches from all the provincial banks, and government statistics. The site also features a message board. Add quotes and a joke page, and you've got a valuable site.

Bondsonline

www.bondsonline.com

$

News and more: Bondsonline provides charts and historical data that compare various bond market sectors. For example, this site offers a comparison of 30-year Treasury bonds, 10-year Treasury notes, and the Dow Jones Industrial Average. You can also find news of the goings-on at the Fed and elsewhere in debt circles.

TradeHistory

www.tradehistory.com

$

Price histories, news, and commentary: Filled with information about thousands of bonds and the various prices at which they're traded, TradeHistory is an excellent resource for keeping current on news of big trades, new issues, and more. You can search by CUSIP, coupon, maturity and state, or any combination of the three.

Other Stuff to Check Out

www.stls.frb.org/fred/data/irates.html
www.moodys.com

Broker Fraud and Complaints

If you suspect that your broker is not as honest as you once thought, you can voice your complaint to the right people using the Internet. Many of these organizations follow up on your complaint and keep you informed of its status.

Better Business Bureau

www.bbb.org

Your complaint will be heard: The Better Business Bureau has an online complaint form. The bureau promises to follow up within two weeks of your complaint.

National Fraud Information Center

www.fraud.org

Help others by reporting fraud: The National Fraud Information Center forwards your complaint to the appropriate organizations and includes it in the Center's Internet fraud statistics (which may not help you get your money back, but may be helpful to other online investors).

Securities and Exchange Commission

www.sec.gov

Check up on your broker: The Securities and Exchange Commission (SEC) has an excellent online complaint process. You can use this site to request any registered broker's disciplinary history, too, free of charge.

If you're thinking about investing in a company, you can do much of your research on the company online. For example, you can read the company's profile or develop your own company profile based on your online research and analysis.

Companylink

www.companylink.com

An all-in-one solution: Companylink provides a compilation Web site for several good research and quote sites, so it's a fine place to start when looking for information on companies traded on U.S. exchanges, plus the largest private U.S. companies.

Hoover's Online

www.hoovers.com

$

Good freebies, great, if you pay the fee: Hoover's Online has free and fee-based information on 8,500 companies. You can search company ticker symbols, locations, and sales at this Web site.

Company profiles include the firm's address, phone numbers, executive names, recent sales figures, and company status.

In a direct public offering (DPO), a company bypasses an underwriter and offers its shares directly to the public. This procedure has both good points and drawbacks. The Internet provides information and materials about many DPOs.

Direct IPO

www.directipo.com

Buy and sell shares directly: Direct IPO provides investor resources, information about traditional IPOs and DPOs, an industry spotlight, an IPO contest, a newsroom, and more. The site is a good place to visit whether you want to buy shares or sell equity in your own company to others.

The Direct Stock Market

www.dsm.com

Companies for sale, info for free: The Direct Stock Market provides information about companies that are issuing direct public offerings. It provides a central online location for the distribution of these companies' prospectuses and documents. You can also find an exchange for over-the-counter and

Bulletin Board shares, and regular Webcasts disseminating investment information.

Internet Capital Exchange

www.inetcapital.com

A nifty independent stock exchange: The Internet Capital Exchange is designed to bring companies and investors together to generate funding capital and investment opportunities. Companies that are already public can allow their stock to be traded by investors using an interactive trading system.

Netstock Direct

www.netstockdirect.com

Netstock Direct is an online source for purchasing shares directly from a company (and not paying brokerage fees). The Web site includes online education about direct investing and company materials about their direct stock purchase plans. Additionally, many of these companies have dividend reinvestment plans that can help you defer taxes and purchase more shares with your dividends.

Other Stuff to Check Out

isp.mousetrap.net/dpo/
www.virtualwallstreet.com

Dividend Reinvestment Programs

Dividend Reinvestment Programs (DRIPs) allow shareholders to purchase additional shares directly from the company (bypassing brokerage fees) and sometimes at reduced prices. Direct Stock Purchase plans (DSPs), sometimes called Direct Purchase Plans (DPPs), allow you to use cash to buy shares directly from issuing companies.

DRIP Advisor

www.dripadvisor.com

It's the DRIPpiest: This site is useful for its apparently complete list of all U.S. companies offering DRIPs and DSPs, plus lots of general information on DRIP investing and some advice on assembling a portfolio of DRIPs.

Netstock Direct

www.netstockdirect.com/

A great starting point: Here, Netstock's managers have assembled a great list of online DRIP and DSP resources. A superb search engine enables you to winnow out the plans that don't fit your plans, based on industry, minimum investment, and other criteria.

Stock1.com

www.stock1.com/

$

Advice and more: Stock1 provides lots of informative material to get you oriented in the world of DRIPs and DSPs, plus loads of links to other sites — you can use this site as a portal. If you pay the fee, you get to look at Stock1's recommended list of DRIP and DSP stocks.

Other Stuff to Check Out

www.natcorp.com/direct.html
www.aaii.com
www.better-investing.org/store/store.html

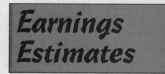

Earnings Estimates

When determining the value of a stock, you often need to estimate the company's earnings. Compare your earnings estimates with the experts' at the following Web sites.

First Call

www.1.firstcall.com

$

A reliable source: The First Call database follows more than 7,500 companies. It also tracks more than 100 industry groups, several commodities and economic indicators, plus the Dow Jones Industrial Average and the S&P 500. Most of the useful stuff here costs you, but it's good stuff.

Reuters Moneynet

www.moneynet.com

$

A money/news portal, and more: Reuters Moneynet provides an S&P evaluation of the company and dividends rank, average quality opinion,

fiscal year ending month, and date of the next expected earnings report. The consensus earnings per share forecast for the next year and statistics about past earnings are included.

Zacks Investment Research

www.zacks.com

$

A long-standing favorite: Zacks provides estimated earnings reports that are based on broker opinions. The site includes a listing of current earnings surprises, recommendations, and the company's annual balance sheet and income statement.

Other Stuff to Check Out

www.nrmcapital.com
www.stocksmart.com

Economic Information

Before you invest, checking out the big picture is always a wise idea. Find out how the economy is doing, both nationally and regionally. For example, if the economy weakens, how will this change affect your investment selections?

Census Bureau

www.census.gov

$

How many, exactly: The Census Bureau provides information about industry, statistics, and general business. *Current Industrial Reports* provide production, shipment, and inventory statistics.

D-10 Industry Information

Census of Manufacturers Industry Series includes industry statistics (some of this information may be outdated). *The Census of Wholesale Trade* contains data about organizations that sell merchandise to retailers, institutions, and other types of wholesalers. The *Survey* provides updates about current and past statistics of monthly sales, inventories, and stock/sales ratios.

GSA Government Information Locator Service

www.gsa.gov

Government Central: The GSA Government Information Locator Service includes many U.S. Federal agency reports in either full-text or abstract forms. Most information resources are cataloged and searchable. Searches can include more than one agency.

Internet Federal Reserve Sites

www.stls.frb.org/other/websites.html

Alan Greenspan's home page: This Web site provides links to all the Federal Reserve home pages and gopher sites. Publications by these organizations include high-quality statistics, analyses, and forecasts of regional, national, and international economic and financial conditions.

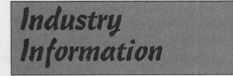

Industry Information

Compare the performance of your investment candidate to the industry standard. How is the company performing? Is the company an industry leader or fighting for market share? Find out by researching the company's industry at the following Internet sites.

American Society of Association Executives

www.asaenet.org

The Plumbing and Drainage Institute, and so much more: The American Society of Association Executives provides links to Web sites for various industries. The Web sites are generally high-quality industry overviews that often include briefings of industry trends, geographic profiles, and statistics for financial performance analysis.

Lexis-Nexis

www.lexis-nexis.com

$

Where talk-show hosts get their background info: Lexis-Nexis has a wide variety of business and legal databases and recently added a new database of 10- to 20-page market summaries of particular industry sectors or demographic markets. Additionally, the Lexis-Nexis database includes the *Market Share Reporter* (from 1991 to the present) and *Computer Industry Forecasts*.

STAT-USA

www.stat-usa.gov

Statistics for all occasions: STAT-USA is sponsored by the U.S. Department of Commerce and provides financial information about economic indicators, statistics, and news. STAT-USA is a relatively friendly way to access deep troves of U.S. government research.

Other Stuff to Check Out

www.fedstats.gov
www.technometrica.com
www.trainingforum.com

Initial Public Offerings (IPOs)

Usually, in an initial public offering (IPO), a company offers shares to the public for the first time. Purchasing shares in an IPO may be one way to get in on the ground floor of a new investment opportunity. Investing in an IPO is also an excellent way to lose your shirt. Take your pick.

Everything About IPOs

www.moneypages.com/syndicate/ stocks/ipo.html

An IPO primer: This Web page contains an informative article about the advantages and limitations of initial public offerings. Start here.

IPO Central

www.ipocentral.com

News of a turbulent field: IPO Central provides the most recent IPO filings, weekly pricing, commentary, and informative articles. This resource is part of the Hoover's empire, so it's reliable.

IPO Maven

www.IPOmaven.com

The best site for the knowledgeable IPO investor: IPO Maven is a portal into online resources for IPO investors. Here, you can find the latest pricing information and news in an attractive, frequently updated format that you can refer to easily.

Other Stuff to Check Out

biz.yahoo.com/reports/ipo.html
cbs.marketwatch.com/news/current/
   IPO_rep.htx
www.ostman.com/alert-ipo
www.investhelp.com
www.ipodata.com
www.ipomonitor.com
www.techweb.com/investor/ipowatch/
   ipostach.html

Interest Rates

The Internet can help you find the best savings rate in the U.S. Some Web sites even include instructions about how to open out-of-state savings accounts.

Bank Rate Monitor

www.bankrate.com

All-purpose loan shopper: Bank Rate Monitor shows the interest rates offered throughout the United States on home mortgages, car loans, small business loans, and more. The Web site even includes a listing of financial institutions that offer special deals to Internet shoppers.

Bank-CD Rate Scanner

www.bankcd.com

$

Rating the rates: This site provides, for $9.95, a list of the top CD rates in the United States, complete with minimum-investment and term information. Bank-CD Rate Scanner guarantees its service; if you can find a lower rate at an FDIC-insured institution that accepts nation-wide deposits, you don't have to pay. Besides, if you're investing enough, this service pays for itself.

BanxQuote

banx.com/banx/rates.htm

Rate quotes, by region: BanxQuote is a good online source for the best rates for money market deposit accounts and various kinds of loans. BanxQuote allows searches by location or terms. Data includes the financial institution's name and contact information and the money market account's rate of return.

Investor Compilation Sites

Investor compilation sites are excellent sources for beginning investors. These investor starting points are also good sources for finding new investor Web sites.

Invest-O-Rama

www.investorama.com

One-stop research: Invest-O-Rama includes more than 2,000 investor-related links sorted into categories. The site has a directory that covers bonds, brokerages, dividend reinvestment plans, futures, mutual funds, and more.

InvestorGuide

www.investorguide.com

A good place to start: InvestorGuide is a well-organized directory with links to thousands of investor-related sites. InvestorGuide includes site reviews, summaries, and an extensive section on initial pubic offerings (IPOs).

Morningstar

www.morningstar.net

Fund research from a leader: Morningstar is a Chicago-based, independent rating company that specializes in mutual funds. The site includes information about both stocks and mutual funds, easy-to-use screening tools, and research sources. Plus, it offers advice to newcomers, reviews of investing books, financial celebrity interviews, and a lot more.

The Syndicate

www.moneypages.com/syndicate

Ask questions, get answers: The Syndicate includes informative articles on investor topics, more than 2,000 links to related investor sites, and information on brokers, bonds, and more.

Wall Street Research Net

www.wsrn.com

$

Share and share alike: Wall Street Research Net focuses on stock market research. The site includes more than 65,000 links to company information, the economy, market news, investor reports, quotes, mutual fund indexes, and more. Some of it is free, too, including a handy stock-of-the-week feature.

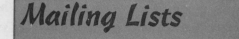

Investor Databases

When researching an investment candidate, investors often use specialized databases to find that elusive piece of data. Here are a few free and fee-based online databases.

FinWeb

www.finweb.com

Free advice from an academic expert: FinWeb is from the University of Texas at Austin. FinWeb has links to the finance and economics departments of many universities, commercial sources, and financial institutions. This financial supersite includes high-quality recommendations, and all links are screened for content.

Govbot

ciir.cs.umass.edu/ciirdemo/Govbot/ index.html

An all-purpose search tool with financial applications: Govbot is sponsored by the Center for Intelligent Information Retrieval (CIIR). The free database allows you to search more than 1,000,000 government and military Web pages, lots of which contain information of interest to investors.

Other Stuff to Check Out

www.asaenet.org/Gateway/
  GatewayHP.html
www.gsa.gov
www.lexis-nexis.com
www.thomasregister.com
www.stat-usa.gov

Mailing Lists

Mailing lists are special e-mail programs that re-mail all incoming mail to a list of subscribers. Get new insights and advice from savvy investors by joining a topic-specific mailing list.

CataList

www.lsoft.com/lists/listref.html

A list of lists: CataList lists more than 21,000 mailing lists and is searchable by site, country, and number of list subscribers. Note that the listed lists aren't all about financial matters — they're about all different subjects.

Holt Stock Report

metro.turnpike.net/holt

Of particular interest to day-traders and options people: The Holt Stock Report provides indexes, averages, information about foreign markets, new stock highs and lows, currency exchange rates, gold prices, interest rates, lists of the most active issues on the NYSE, NASDAQ, and AMEX, stocks with today's volume up more than 50 percent, and stocks that have reached new highs and lows. You can access a Web site, too.

Reference.Com

www.reference.com

Another list of lists: Reference.Com searches 150,000 Usenet newsgroups and mailing lists for the information you want. Instructions about basic and advanced searches are available.

Municipal and Treasury Information

State or local units of the government often issue municipal bonds (sometimes called *munis*). Treasury securities (sometimes called *Treasuries*) are issued by the U.S. Federal government. Both types of investments can help you diversify your portfolio, providing some tax protection and predictability in the process.

Capital Markets Commentary

www.intdata.com/capital.htm

Informed commentary: Capital Markets Commentary is a weekly fixed income (bond) market review provided by Interactive Data Corporation, a Financial Times company. The Capital Markets Commentary includes market information about U.S. government agency bonds, U.S. corporate bonds, international bonds, U.S. municipals, and commercial mortgage-backed bonds.

Treasury Direct

www.publicdebt.treas.gov/sec/ sectrdir.htm

Government instruments on the cheap: Avoid brokerage fees by purchasing Treasury bills, notes, and bonds directly from the Federal government. Find out all about it from the Federal Reserve Bank of San Francisco.

Other Stuff to Check Out

www.economeister.com
www.govpx.com

Mutual Funds: Automatic Investment Plans

Even if you only have $50 to invest, you can purchase shares in a mutual fund. Automatic Investment Plans (AIPs) allow you to avoid hefty initial minimum investment requirements.

Strong Automatic Investment Plan

www.strong-funds.com/strong/ LearningCenter/aipbroch.htm

How Strong's program works: Strong has an automatic investment plan for 36 of its no-load funds. The program allows you to invest at predetermined intervals for as low as $50. No charges are required to establish or maintain this service.

T. Rowe Price

www.troweprice.com

Load up on no-loads: T. Rowe Price has two no-load funds in its automatic investment plan that allow monthly, bimonthly, quarterly, semi-annual, and annual automatic payments. Minimum payments can be as little as $25.

Vanguard Fund Express

www.vanguard.com/catalog/service/ 5_3_1_2.html

A disciplined savings plan: The Vanguard Fund Express plan allows monthly, bimonthly, quarterly, semi-annual, and annual automatic payment to be transferred to your Vanguard account. The maximum amount of investment is $100,000 and the minimum amount is $25.

Mutual Funds: Companies and Funds

In this section, I list mutual fund companies that manage many mutual funds. Purchasing a mutual fund from a company that manages many mutual funds has some advantages. One such advantage is that some mutual fund companies allow you to swap your investment in one of their funds for another of their mutual funds at no charge.

Fidelity

www.fidelity.com

A titan on the Web: Fidelity is the largest mutual fund house around, with 35 percent of the total market. This Web site has news about Fidelity investments, a mutual fund library, online prospectuses, online investment and retirement planning advice, and more.

Invesco

www.invesco.com

A good corporate site: If you're a beginning investor, you'll appreciate Invesco's useful advice. This Web site includes online prospectuses, charts to compare rates of return, and a list of the firm's financial services. If you register with this service, you can access your investment account balances through this site.

Janus

www.janus.com

Two faces: Janus has a family of no-load funds. The site provides account access, brief overviews of fund performance, application forms, investor chats, and articles.

T. Rowe Price

www.troweprice.com

Price quotes and more: T. Rowe Price provides daily mutual fund prices, brief updates of fund performance, and more. You have the option of downloading a prospectus or having one sent to you by mail.

Vanguard

www.vanguard.com

On the cutting edge: Vanguard has about 90 funds that do not charge sales fees. Vanguard is one of the largest mutual fund companies. The site includes fund descriptions, downloadable prospectuses, an education center for investors, and more. You can also sign up to receive your statements by e-mail.

Mutual Funds: Information Services

Uncertain about which mutual fund is best for you? The Internet provides lots of mutual fund information sources.

CBS MarketWatch — Super Star Funds

cbs.marketwatch.com

Eye on funds: CBS MarketWatch provides articles, news, market data, fund research, links to fund sites, mutual fund tutorials for new investors, market data, portfolios, and a stock chat room. Click the Super Star Funds box to see the fund information.

The Mutual Fund Channel

www.mutual-fundchannel.com

The Mutual Fund Channel uses special software to bring you one-stop mutual fund shopping. Using push technology, the Mutual Fund Channel delivers quotes, valuations, market and business news, fund profiles, historical data, and market analyses for more than 5,400 funds.

Mutual Fund Magazine

www.mfmag.com

🕮 $ 🛒

A complete toolkit, for a price: Mutual Fund Magazine offers two levels of membership: you can be a registered user (it's free) and get some service or you can be a charter member (it costs $9.95 a month) and get full access to a wide variety of features, departments, screens, reports, online calculators, and tools to assist you in making your mutual fund selections.

Mutual Funds Interactive

www.fundsinteractive.com/ profiles.html

An excellent center of information: Mutual Funds Interactive has recommendations, analysis tools, and links to other useful sites. Plus, you can find profiles of many top money managers.

Other Stuff to Check Out

www.fundalarm.com
www.mfea.com
www.stocksmart.com

Mutual Funds: Performance

Check out how your mutual fund stacks up against the competition with these Internet sources.

InvestorSquare

www.investorsquare.com

News, graphs, and commentary: InvestorSquare ranks more than 9,500 funds on 100 different variables. This Web site also includes a detailed profile of each fund. The site covers stocks, too.

The Street.com

www.thestreet.com/ mutualfundprofiles/funds.asp

🕮 $

Search by symbol: The Street provides fund profiles and scorecards. You can search free and fee-based areas. One free area is Lipper Analytical's latest top performers for the week.

Other Stuff to Check Out

www.investorama.com
www.stockmaster.com

Mutual Funds: Prospectuses

The first rule in purchasing mutual funds is to read the prospectus before you buy any shares. Here are a few great online sources for mutual fund prospectuses. Don't forget to look at the fund companies' sites, too.

EDGAR for Mutual Funds

edgar.stern.nyu.edu/mutual.html

Quick and dirty (and free) searching: EDGAR for Mutual Funds is a Web site that provides prospectuses for more than 7,000 mutual funds. If you know the name of the fund you are interested in, you can investigate the fund's activities at this site.

Mutual Fund Resource Center

www.fundmaster.com

Education and data: The Mutual Fund Resource Center provides free information, prospectuses, and applications for more than 75 mutual funds.

Mutual Funds: Screens

Out of the 9,500 available mutual funds, which one meets your financial objectives? Use a mutual fund screen to help you find likely candidates. Mutual fund screens are on the Internet, easy to use, and often free.

Investor Square

www.InvestorSquare.com

Limit by criteria: The Investor Square mutual fund screen is particularly useful for beginning investors. The screen is designed to help you find the best 25 performers by category, detailed objective, and specific category (such as short-term or long-term bond fund).

Morningstar

www.morningstar.net

Take it from the experts: Morningstar uses a few sensible preselected variables in its screen of 6,500 mutual funds. Each broad fund category contains narrower categories within it. For example, if you're interested in the technology sector funds that have the highest Morningstar Ratings, you can first check out the screen on U.S. Stock Funds with the highest Morningstar Rating. Once you get your results, you get a new pull-down list of narrower fund-category choices, and Technology becomes one of your new options. Choose it, and click View Results to view more choices on-screen.

MSN MoneyCentral Investor

investor.msn.com

Investment wizardry: Now free, MSN MoneyCentral Investor includes the Fund Research Wizard, which can help you identify mutual funds that meet your needs. The Wizard provides several options. First you can select one of almost a dozen pre-built screens. Second, you can build a mutual fund screen that includes all the variables you feel are important. Each type of mutual fund screen is easy to use, and you can copy the results to your spreadsheet.

Quicken.com

www.quicken.com

The online presence of a personal finance software leader: Quicken provides three types of mutual fund screens free of charge. Each screen is more complex than the one before it. If you're a beginning investor, this site may be the place to start. The screen's values are updated on a monthly basis.

Other Stuff to Check Out

www.researchmag.com
www.thomsoninvest.net

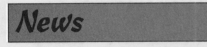

News

The Internet offers online news from many large news organizations. Often these organizations will send brief versions of the daily business and investor news or breaking news directly to your e-mailbox free of charge.

ABCNews.com

www.abcnews.com

Features business and industry news, market commentary, and personal finance articles: Catch up on the latest investment issues with the Laughing StockBroker, The Street, and S & P's Personal Wealth.

Bloomberg Personal Finance

www.bloomberg.com

$

Bloomberg Personal Finance is loaded with timely news, data, and analyses of financial markets and businesses: Find data on securities, statistics, indices, and research for free. As of this writing, access to the member area of the Web site is $49 per year. Additional levels of service are available, including portfolio tracking, online stock quotes, company news, mutual fund information, and at-home delivery of the monthly magazine.

CBS MarketWatch

cbs.marketwatch.com

$

CBS MarketWatch combines the resources of CBS News and Data Broadcasting Corporation: This Web site has many free and fee-based services. The free edition offers delayed stock quotes, feature articles, and breaking news targeted for individual investors. CBS MarketWatch RT is a $34.95/month service offering real-time quotes, company snapshots, deeper historical and fundamental data, and research tools for active investors. CBS MarketWatch LIVE is a branded version of DBC's new StockEdge Online ($79/ month). This service gives the user a virtual trading desk on any or all of his/ her computers. Using proprietary *active push* software, CBS MarketWatch LIVE allows the user to set up dynamically updated charts, tickers, and quote screens. (Push technology "pushes" the information you preselect to your desktop computer, as opposed to the usual "pulling" of information from different search engines and other sources.)

CNNfn

www.cnnfn.com

CNNfn offers news, articles on investment topics, and professional advice on money management: Major global stock indices, stock quotes, currency rates, commodities, and interest information are also available. CNNfn offers links to official company Web sites, a glossary of business terms, general references, and government resources. At your request, free daily news briefings are sent to your e-mailbox.

Dow Jones

www.dowjones.com

$

An old standby: Dow Jones information technology has been on the Internet forever with a wide variety of products and services designed for individual investors who want to manage their own portfolios and make their own investment decisions. A few examples of its products are Smart Money (www.smartmoney.com), CNBC (www.cnbc.com) Far Eastern Economic Review (www.feer.com), Barron's Online (www.barrons.com), and The Wall Street Journal (www.wsj.com).

MSNBC's Investment Toolkit

www.msnbc.com/modules/commerce/ newtoolkit/default.asp

The MSNBC Investment Toolkit is designed for online investors: The toolkit includes market news; mutual fund, stock, and bond indexes; commodities; quotes; historical charts; corporate news; information about world markets; and personal finance features.

Reuters moneynet.com

www.moneynet.com/home/moneynet/ homepage/homepage.asp

moneynet.com is sponsored by Reuters and specializes in financial data: moneynet.com is a convenient Web site for quotes, financial and company news, charts, research, and market snapshots. If you're looking for free online portfolio management, this site has Portfolio Tracker, one of the better portfolio management programs on the Web.

Newsgroups

Newsgroups contain discussions about different subject areas. The content of these discussions ranges from the ridiculous to the sublime. By using the search engines I list in this section, you may find a newsgroup that's a good source for opinions on different investments.

DejaNews

www.dejanews.com

Usenet without the hassle: You can use this site to search more than 25,000 Usenet newsgroups (including those directly, indirectly, and not at all related to investments) for the information you are seeking. Searches can be by group, author, subject, or dates.

Usenet Info Center Launch Pad

sunsite.unc.edu/usenet-i

Beginners' information: If you're new to Usenet, the resources here can help you get up to speed.

Newsletters

If you subscribe to an online newsletter, you may receive issues several times a day, daily, weekly, biweekly, monthly, or quarterly. Investor newsletters may be free or costly, and they may have hard facts and breaking news or chatty items about the market's latest events. Or they may be completely full of hot air. These are some of the better ones.

GS Research on Demand

www.gsnews.com

 $

Good information, for a price: GS Research on Demand is a high-end service from Goldman Sachs. Research on Demand offers *Research Headlines,* a daily update of rating and estimate changes, and *U.S. Research Viewpoint,* a weekly review of the impact of earnings and rating changes.

Holt Stock Report

metro.turnpike.net/holt

All-encompassing news and comment: The Holt Stock Report can be delivered to your e-mailbox daily. This newsletter provides all the market statistics you need for your investment decision-making.

InvestorGuide Weekly

www.investorguide.com/weekly.htm

Internet for fun and profit: InvestorGuide Weekly is designed to keep you informed of new Web-related developments in the areas of investing and personal finance. It includes links to articles on how to use the Internet for investing, new and improved Web sites, investing in Internet companies, and electronic commerce.

Kiplinger Online

www.kiplinger.com

 🛒 $

The electronic version of a popular print mag: Kiplinger Online provides news of the day, business forecasts, personal finance, stock quotes, lists of top funds, online calculators, retirement advice, listings of great Internet sites, and financial FAQs.

Newspapers

Get the news in quick summaries and then read the full story at your leisure, all online. Many online newspapers let you customize your paper so you get just the news that interests you.

Ecola's 24-hour Newsstand

www.ecola.com/news

Newspaper central: Ecola's 24-hour Newsstand contains links to more than 1,500 Web sites for published material from local and specialty papers, magazines, and major news services. You can search titles by keyword.

Individual NewsPage

www.newspage.com

 $

News you care about: Individual NewsPage provides free and fee-based information. You can set a personal profile that makes this online newspaper your personal clipping service. Its home page provides breaking news, company links, news searches, and quotes.

InfoBeat

www.infobeat.com

Tailored news: InfoBeat enables you to select user profiles that highlight finance, news, weather, sports, entertainment, or snow. To subscribe, just go to the Web site and enroll. You can also get updates sent to you by e-mail.

Newspaper Association of America

www.naa.org/hotlinks/index.asp

All online papers: The Newspaper Association of America offers comprehensive indexes to the online versions of major newspapers, searchable and browsable.

Other Stuff to Check Out

www.nyt.com
www.sjm.com
www.wsj.com

Online Brokerages

Electronic brokerages often charge the lowest commissions available. Each commercial enterprise charges a different fee and has its own unique features. Online brokerages are generally as accurate as their full-service counterparts.

Ameritrade

www.ameritrade.com

$

Do-it-yourself, online: Ameritrade features equity and option trading, retirement accounts, and trading on margin.

DLJdirect

www.dljdirect.com

$

The online version of a well-known company: Donaldson, Lufkin and Jenrette offers a wide variety of brokerage services, downloadable software, and investment information.

E*Trade

www.etrade.com

$

Fast and competent: E*Trade charges a flat rate for online trades. It's one of the best online brokerages.

National Discount Brokers

www.ndb.com

$

Trading plus information: National Discount Brokers is a Chicago-based firm that charges a flat fee for basic transactions. The firm offers portfolio accounting, technical analysis, and more.

Schwab

www.schwab.com

$

A long-time discount house goes online: Schwab's Internet trading site (sometimes called eSchwab) offers downloadable trading software, online trading, account information, quotes, and more.

Other Stuff to Check Out

www.computel.com
www.datek.com
www.fidelity.com
www.lombard.com
www.jboxford.com
www.protrade.com
www.quick-reilly.com
www.msiebert.com
www.waterhouse.com

Online Calculators

If you have a hard time with the math of personal finance, the Internet can help you. The Net provides many online financial calculators that can do all the math you require.

Altamira Resource Center Net Worth Calculator

www.altamira.com/icat/toolbox/ netcalc.html

What you're worth, dollar-wise: The Altamira Resource Center suggests that one of the primary financial goals in life is to increase net worth. Therefore, this site provides an online calculator that's designed to help you determine your current net worth.

Bank of American Investment Services

www.bankamerica.com/tools/ sri_assetall.html

Get a grip: This page from the Bank of America Web site provides a survey of 12 questions. Enter your answers and the online calculator suggests an investment allocation strategy that suits your current needs and situation.

FinanCenter

www.financenter.com

Calculators by the bagful: The FinanCenter provides many online calculators that can help you with your personal finances and investment decision-making. Just click an icon (budget, investments, retirement, and so on) and select the appropriate calculator.

Star Strategic Asset Allocation

www.io.org/~nobid/star.html

Investment by Q&A: Answer the questions, and the online calculator suggests the types of investments that are good matches to your risk-tolerance level.

Portfolio Management: Online Tools

Many online portfolio management programs exist that can monitor your investments, track their performance, and send you end-of-the-day messages to notify you of major changes. This section lists just a few examples.

Stockpoint Portfolio Management

www.stockpoint.com

A favorite of Barron's: Stockpoint provides a free personal portfolio tracking program. Other Web site offerings include quotes, analysis, stock news, and end-of-the-day e-mail portfolio updates. You can also download this information to your Quicken personal finance program.

Thomson Investors Network

www.thomsoninvest.net

Tracking, by e-mail and on the Web: Thomson Investors Network provides free and fee-based services. Subscribers and registered guests can use the Web site's portfolio tracking services (which include end-of-the-day quotes sent to your e-mailbox).

Yahoo!

edit.my.yahoo.com/config

Do you Yahoo: Yahoo! has a personalized portfolio program. To create portfolios, just enter a portfolio name and then add the ticker symbols of your investments separated by commas.

Other Stuff to Check Out

> www.moneynet.com
> my.excite.com
> www.quicken.com
> www.wsj.com

In the past, you had to laboriously search the Internet for that one vital piece of missing investment information. Now you can use push technology to bring that needed information directly to your desktop computer.

BackWeb

www.backweb.com

Intelligent screen savers: BackWeb flashes the news you select across your screen when you're not using your computer. BackWeb has a total of 50 channels to select from, and is free and downloadable.

Marimba

www.marimba.com

Use Java technology: Marimba can distribute software updates and corporate information directly to your computer. When Marimba detects new or updated information that you're interested in, it retrieves the data and saves it on your hard disk. You can view it at your leisure. The program is free and downloadable.

PointCast

www.pointcast.com

A popular choice: PointCast delivers the information you select to your computer. The company's smart screen acts as a screen saver. You can customize the program so the most current prices of your investments scroll across the screen. The PointCast program has more than 200 information *channels*. About 40 of these channels are money and investment topics. The program is free and downloadable.

The Internet provides many quote servers that provide real-time and delayed stock, mutual fund, bond, option, and Treasury security prices. Here are a few examples of online quote services and their features.

Data Broadcasting Online

www.dbc.com

$ ↘ 🛒

Quickie quotes: Data Broadcasting Online retrieves up to seven ticker symbols at one time. Quotes include last price, change, currency, percent change, opening price, today's low, today's high, previous day's closing price, and volume.

Interquote

www.interquote.com

↘ 📖 $

Real-time quotes: Interquote provides real-time, continuously updated quotes with the help of a special Windows program.

PC Quote

www.pcquote.com

📖 $ ↘

Quotes, now: PC Quote offers many free services and five levels of fee-based service. Free services include ticker symbol lookup, current stock prices, portfolio tracker, company profiles, and Zacks Investment Research broker recommendations.

Other Stuff to Check Out

quote.pathfinder.com/money/quote/qc
quotes.quicken.com
www.cnnfn.com
www.stocksmart.com
www.thomsoninvest.net
www.quote.com

Retirement Planning

Can you retire early? Check out the helpful guidance that the Internet offers, and maybe you can say good-bye to your day job earlier than you think.

Deloitte & Touche LLP

www.dtonline.com/promises/cover.htm

Tax law, translated: Deloitte & Touche LLP provides help interpreting the IRS tax language with a summary of new tax laws and Individual Retirement Accounts (IRAs). Following each tax law change, this site offers suggested action steps that you may want to consider.

Independence Life and Annuity Company FAQ

www.websaver.com/WSfaq.html

Annuity how and why: Independence Life and Annuity Company answers the most frequently asked questions about annuities, costs, and income options.

Retirement.com

www.retirement.com

IRA questions, answered: Sponsored by Strong Funds, this site attempts to answer your questions about traditional IRAs, Roth IRAs, SEP IRAs, and other retirement savings vehicles.

Retirement Planning: Online Worksheets

Need to do a few calculations for your retirement planning? The following Web sites can do the math for you.

BYG Publishing

www.bygpub.com/finance/RetirementCalc.htm

High-level planning: This site's retirement planning calculator can assist you in determining what sort of lifestyle you can expect during retirement by showing your 401(k) account balance before and after retirement. You can experiment with different savings amounts so that you can see the effect these amounts will have on your retirement lifestyle.

Fidelity Investments

personal.fidelity.com/toolbox

Retirement calculators, among others: Click the toolbox icon and go to a page with lots of links to online calculators. One of these calculators is for retirement planning. Use the calculator to determine the value of your nest egg at retirement, estimated savings surplus or shortfall, and estimated additional annual savings needed.

Other Stuff to Check Out

www.troweprice.com/retirement/retire.html
www.waddell.com

Savings Bonds

You can purchase savings bonds at banks, thrifts, or credit unions. Also, many employers offer payroll deduction plans that allow you to purchase savings bonds. For many people, purchasing savings bonds is the only way they can save money.

The Bureau of Public Debt

www.publicdebt.treas.gov/sav/savbene.htm

The government promotes its bonds: The Bureau of Public Debt provides information on the benefits of savings bonds and covers interest rates and maturity periods. You can either purchase (for the cost of the shipping and handling) or download Bond Wizard, a software program that calculates the value of your savings bonds.

Market Analysis of Savings Bonds

www.bondinformer.com

Easy for anyone to understand: One expert provides a market analysis of short- and long-term interest rates for savings bonds.

Stocks: Historical Prices

As part of your investment research of equities, you likely want to know the historical stock prices. This information is valuable for your forecasts of future stock prices.

Historical Stock Data for S&P 500 Stocks

kumo.swcp.com/stocks/

For hard-core analysts: Here, you can download files containing historical information for the stocks that make up the S&P 500-stock index (as well as those that were part of it in the past). The files can be used with analysis software.

Quote.Com

www.quote.com

Not just current quotes: Quote.Com provides historical data files as an additional service ($1.95) for current subscribers.

Other Stuff to Check Out

www.prophetdata.com
www.stockwiz.com/stockwiz.html

Stock Screens: Online

Stock screens can help you whittle down your list of investment candidates. Your creative searches can reveal stocks that have just the characteristics you're looking for.

Market Guide's NetScreen

netscreen.marketguide.com

$

Do your own sifting: Market Guide's NetScreen allows you to screen for stocks using any of 20 variables. The database is updated weekly.

MSN Investor

investor.msn.com

Loads of data: MSN Investor has a stock screen called Investment Finder that searches 8,000 companies to find securities that meet your specific criteria. The program uses dozens of variable combinations. You'll have better luck with this site (surprise, surprise) when you use the latest version of Microsoft Internet Explorer.

ResearchMag

www.researchmag.com

Applied research: The stock screen has 12 basic variables that screen more than 9,000 stocks. To use the advanced stock screen, you must be a subscriber. The subscription cost is based on the number of reports you use per year.

Stock Screens: Prebuilt

Online prebuilt stock screens can assist you in finding the stocks that are worthy of your additional analysis. (Remember, the best prebuilt screen is the one that screens for the things that you believe are important.)

Market Player

www.marketplayer.com

Power tools: Market Player provides a relatively advanced stock screening engine. Instructions about how to use the engine are easy to understand, but you should allow some time for figuring out the program. Market Player has many prebuilt screens that you may find useful. You can also play stock-picking games here.

The Motley Fool

www.fool.com

The original stock chat site: Motley Fool offers a weekly discussion of its stock screens. Motley Fool provides screen results that pick out companies that missed or beat analysts' consensus estimates by 9 percent or more. Stocks are listed alphabetically as well as by descending percentages.

Wall Street Voice

www.wsvoice.com

Solid criteria: Wall Street Voice provides easy-to-use, prebuilt stock screens with only two variables. The first variable is the stock's beta. *Beta* is a measure of the sensitivity of an investment's return compared to the market. The second variable is rank, as determined by Standard & Poor's analysts. The database of 1,100 stocks in 103 industry groups is updated weekly.

Tax Preparation and Online Assistance

If you're struggling with your taxes, the Internet can help you complete your tax return and file it electronically.

Income Tax Preparation Online

taxreturns-online.netgate.net

$

Help with your taxes: Income Tax Preparation Online provides fast, accurate, low-priced services. This site includes a *Tax Organizer* to help you gather all the information you need to complete your income tax report.

The Internal Revenue Service

www.fourmilab.ch/ustax/ustax.html

An IRS-authorized e-file provider: This Web site enables you to access the complete text of the United States Internal Revenue Code. It has a powerful search engine that can save you hours of time.

D-28 Tax Preparation and Online Assistance

Secure Tax

www.irs.ustreas.gov

Straight from the horse's mouth: A surprisingly well-organized and reasonably helpful tax guide. Get your tax forms here in Adobe Acrobat format.

Tax Systems

www.taxsys.com/1040ez.htm

$

Tax Systems can assist you in completing 1040EZ, 1040A, and 1040 forms online and filing your return electronically.

U.S. Tax Code Online

www.fourmilab.ch/ustax/ustax.html

An IRS-authorized electronic filing center: This Web site enables you to access the complete text of the United States Internal Revenue Code. It has a powerful search engine that can save you hours of time.

Other Stuff to Check Out

www.1040.com
www.dtonline.com/promises/cover.htm
www.hrblock.com
www.netcpa.com/forms/orglinks.htm
www.quicken.com/taxes/
www.maxwell.com/tax/
www.tax.org/TodaysTaxNews
www.taxsites.com/federal.html
www.taxweb.com
www.turbotax.com

Part III
Paying the Right Price

The 5th Wave   By Rich Tennant

"The book value of our stocks went way down when I discovered missing pages."

In this part . . .

The Internet offers plenty of resources that can help you turn your hunches into investment strategies. The chapters in this part of the book show you how to use the Internet to locate hard-to-find financial information so that you can analyze investment candidates. This part of the book shows you how to buy and sell mutual funds online, as well as how the World Wide Web can assist you in finding annual reports and other data about companies that you fancy. In this part, you find out how to evaluate stock prices like a pro, explore one of the easiest ways available to value bonds, and see how to purchase Treasury securities online. You also discover how to reduce the purchase costs of buying your favorite stocks by using direct purchase and dividend reinvestment plans.

Chapter 10

Online Analysis, Buying, and Selling of Mutual Funds

*W*hen selecting a mutual fund, investors often look for relative performance over the last ten years, five years, and three years to see how the fund reacts to different economic conditions and stock market environments. Other factors in selecting a mutual fund include evaluating the fund manager's experience and record, the fund's level of consistency, and the fund's major investment holdings.

In this chapter, I show how you can match your financial objectives and risk-tolerance level to the right mutual funds. As a result, you can decide how much you should invest in a particular type of fund. This chapter includes instructions about how to read an online mutual fund listing. I also describe how you can use online mutual fund ratings to assist you in selecting the very best mutual funds for your personal portfolio. I compare three different mutual fund rating systems and provide a short list of online mutual fund companies that you can purchase without a broker. I conclude with step-by-step directions on how to purchase mutual funds with a broker and how to tell when it's time to sell.

Going Online with Mutual Funds

Mutual funds are great for investors who lack capital, technical knowledge, and the time to establish and maintain a diversified stock or bond portfolio. The advantages of mutual funds are easy access to your assets, the ability to sell the funds if you need to, and professional management.

The secretary of state for Montana offers a short online guide for beginning mutual fund investors at mos1.sos.state.mo.us/sos-sec/mufunds.html

A wide difference exists in the kinds of mutual funds available. Many large mutual fund companies manage *families* of funds. A mutual fund family is a group of mutual funds all under the same management. Today, you can select from more than 9,600 different mutual funds from over 700 fund families. Most likely, one of these funds meets your personal objectives and risk-tolerance level. If you aren't satisfied with the fund you select, you can always switch from one fund to another in the same fund family (often without any additional exchange costs).

You can find information about a fund's goals, strategies for reaching those objectives, performance, management, and fee structures in the fund's prospectus. Prospectuses are often located at the fund's Web site (for example, T. Rowe Price's site at www.troweprice.com), and they're also filed at the Securities and Exchange Commission's Web site at www.sec.gov.

Mutual funds fall into two main categories: *open-end funds* (which can continuously acquire new funds for investment through the sale of additional shares) and *closed-end funds* (which initially raise capital by selling a fixed number of shares, and then those shares are bought and sold on a stock exchange).

Different funds have different fees. Some funds have *up-front loads* (a sales commission when you buy the fund) or *back-end loads* (a sales commission when you sell the fund), and some funds have *no loads* (no sales commissions).

For a list of a few no-load mutual funds, see www.noload.com.

All funds have fees and expenses, but the amounts vary. In addition to sales and redemption fees, the mutual fund's prospectus indicates the fund's management and administration expenses. The fund's investment advisor generally receives 0.5 to 1.0 percent of the fund's average daily net assets. Administrative expenses include legal, auditing, and accounting costs, along with the fees for directors and the costs of preparing the annual report and proxy statements. These administrative expenses are added to the investment advisory fee. The total costs often average between 0.75 percent and 1.25 percent of fund assets. Savvy mutual fund investors are wary of funds that charge more than 1.25 percent.

In 1980 the SEC passed Rule 12b-1, which allows mutual fund companies to charge fund assets with advertising and marketing expenses. These costs typically range from 0.25 percent to 0.30 percent and can be as high as 1.25 percent. Some mutual funds charge these fees and others don't, so read the prospectus carefully.

Figure 10-1 shows the Mutual Fund Investor's Center (`www.mfea.com`). You may be interested in what it has to say about its membership. The site provides links to profiles on performance data for no-load mutual funds, lists of funds with the lowest initial minimum deposit, lists of funds with the lowest expenses, comparative indexes, and other relevant mutual fund information.

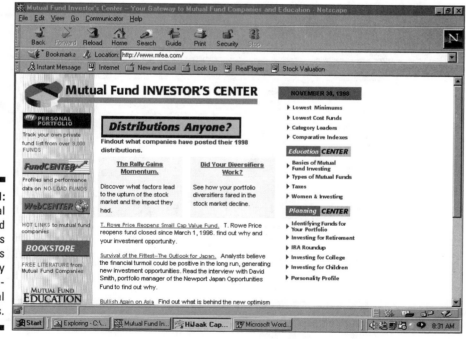

Figure 10-1:
The Mutual Fund Investors Center has much to say about no-load mutual funds.

Finding the Right Mix of Investments

Asset allocation is the specific amount of money that you spend for each type of investment. In Wall Street-speak, the term describes how you diversify your financial assets (stocks, bonds, and cash) by amounts that you determine. Asset allocation also means trying to squeeze every bit of return out of each asset type, given the level of risk. Overall, the right asset allocation approach is the one that works best for you. It should take into consideration your age, the amount of time you can invest your money, your financial goals, your risk-tolerance level, and the impact of taxes on your investment decisions.

Table 10-1 shows all the ingredients for finding the combination of assets that may be just right for you. The source of this guideline is Value Line (www.valueline.com). The table shows Value Line's definitions of nine investor types. The types are categorized as conservative, moderate, and aggressive. The investment time frame fills out the picture. The investment period can be short-term, medium-term, or long-term.

Table 10-1	**Mutual Fund Asset Allocations Based on Investor Risk-Tolerance Levels**		
Risk	*Time Frame*		
	Short-term (0 to 2 years)	*Medium-term (3 to 5 years)*	*Long-term (6 years and greater)*
Conservative	#1	#2	#3
Stocks	0%	30%	50%
Bonds	0%	25%	50%
Cash	100%	45%	0%
Moderate	#4	#5	#6
Stocks	10%	55%	65%
Bonds	30%	35%	35%
Cash	60%	10%	0%
Aggressive	#7	#8	#9
Stocks	30%	70%	100%
Bonds	30%	30%	0%
Cash	40%	0%	0%

Source: Value Line Mutual Fund Survey, *How to Invest in Mutual Funds* (1995), Value Line Publishing, Inc., New York, NY.

Many mutual funds match the asset allocation table shown in Table 10-1. You can start with one mutual fund or you can purchase a mutual fund for each allocation. If you purchase several mutual funds, you can diversify your risk even more. For example, to complete your portfolio, you may want to buy a money market fund, a stock mutual fund, and a fixed-asset (bond) mutual fund. It's your money and your choice.

Matching Mutual Funds to Your Financial Objectives

Table 10-2 shows how you can match mutual fund categories to your financial objectives and risk-tolerance level. After you read Table 10-1, decide which of the nine-investor types most closely matches your personal financial plan and risk-tolerance profile. For more detail about the investor types, visit the Value Line site at www.valueline.com. Table 10-2 shows what categories of mutual funds are right for your investor type. The percentages listed in Table 10-2 match the recommended allocations shown in Table 10-1. (For details about fund types, see Chapter 6.)

Table 10-2	Suggested Mutual Funds for Nine Types of Investors		
Investor Type	**Cash**	**Stocks**	**Bonds**
1	(100%) Money market fund		
2	(45%) Money market fund	(30%) General equity	(25%) Intermediate fixed income partial equity funds (asset allocation), Tax-free fixed income funds (municipal bonds)
3	(0%)	(50%) General equity funds (income, growth)	(50%) Taxable fixed-income funds (government agency, and income) Fixed-mortgage income, partial equity funds (asset allocation)

(continued)

Table 10-2 *(continued)*

Investor Type	Cash	Stocks	Bonds
4	(10%) Money market fund	(30%) General equity funds income	(60%) Short-term Fixed-income funds (diversified), Fixed-income partial equity funds (asset allocation and balanced)
5	(10%) Money market fund	(55%) General equity funds (growth income)	(35%) Intermediate fixed-income funds (diversified), Intermediate fixed-income partial equity funds (balanced), Tax-free fixed-income funds (municipal bonds)
6	(0%)	(65%) General equity funds (growth, growth and equity)	(35%) Fixed-income bonds (diversified, corporate), Fixed-income partial equity funds (balanced), Tax-free fixed-income funds (municipal bonds)
7	(40%) Money market fund	(30%) General equity funds (aggressive growth, small cap)	(30%) Short-term fixed-income funds (corporate high-yield), Short-term fixed-income partial equity funds (convertible)
8	(0%)	(70%) General equity funds (aggressive growth, small cap), Specialty equity (technology, other)	(30%) Intermediate fixed-income (corporate high yield), Intermediate fixed-income partial equity funds (flexible), Tax-free fixed-income funds (municipal bonds)

Investor Type	Cash	Stocks	Bonds
9	(0%)	(100%) General	(0%) equity funds (aggressive growth, growth, and growth and income), Small cap equity funds, Specialty equity (technology, other), International equity (European, foreign, global, or Pacific stock)

Interested in finding specific mutual funds in the categories that match your personal finance profile? Stock Smart (www.stocksmart.com) can assist you in finding the mutual fund that's right for you. When you reach the Stock Smart home page, click on the Fund icon at the top of the screen. Next, click on the Smart Stock Fund Wizard icon. On the questionnaire that appears, answer the questions about what you're looking for in a mutual fund. The Wizard uses your preferences to find funds that best match your specific needs.

Using the Internet to Help You Choose the Best Funds in Each Class

Past performance doesn't guarantee future performance. However, annualized returns are often used to compare funds. The Internet offers tables of fund comparisons for each month and for periods ranging from one month to ten years or more. For example, Business Week (www.businessweek.com) has a Mutual Funds Corner that provides listings of the returns for the best funds, bond fund leaders, the worst funds, and so on.

Comparing a fund to similar funds is a good way to examine a fund's performance. Organizations such as Morningstar (www.morningstar.net) have mutual fund tables that make comparisons easy by grouping fund classes (see the section "A Fund for You, a Fund for Me," in Chapter 6 for details about fund classes) and including the averages for each category. A fund's capability to consistently outperform similar funds is one sign of good quality. In contrast, you should avoid funds that have consistently underperformed for three years or more.

Make certain that the funds you're comparing are similar. A big difference exists between an aggressive growth fund and a growth fund. To verify your analyses, check the prospectus of each fund. The fund's investment objectives are listed in the first paragraph. You may discover that the fund that looked so attractive at first is too risky for you.

Following a mutual fund checklist

As you select your first mutual fund, consider several factors, which I describe in the following checklist:

- ✓ **The fund manager:** Often a fund is only as good as its management. If the fund manager has shown great performance in the past, future performance is likely to be above average. If the fund manager has been replaced, past performance becomes less meaningful and may even be worthless. A poor-performing fund that gets a new fund manager may turn around and become a top performer.

- ✓ **The stability of the fund's philosophy:** If the fund seems unclear about its financial goals and is switching investment methods, it may be in trouble.

- ✓ **The size of the fund:** Good fund candidates have at least $50 million under management and should be large enough to keep up with institutional investors. At the opposite end of the spectrum, funds with more than $20 billion tend to have problems with being too large.

- ✓ **The objectives of the fund:** Some funds focus on specialty or sector funds (gold funds, biotech funds, and so on) and often offer great returns. However, they aren't good funds for the online investor who wants to own just one mutual fund. If you own just one specialty fund, you lose the advantage of diversification.

- ✓ **Fees:** A debate has raged during the last ten years about which is better: no-load or load mutual funds. All the studies indicate that paying a sales commission doesn't ensure a greater return. However, investing in a fund with high fees and high returns is better than investing in a fund with low fees and poor performance.

- ✓ **Purchase constraints:** Although some funds require a minimum initial investment of $5,000, many good funds don't have this requirement. Additionally, if you enroll in a fund's automatic investment program, the minimum initial investment amount is usually waived. Additionally, many fund minimums are waived or substantially reduced for IRA investments.

For additional information about selecting mutual funds, see Morningstar (www.morningstar.net). Morningstar has a learning section (just click on Learn) and helpful articles. One such article is titled "Select Your First Fund."

How to read an online mutual fund listing

As a general rule, mutual fund listings are slightly easier to read than stock listings. (See the section "How to Read a Stock Chart or Table" in Chapter 7 to find out about stock listings.) Some online sources and newspapers list mutual funds differently. Table 10-3 shows how the Wall Street Journal Interactive Edition (www.wsj.com) shows the performance of a mutual fund profile. The name and ticker symbol of the mutual fund is listed first.

Table 10-3 How to Read an Online Mutual Fund Listing			
Title of Fund:		Dreyfus Growth Opportunity Fund, Inc.	
Symbol:		DREQX	
Net Asset Value:	9.97	52-Week High	10.94
Change:	+0.12	52-Week Low	8.51
Performance			
	Total Return		Percentile within Objective
Year-to-date	3.9%5	D	34
1-Year	4.5%	D	26
3-Year (annualized)	16.0%	D	27
5-Year (annualized)	11.5%	E	15
Fund Information			
Investment Objective:		Growth Funds	
Fund Manger (Tenure):		Timothy M. Ghriskey (since 1995)	
Minimum Initial Investment		$2,500	
Maximum Sales Charge:		0%	
Maximum Redemption Charge:		0%	
Total Expense Ratio:		1.06%	
Total Net Assets:		$406,200,000	
Phone:		800-383-9387	

Source: Wall Street Journal Interactive (www.wsj.com)

You can use a company look-up to find the ticker symbol of the mutual fund you're researching. Many online sources, such as the Wall Street Journal (www.wsj.com) have company look-ups. These handy tools are often listed next to the quote server tools so that you don't have to change to another Web site. Enter the full or partial name of the fund you are interested in. The company look-up tool provides a hyperlinked list of potential matches. Click on the ticker symbol that you think matches the fund you are researching. If the symbol doesn't represent the correct fund, click the Back button and try another candidate.

The Net Asset Value (NAV) of the fund and the changes in the fund's value for that day appear under the ticker symbol information (refer to Table 10-3). The NAV is the sales price of one share of the fund. (The NAV is calculated by dividing the value of the fund by the number of shares.) Below that appears the change in price for the day, and is the *bottom line* for investors. Table 10-3 indicates that the example fund increased by $0.12. In the next column are the fund's NAV 52-week high and low.

The *Performance* section of Table 10-3 indicates the total performance of the fund for the time periods of year-to-date, one year, three years (annualized), and five years (annualized). A total return assumes that all dividends have been reinvested at the share price on the day of payout. The annualized returns are the compounded annual rate of investment return expressed as a percentage. These amounts are also important to investors. They indicate how much the fund has gained or lost in a specific time period. (These figures are calculated before subtracting for sales fees.)

The Wall Street Journal has its own rating system. The percentile within objective is a comparison of the fund to other like funds (aggressive funds to aggressive funds, growth funds to growth funds, and so on). The fund is ranked in two ways. First, the letter score shows the ranking of the fund. A score of "A" indicates that the fund is in the top 20%, B is the next 20%, C is the middle 20%, and D is the next 20%. A score of "E" indicates that the fund was in the bottom 20% of the objective in that time period. The fund illustrated in Table 10-3 has a year-to-date rank of D, indicating that at this time the fund is below the middle rating and in the bottom 40% of the objective.

Percentile scores are the actual ranking within the objective. Table 10-3 shows that the year-to-date performance of the fund has a score of 34, which indicates that the fund did better than 34% of the funds in its category in the same time period. This information means that 66% of the funds performed better than our example did.

The *Fund Information* section of Table 10-3 shows basic fund information. Investment objective data indicates how the fund is categorized by its investment objectives. (The Wall Street Journal uses 28 categories.) Click the Investment Objective link to see the definition of this category and a listing of the top winners and losers in this investment objective. Other fund information includes the fund manager's name and length of tenure, minimum initial investment amount, maximum sales and redemption charges, expense ratio (which is the percentage of average net assets devoted to expenses and distribution (12b-1 fees) as reported in the annual report), and total asset size of the fund.

Assessing mutual fund performance

No hard-and-fast rules exist about how to assess a mutual fund. However, the following list provides easy-to-use guidelines to assess the performance of your mutual fund investment candidates. After your assessment, each fund will require additional analysis. Only funds that meet all of the criteria should be selected for further research. Funds that meet all the following criteria are likely to reduce your chances of losing money without lowering your mutual funds returns.

Tax liabilities and returns: All mutual fund performance is shown on a pre-tax basis. This is reasonable because different investors are in different tax brackets. If you are investing through taxable accounts (which are different than non-taxable accounts that might include your IRA or other tax-exempt investments), you should only compare the after-tax returns of the funds you are analyzing. This comparison allows you to compare apples to apples instead of apples to oranges.

The impact of short-term performance: Ignore short-term performance. Short-term returns are heavily influenced by fluctuations in the market and are valueless.

Inconsistent returns: Avoid funds that have inconsistent returns when compared to unmanaged indexes. In other words, when you compare your fund to the appropriate benchmark, take into consideration the consistency of the two funds. If your fund is more volatile than the benchmark, it may have more risk than you expected. For a quick list of mutual fund benchmarks, see www.centrepost.com/concept9712.htm.

Fund ranking when compared to like funds: The fund's performance is ranked within the top 20% to 50% of its type. Make certain that your analysis compares growth funds to growth funds and value funds to value funds, etc.

Fund ranking when compared to unmanaged indexes: The fund's performance and risk level is better than an unmanaged index for 1-, 3-, and 5-year time periods. Compare the fund's performance (before mutual fund costs). A broad-based U.S. stock fund should be compared to the S & P 500 (www.stockinfo.standardpoor.com) or the Wilshire 5000 Index; small company funds should be compared to the Russell 2000 Index, and so on.

The fund's price/earnings (P/E) ratios are 15 to 25: P/E ratios above 30 tend to be high-risk.

The fund's standard deviation: The fund's Morningstar standard deviation for 3 years is 17 or lower. If you are using the Value Line calculated standard deviation (which is different), the standard deviation for 3 years is 12 or lower.

The fund's risk value: Value Line rankings range from 1 (low risk) to 5 (high risk). The fund's Value Line risk value is 1.0 or lower. Morningstar uses its own *Morningstar Risk Values*. A ranking of 1.0 means that the fund is as risky as comparable funds. The Morningstar Risk Value should be .90 or lower.

The evaluation criteria in the preceding list are a good starting point for your analysis. As you become a more sophisticated investor, you're likely to modify, delete, and add criteria. This customization ensures that your mutual fund selections meet your individual risk-tolerance level and financial objectives.

The Ratings War

Mutual fund companies don't show you the standard deviation and the betas (a measurement of the volatility of a security with the market in general) of their mutual funds. However, you don't have to make your investment decision without these bits of vital information. Many Web sites offer information on the ranking of mutual funds. Rankings are useful because they help you digest important performance and risk statistics into one measure. Here are a few examples of Web sites that offer information on the ranking of mutual funds:

- **Barron's** (www.barrons.com)
- **Business Week** (www.businessweek.com)
- **Forbes** (www.forbes.com)
- **S&P Mutual Fund Profiles and Stock Guides** (www.stockinfo.standardpoor.com)
- **Wall Street Journal** (www.wsj.com)

Two of the most popular online rating services are Morningstar and Value Line. Morningstar (www.morningstar.net) is a free service. Value Line (www.valueline.com) is a fee-based service.

The Morningstar rating system

Morningstar is an independent, Chicago-based firm that has been evaluating mutual funds and annuities since 1984. The organization currently evaluates more than 7,500 mutual funds.

Morningstar uses historical data to develop its ratings. The unique feature of the rating system is that it penalizes mutual funds for excess risk that doesn't result in excess returns. Morningstar rates funds for consistently giving the highest returns and adjusts for risk as compared to funds in the same category.

Morningstar's five-star system is as follows:

- ✔ **Five Stars:** In the top 10 percent of performance; produces substantially above-average returns

- ✔ **Four Stars:** In the next 22.5 percent of performance; produces above-average returns

- ✔ **Three Stars:** In the middle 35 percent of performance; produces average returns

- ✔ **Two Stars:** In the lower 22.5 percent of performance; produces below-average returns

- ✔ **One Star:** In the bottom 10 percent of performance; produces substantially below-average returns

The Value Line dual rating system

Value Line uses a dual rating system that includes overall rank and measures various performance criteria, including risk. Funds are ranked from 1 to 5, with one having the highest rank (the best risk-adjusted performance) and the best risk ranking (the least risky). For more details about Value Line, see *Investing For Dummies* by Eric Tyson, MBA (IDG Books Worldwide, Inc.).

Value Line uses historical data to develop its ratings. The five-number system is as follows:

- ✔ **1:** In the top 10 percent; highest overall performance and lowest risk

- ✔ **2:** In the next 20 percent; above-average performance and lower risk

- ✔ **3:** In the middle 40 percent; average performance and average risk

- ✔ **4:** In the lower 20 percent; below-average performance and higher risk

- ✔ **5:** In the lowest 10 percent; lowest average performance and highest risk

Value Line has a software package that includes no- and low-load versions of Value Line's fund-analysis software. Launched as a less extensive alternative to the full Mutual Fund Survey for Windows, the program features the same sophisticated sorting, screening, filtering, portfolio analysis, and graphics capabilities. Its database presents essential information on more than 3,000 no- and low-load funds. The program is available on CD-ROM or 3 ¹/₂-inch disk. One-year subscription prices are $149 for the monthly service and $95 for quarterly updates. A two-month trial subscription is available for $29. You can download updates from Value Line's Web site at www.valueline.com. A free, downloadable demo version of the software and database is available.

When using mutual funds ratings, you must keep two things in mind. First, past performance does not predict future performance. Second, comparing the ranks of two different mutual fund categories is meaningless. For example, you can't compare the ranks of a municipal-bond fund against an aggressive-growth fund.

Using Scoreboards and Ratings

In this chapter, I present three different rating systems: The Wall Street Journal, Morningstar, and Value Line. The Wall Street Journal (www.wsj.com) ranks mutual funds from A to E, with A the top scorer. Morningstar (www.morningstar.net) rates mutual funds from five to one star, with five stars the top performers. And Value Line (www.valueline.com) categorizes mutual funds from 1 to 5, with 1 taking top billing.

In the best of times, the same fund can be ranked a five-star Morningstar winner and a number one mutual fund by Value Line. Sometimes a mutual fund's score can indicate a top performer by one mutual fund rating service and a loser by another mutual fund rating service. Why the difference?

Some mutual funds scores are *risk adjusted* and some are *absolute*. Risk adjusted scores punish mutual funds for inconsistent returns and rewards others for stability. For example, the risk adjusted mutual funds rating can:

- ✔ Penalize a fund for radically changing from its previous performance. Additionally, a fund can be penalized for *exceeding* its previous performance. In other words, the fund can receive a lower rating because of unexpected increases in returns. This rating penalty can be just as bad as an unexpected decrease in returns.

- ✔ Reward mediocre fund performers. They can receive a higher rating because of their stability.

Conservative investors prefer to use risk-adjusted scores. Other investors prefer to use the absolute numbers. However, the best approach is to have a clear understanding of the differences in the ranking systems.

The analysis of mutual funds includes more research than selecting a fund by its rating. Remember that the more informed you are, the better your decision-making will be.

Forecasting Your Mutual Fund's Future

Selecting mutual funds based on past performance may not be the best way to pick next year's winners. Past returns don't guarantee future performance. Additionally, factoring in risk using standard deviation methods may not be helpful. After all, the information used for the standard deviation calculations are also based on historical returns. To solve this dilemma, in January 1998, Worth Online (www.worth.com/articles/Z9801M01.html) developed a forward-looking mutual fund rating system. The goal of the system is to help the investor select today's and tomorrow's top performers.

You may find that locating the Worth Mutual Fund Ratings Guide is sort of tricky. First, go to its homepage at www.worth.com. Then click Archives and then click Archives By Date. Click December/January 1998 and then click the title "A New Way to Rate Mutual Funds." At the end of the article you find the hyperlinks to the Mutual Fund Ratings and a link to information about how to read the listings. Don't forget to bookmark this page — it will save you time in the future.

Worth Online slices entity funds into five classes based on stock types: global, small-company value funds, small-company growth funds, large company value funds, and large company growth funds. Worth Online doesn't rate funds for historical performance and new forward-looking measures of Regret (decline) and Reward (appreciation).

The authors of the guide state that it's designed for 401(k) plans, IRAs, or other retirement accounts. If you aren't selecting funds for a tax-advantaged plan, refer to Morningstar (www.morningstar.net) for information about a fund's turnover and sales charges. Additionally, individuals investing late in the year may experience an unexpected tax burden when annual capital gains distributions are paid in November and December. Just for the "fund" of it, check out the A. Bull & Co. Power Ratings for 600+ No-Load Funds at www.angelfire.com/biz/mutualfunds/POWER.html.

The company provides free analyses of the 600 most popular no-load mutual funds in the U.S. Each analysis includes a listing of a fund's total returns for the last three months and the last month as well as forecasts of the mutual fund's annual return. The forecast is based on price changes and weighted returns (including distributions) for the next year.

A. Bull & Co. also provides a free current update of its forecasts for 600 well-known no-load mutual funds in a generic spreadsheet format that allows you to sort and screen funds by using your own criteria. In addition to the data shown at the company's Web site, you can order a full report that includes ticker symbols, risk measurements based on three-year standard deviations, and more. To receive the full free update by e-mail, just send your request to mutualfunds@mailexcite.com.

Buying Mutual Funds Online: No Broker Needed

You can purchase a mutual fund without a broker. All you have to do is contact the company directly. Table 10-4 lists a few online mutual fund companies. The table shows the name of the mutual fund company, its Internet address, the minimum investment required, the number of funds the mutual fund company has (as of this printing), and whether the company has an automatic investment program. Usually, if you enroll for the automatic investment plan, you don't have to deposit the required initial minimum investment amount.

Table 10-4	Examples of Online Mutual Fund Sources			
Company	*Internet Address*	*Minimum Investment (Non-IRA Accts)*	*No. of Funds*	*Automatic Investment Plan?*
AIM Funds	www.aimfunds.com	$500	45	Yes
Alliance Funds	www.alliance-capital.com	$250	118	Yes
American Century Funds	www.american-century.com	$2,500	60+	Yes
Columbia Funds	www.columbia-funds.com	$1,000	12	Yes
Dreyfus Funds	www.dreyfus.com	$2,000	150+	Yes
Evergreen Funds	www.evergreen.com	$1,000	70+	Yes
Fidelity Funds	www.fidelity.com	$2,500	253	Yes
INVESCO Funds	www.invesco.com	$1,000	48	Yes
Janus Funds	www.janus.com	$2,500	19	Yes
John Hancock Funds	www.jhancock.com	$1,000	71	Yes
Kemper Funds	www.kemper.com	$1,000	43	Yes

Company	Internet Address	Minimum Investment (Non-IRA Accts)	No. of Funds	Automatic Investment Plan?
Merrill Lynch Funds	www.plan.ml.com/ products_ services	Varies	100+	Yes
Nations Funds	www.nationsbank. com	$1,000	44	Yes
Oppenheimer Funds	www.oppenheimer- funds.com	$1,000	49	Yes
Paine Webber Funds	www.painewebber. com	$25,000	86	No
Prudential Funds	www.prudential.com	Varies	168	Yes
Putnam Funds	www.putnaminv.com	$500	209	Yes
Schwab Funds	www.schwab.com	$1,000	29	Yes
Scudder Funds	funds.scudder.com	$2,500	47	Yes
Smith Barney Funds	www3.smithbarney. com	$1,000	60+	Yes
Stein Roe Funds	www.steinroe.com	$2,500	21	Yes
Strong Funds	www.strong.com	Varies	30	Yes
Vanguard Group	www.vanguard.com	Varies	90	Yes

Buying Mutual Funds Online: Using an Electronic Broker

You can purchase mutual funds through registered representatives of banks, trust companies, stockbrokers, discount brokers, and financial planners. To purchase mutual funds via the Internet, go to an online broker's Web site. (I list a few examples later in this section.)

Register by completing the online application form. You have to provide information about your income, net worth, social security number, and the type of account you desire. Sometimes you can open an account based on the quality (creditworthiness) of your information.

However, to have a fully functioning account, brokerages are required to have your signature on file. After they have your signature on file, you can buy or sell as much as you want.

After you open your account, you can log on to the Internet, go to your brokerage Web site, and enter orders by completing the online form. You can access your account at any time, check all your investments, and monitor your investments by using online news or quote services.

You have the following options for selecting an electronic broker:

- ✔ **A deep-discount broker:** The least expensive type of broker ($7 to $15 per trade); offers no recommendations; contacting a human if an error occurs is often difficult. For a partial list, see Web Investor at www.thewebinvestor.com/stocks-dddiscount.html

- ✔ **A discount broker:** Less expensive than full-service brokerages; no recommendations; minimum human contact

- ✔ **A full-service broker:** Full commissions, recommendations, advice, and personal service

Here are a few examples of online deep-discount brokers:

- ✔ **American Express Financial Direct** (www.americanexpress.com) requires an initial investment of $2,000 to open an account. This firm trades stock and mutual funds for a flat rate of $24.95.

- ✔ **Ameritrade** (www.ameritrade.com) is a New York-based firm that charges a flat rate of $8.00 per trade. This firm trades stocks, funds, and options. An initial investment of $2,000 is required to open an account. If you're wondering where this firm came from, the organization is a consolidation of Ceres, Aufhauser, and eBroker.

- ✔ **Discover Brokerage Direct** (www.lombard.com) is a San Francisco-based firm that requires an initial investment of $2,000 to open an account and charges $14.95 per trade. The firm trades stocks, funds, and options.

- ✔ **Donaldson, Lufkin, & Jenrette (DLJ Direct), formerly PC Financial Network,** (www.dljdirect.com) is based in New York. Trades are $20 for up to 1,000 shares. Trades of over 1,000 shares add $.02 per share. The company trades stocks, funds, bonds, and options.

- ✔ **E*Trade** (www.etrade.com) is a Palo Alto, California-based firm that charges a flat rate of $19.95 for the first 5,000 shares traded and then $.01 per share for shares above that amount. It's also available on America Online and CompuServe.

✔ **Investexpress** (www.investexpress.com) doesn't require an initial investment to open an account. The firm trades stocks, funds, and options, and charges $13.95 per trade.

✔ **National Discount Brokers** (www.NDB.com) is a Chicago-based firm that requires an initial investment of $2,000 to open an account, and charges $14.75 per trade. The firm trades stocks, funds, and options.

✔ **Net Investor** (www.netinvestor.com) is a Chicago-based firm that requires an initial investment of $5,000 to open an account. Trades are $19.95 plus $.01 per share and a $4.45 transaction fee. The company trades stocks, funds, bonds, options, and CDs.

The Right Time to Sell Your Mutual Funds

If your fund becomes one of the worst performers, consider selling. However, you need to look at more than just the fund's rating. Here are a few guidelines for determining when to sell a fund:

✔ Look at the performance of comparable mutual funds. If a similar fund's overall performance is down 10% and your fund is down 16% and its performance consistently trails its peers, it may be a loser.

✔ If your fund has *drifted* from its original investment objectives, then it's not meeting your asset allocation goals. You'll lose all the benefits of diversification if you have two mutual funds investing in the same asset class.

✔ Keep track of changes in your fund's management. If the fund hires a new money manager, that person may have a different investment strategy.

✔ You may want to sell if your mutual fund's expenses have been creeping up, you inherited the fund, or your old broker sold you a fund with a high 12b-1 fee. High fund fees reduce your returns and make the fund less profitable than similar funds with lower expenses.

✔ In a volatile market, you may discover that you are a more conservative investor than you imagined. If you can't sleep at night, sell your fund.

✔ You are going to pay taxes on your capital gains. One of your mutual funds is posting negative returns. You may want to consider selling the losing fund to offset your tax liabilities.

✔ If the fund increases by three or four times its original size in a short time period and its performance starts to decline, you may want to sell. As the fund keeps growing and growing, the professional money manager can't invest in the securities he or she knows and loves best, so the fund may start to acquire poor or average performing assets.

✔ Consider your needs. If you purchased the fund for a specific purpose and your life circumstances change, you should sell the fund and purchase one that meets your needs — even if the fund is doing well.

Figure 10-2 shows FundAlarm (`www.fundalarm.com`), a free, noncommercial Web site. FundAlarm provides objective information to help individual investors decide whether to sell a mutual fund. For details about how you can be automatically notified about when it's time to sell your mutual funds, see the Web site.

Funds that under-perform in the short term can still be sound investments. For example, Fidelity Magellan and Janus Income and Growth funds didn't outperform the market in the last three years; however, their average total returns over the last three years were 21.7 percent and 27 percent, respectively.

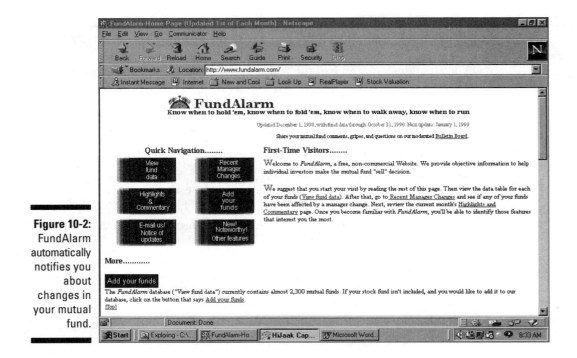

Figure 10-2:
FundAlarm automatically notifies you about changes in your mutual fund.

Chapter 11

Researching Individual Stocks

● ●

● ●

*I*n the past, only large financial institutions had access to high-quality financial data. Clients didn't have anywhere else to go for stock advice, which meant that bankers and stockbrokers charged customers hefty commissions for their research and recommendations. Much of this data is now available on the Internet. Some of the databases are free, and some are fee-based. Databases that charge fees require subscription fees — payment by the month, by database, or by document.

Even with free or low-cost information, researching stocks is still hard work. Doing so requires good judgment, the ability to fit all the bits and pieces of information together, and excellent decision-making skills. If you're thinking about investing in stocks, you need to research the following information:

✔ **Companies:** Profiles, management, financial health, insider trading, potential mergers, and acquisitions

✔ **Industries:** Industrial markets, industrial standards, and trends

✔ **Economic indicators:** The national, regional, and local economics

✔ **Other factors:** New legislation, technological breakthroughs, and new stock offerings

Often the best starting point for researching the stock of a certain company is the annual report. The best place to find annual reports is on the Internet. This chapter shows you how to locate annual reports by using a search engine, special company locator sites, investor supersites, and EDGAR — the Securities and Exchange Commission's online database.

Publicly traded companies are required to file quarterly reports with the Securities and Exchange Commission (www.sec.gov). These reports provide updates of the company's activities since it filed its annual report. If the company is going through a momentous change (such as a merger or acquisition), it's required to file more often.

You can find important information about a company in the annual report, but annual reports require careful reading. This chapter shows you how to download an annual report and analyze any publicly traded company. After all, reading a company's annual report is a little like kicking the tires of a used car. You want to make certain that you get what you think you're buying.

Finding Financial Statements Online

If you're a stockholder, you automatically receive the company's annual report. Annual reports are also free for the asking to anyone else. All you have to do is call the firm's investor relations department and request that they mail you a copy.

For online investors, getting annual reports is even easier. The Internet provides four sources for annual reports:

- ✔ **Annual Report Web sites:** These Web sites are designed for investors, shareholders, and money managers who want instant access to company annual reports. Many sites include additional company quarterlies, fact books, and press releases.

- ✔ **Company Web sites:** Many companies have sites on the Internet that include their annual reports. You can use special corporate linking sites and commercial search engines to find these on the Internet.

- ✔ **Investor compilation sites:** These Internet investor supersites often include annual reports, company news, earnings forecasts, and other useful information.

- ✔ **Securities and Exchange Commission (SEC) filings:** The SEC does a good job of making electronically filed company reports available online to the public.

In the following sections, I show you how to find annual reports using these sources.

Accessing Web sites that specialize in annual reports

The Internet features Web sites that focus on the individual investor's need for company information. These sites deliver annual reports in a variety of ways. For example, you can order hard copies of the original reports, immediately access online annual reports, or view annual reports in their original formats using free Internet plug-ins. The following are a few examples of information services on the Internet:

✔ **Disclosure** (www.disclosure-investor.com): This site, shown in Figure 11-1, provides SEC filings, financial information on over 12,000 U.S. public companies, financial data on over 13,000 global companies, and company press releases. The SEC information, corporate snapshots, and company PRNewsire press releases are free. Profile and investment tearsheets are $3.00 each. (*Tearsheets* are one-page reports that consolidate company financial information.)

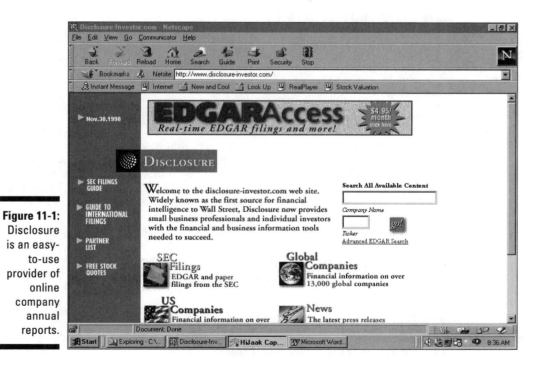

Figure 11-1: Disclosure is an easy-to-use provider of online company annual reports.

- ✔ **Investor's Relations Information Network (**www.irin.com**):** The Network offers over 2,500 free company annual reports in their original formats. That is, annual reports include photographs, graphs, and text. You use the Adobe Acrobat pdf format to read the information. (Reports are readable on Windows, Macintosh, DOS, and UNIX operating systems.)

- ✔ **Public Register's Annual Report Service (**www.prars.com**):** This service is free and provides both online annual reports and hard copies of company annual reports. Some annual reports are in the Adobe Acrobat format. You can download a free copy of the Adobe Acrobat Reader at the Web site.

- ✔ **The Annual Reports Library (**www.zpub.com/sf/arl/index.html**):** Founded in 1983, the Annual Reports Library includes more than 1.5 million original annual reports from corporations, foundations, banks, mutual funds, and public institutions located throughout the world.

Using a search engine to find an annual report

Many publicly traded companies have Web sites on the Internet. These sites often include the company's annual report as part of the firm's public relations and investor services.

To find these annual reports, you can start with a commercial search engine, such as AltaVista (www.altavista.digital.com), Infoseek (www.infoseek.com), or Excite (www.excite.com). After you access one of these *search engines* (Web-based tools that enable you to hunt for Web sites on topics that you specify), you simply enter words or phrases that describe the information you want to find, and then you click the Search button. To find a company report, you enter the company name, a plus sign (+), and the words *annual report* in quotation marks, as in the following example:

```
Microsoft + "annual report"
```

Using Boolean operators (which I discuss in Chapter 2) forces the search engine to stack all the annual reports on top of the retrieved Web pages.

Using Web sites that link to company home pages

Many Web sites provide links to the home pages of large businesses. Here are two examples of these sites:

✔ **Global Securities Information, Incorporated (**www.gsionline.com**):** This site provides links to the home pages of large corporations.

✔ **Web100 (**www.w100.com**):** Figure 11-2 shows Web100, a site that provides links to the 100 largest U.S. and international businesses on the Internet. You can sort the database by industry and Fortune 500 rankings.

Finding online annual reports: Investor supersites

If using a commercial search engine or a special business Web site locator doesn't lead you to the annual report you desire, try an investor supersite. You can find many such investor directories on the Internet. Following, I list a few examples:

✔ **Hoover's Online Company Profiles (**www.hoovers.com**):** This site includes company profiles and annual report information on more than 25,000 publicly traded, private, and international firms. You can get capsule information for free; you pay a fee for access to the entire database.

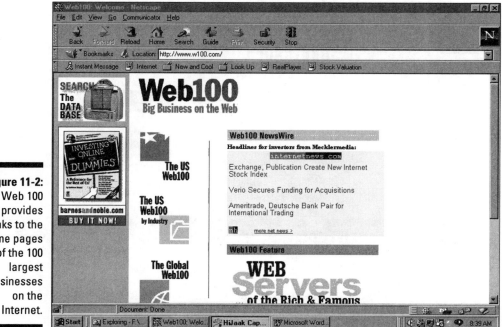

Figure 11-2:
Web 100 provides links to the home pages of the 100 largest businesses on the Internet.

- **Invest-O-Rama's Publicly Traded Corporations Online** (www.investorama.com/corp.shtml): This site provides links to more than 1,000 publicly traded companies. Many of these pages include links to the firms' annual reports.

- **SmallCap Investor** (www.smallcapinvestor.com): The site is a compilation site that is geared for individuals interested in investing in small companies. The research center includes small company stock research reports and company profiles, stock quotes and graphs, company news, and links to SEC filings.

- **Wall Street Research Net** (www.WSRN.com): This site provides the annual reports for more than 16,000 publicly traded firms.

- **Zacks Investment Research** (www.zacks.com): Figure 11-3 shows the Web site for Zacks Investment Research. This firm's database includes more than 7,000 U.S. and Canadian companies. The site also tracks 200 industry groups.

Figure 11-3: Zacks Investment Research includes company data on more than 5,000 U.S. and Canadian companies.

Researching a company's SEC filing

In the United States, publicly traded companies are required to file business and financial information with the Securities and Exchange Commission (SEC). These reports are entered into a government-sponsored database called EDGAR (www.sec.gov). The SEC's EDGAR service provides downloadable data that can be accessed by individual investors. You also can save SEC reports on a disk and read them at a later time. One disadvantage of this free service is that financial data can't be downloaded to your spreadsheet program.

Annual reports may include more than 50 pages and often exceed 100 pages. For example, the 10-K annual reports include descriptions of the business, business properties, legal proceedings, stockholder voting matters, selected financial data, management's discussion of the firm's financial condition and results of operations, financial statements and supplementary data, changes in accounting procedures and financial disclosures, insider transactions, executive compensation, and leasing agreements.

When you search the EDGAR database, you're asked for the report number of the document you want. The reports are numbered in the following manner:

- **10-K Reports:** Annual reports that include shareholder information covering the firm's fiscal year

- **10-Q Reports:** Quarterly reports that include shareholder information for the firm's last quarter

- **8-K Reports:** Interim reports covering an odd period due to a merger, acquisition, or other event

- **S-1 Registration:** Forms required for businesses that want to offer stock to the public; often used for initial public offerings

- **S-3 Registration:** Registration of a secondary offering; necessary form to offer stock to the public after an initial public offering

- **14-A Form:** Information about voting matters and candidates seeking election to the board of directors; this form is also called a proxy

Downloading SEC filings in just three clicks

When you find the annual report you want, save it to a floppy disk or your computer's hard disk. After you download the report and save it on your computer, you can read the file at your leisure. You can also use your word processor's snappy text search features to find the important information you need.

Trivia from the Annual Reports Library

Can you name...

1. The oldest library in the world still operating?

2. The first people who used handwriting?

3. Who founded the first "members only" library? and when?

4. Where and when was the first tax-supported library?

5. Who said, "Never judge an annual report by its movie"?

6. The oldest printed annual report?

7. The world's longest printed annual report?

8. The first annual report with CD-ROM and diskette copies?

9. The annual report with sunflower seeds?

10. The annual report that included a saliva drug screening kit?

11. The smallest/shortest annual report?

12. The annual report that had a penny glued to the cover?

13. The annual report that smelled of spices?

14. The annual report that came wrapped in a reusable canvas sack?

15. The annual report that included water?

16. The first annual report that included coupons for all the company's products?

17. Who said, "The real purpose of a library is to trap the mind into doing its own thinking"?

18. The annual report cut into the shape of a deck of playing cards?

19. The annual report that's covered with a laced-up sleeve that you have to unlace before you can read the report?

20. The annual report that reads like and follows along like a game of monopoly?

21. The annual report that put a warning on its front cover stating, "WARNING: This Report is NOT interactive NOR entertaining"?

22. The annual report that came inside a bank coin bag which, when unzipped, revealed a simulated checkbook and $100 bills all wrapped together and, when opened, revealed the annual report?

Give up?

For the answers, see The Annual Reports Library at www.zpub.com/sf/arl.

After you find the report you want, you can save the data in just three clicks:

1. **Click the File menu at the top-left corner of your Internet browser screen.**

2. **Click Save.**

   Your browser displays a dialog box asking you which drive you want to save the data on and which name you want to file it under.

3. Enter a name for the file and specify where you want to save the file.

Use the company's name, initials, or ticker symbol for the filename and a file extension of .txt or .doc.

4. Click Save.

You're finished downloading a 50-page document from the Internet.

To read the file, just start your word processing program and open the file.

If the columns are out of alignment, you may need to adjust the font size for the entire document.

Analyzing a Financial Statement

Companies often use their annual reports to attract new investors; you can guess that these reports contain some marketing fluff and exaggerations. Most of this embellishment is self-evident. Analyzing a company with a calculator, paper, and pencil will take you about an hour, and the results of this examination can help online investors make investment decisions. Buying stock in a company without reading the annual report is like buying a used car without seeing it. Here's a checklist of the information you need to consider while you review a company's annual report:

- ✔ **Profitability:** How much money did the company make last year?

- ✔ **Survivability:** How is the company coping with competition?

- ✔ **Growth:** Is the company expanding? How fast is this expansion?

- ✔ **Stability:** Is the company subject to radical changes from year to year?

- ✔ **Dividends (if any):** Is dividend growth constant? How does it compare to the industry averages?

- ✔ **Problems:** Does the company have any pending lawsuits? Any other problems?

- ✔ **Risks:** Is the company subject to any environmental, political, or exchange rate risks?

- ✔ **Other factors:** Is the management team experienced? Does the company need more executive talent?

EDGAR Online (www.edgar-online.com) is a value-added SEC database provider. Free services include, among other things, access to the SEC database back to 1994, exclusive of today's filings. The EDGAR Online search engine allows you to search by date, company, ticker symbol, people, type of filing, industry, and location. You can import reports to word-processing programs and financial data to Lotus or Excel spreadsheet programs. The premium service is $9.95 per month, which includes all the free services, plus a Watchlist that notifies you when companies that you select file SEC documents. In addition, EDGAR provides features that allow you to discover executive salaries, stock options, corporate board memberships, and individual insider trading. (You may want to know whether the company CEO gave himself a big salary increase as sales revenues dropped and profits dwindled.)

Dissecting the Annual Report

Despite their glossiness, annual reports often present many unglamorous but truthful statements about a company. Corporate challenges are often treated with amazing frankness.

The National Association of Investors (NAIC) (www.better-investing.org) is a non-profit educational organization that supports individual investors and investment clubs. The Association offers downloadable demos of its investment analysis, stock screening, and portfolio management software programs. The programs are designed for computer novices. If you are math adverse, using these demos may be a good way to approach the ratio analysis tasks described in this section.

In general, annual reports consist of nine sections:

- ✔ Letter to the shareholders
- ✔ Company overview
- ✔ Ten-year summary of financial figures
- ✔ Management discussion and analysis of operations
- ✔ Independent auditor's report
- ✔ Financial statements
- ✔ Subsidiaries, brands, and addresses
- ✔ List of directors and officers
- ✔ Stock price history

As you start analyzing annual reports, you're likely to notice that each company has its own style and approach. Additionally, writing the annual report is often an ongoing company project and not something that happens just at the end of the fiscal year. As you read the annual report you may notice that some sections are clear and straightforward. Other sections may be almost indecipherable and require your close attention. Several sections may be lengthy and others provide just a brief overview. These inconsistencies are normal because different company departments and individuals write different sections of the annual report.

Reading the letter to the shareholders

Although you usually find the letter to the shareholders within the first couple of pages of the annual report, save reading this letter for last and then compare it to the facts you uncover about the company. Is the CEO being truthful with the shareholders? What is the CEO's view of the company's operations? What does this letter tell you about the character of the CEO? As you read the letter to the shareholders, consider the following questions:

- What changed in the last year?
- Are conditions continuing to change?
- Which goals weren't achieved?
- What made the company miss the mark?
- What are the company's goals for next year?
- Are these goals realistic, given current economic conditions and the company's resources?
- What is the time schedule for specific actions?
- Does the letter apologize for anything?

Viewing the company overview

After the letter to the shareholders, the annual report usually presents an overview of the company, which includes a description of the company's products and its channels of distribution. This section should provide answers to the following questions:

- What product or service does the company sell?
- Is the company introducing any new lines of business?
- How, where, or when does the company sell its products or services?
- Where (geographically) does the company make most of its money?
- Does the company divide its various lines of business into logical groupings, such as global sales, continental sales, national sales, and regional sales (or electronics, computers, and software sales)?

Figuring out the ten-year summary of financial figures

Companies often provide selected financial data. The ten-year summary of financial figures should indicate the steady growth of the company, if there was steady growth. As you review the annual report, ask yourself the following questions:

- ✔ Is information on steady growth included? (Does the company provide the financial data needed?)

- ✔ What's the growth in profits? (Often the year-to-year percentage of growth is calculated for you.)

- ✔ What's the growth in operating income? (The company may have calculated this number for you. If not, you'll have to download the data to your spreadsheet program and do the analysis yourself.)

Investor Relations at Microsoft (microsoft.com/msft/tools.htm) provides annual reports, earnings reports, stock information, SEC filings, and investment and acquisition data, in addition to many online annual report analysis tools. These tools allow you to download several spreadsheets with macros that help you analyze specific company data. For example, you can click on a hyperlink, and the company's financial history from 1985 to the current statement appears in a free, special Excel spreadsheet program that allows you to manipulate the numbers. A second analysis tool lets you look at the sources of revenues by sales area or product group (for example, you can look up sales revenue in Europe). A third financial model allows you to perform "what if" analysis, which lets you forecast future income statements for Microsoft in a free Microsoft Excel Viewer.

Analyzing the management discussion and analysis of operations

The management discussion, which is one of the most significant sections of the annual report, usually focuses on corporate operations. This section addresses such issues as how technology has impacted the company, how the company copes with competition, and what management expects to accomplish in the next year. Consider the following questions when you review this section of the annual report:

- ✔ Does the management discussion offer a clear analysis of significant financial trends over the last two years?

- ✔ Is the discussion candid and accurate?

- ✔ Has the company sold any parts of its business?

- ✔ Have any products been discontinued?

Scrutinizing the independent auditor's report

Toward the back of the annual report you generally find an opinion letter with a title like *Report of Independent Auditor* or *The CPA Opinion Letter*. Keep in mind that the company pays the auditor, a fact that may sometimes lead to a biased annual report. (During the savings and loan crisis, for example, the annual reports of many thrifts didn't reveal their shaky financial situations.)

The first part of the auditor's opinion is standard. The key words you're looking for are "in our opinion, the financial position stated in the annual report has been fairly stated in all material aspects and in conformity with generally accepted accounting principles," or something to this effect. If this statement isn't used, a problem may exist. As you read the independent auditor's report, ask the following questions:

✔ What are the qualifications of the CPA firm? (Is this a Big Six accounting firm, like Price Waterhouse or Deloitte & Touche, or an accounting firm you've never heard about?)

✔ Are the firm's accounting procedures standard for the industry?

Examining financial statements

Many companies belong to conglomerates that operate in numerous industries and countries. In such cases, it isn't possible to compare company performance to any industry average. The only way you can judge whether the company's performance is improving or declining is by comparing current financial ratios to the firm's previous ratios.

Often, the notes to the financial statements are the most revealing part of a financial statement. Notes define accounting policies and disclose any pending litigation and environmental issues.

The company's financial statements consist of four separate documents:

✔ **Balance sheet:** A snapshot of the company's assets and liabilities

✔ **Income statement:** The results of operations for the last year

✔ **Statement of cash flows:** How the company made its money and spent its cash

✔ **Statement of retained earnings:** How company profits were distributed to shareholders

Entrepreneurial Edge Online (`www.edgeonline.com/main/bizbuilders/ biz/financialmgmt/balsheet.shtml#analyze`) is an online resource that can assist you in analyzing a balance sheet. This Internet source provides an introduction to accounting terminology and examines the concepts of assets, liabilities, and net worth in a way that helps you relate them to your investments. It explains the step-by-step process of creating a balance sheet and shows you how to use a balance sheet to analyze a company's liquidity and leverage.

When analyzing the financial statements and developing ratios, you should note the following information:

- **Growth in sales:** Are sales increasing or decreasing?

- **Growth in profits:** Are profits growing as fast as sales? Are high interest payments eating away at profits?

- **Profits:** Have earnings per share increased every year? (If not, why not? There may be a logical answer. For example, an aluminum company's profits may not rise every year because the commodity price of aluminum fluctuates.)

- **Research and development spending:** Does the company spend the same amount on research and development as similar firms?

- **Inventory:** Are inventories going up or down due to a change in accounting procedures?

- **Debt:** Are debts increasing?

- **Assets:** Are most of the company's assets leased?

- **Litigations:** Are there any pending litigations (lawsuits)?

- **Pension Plan:** Is the pension plan in bad shape?

- **Changes in Procedures:** Is the company using accounting changes that may inflate earnings?

You may want to calculate several ratios that you can then compare to the company's previous ratios and to industry averages. Industry averages provide a benchmark for your analysis.

Investor ratios include:

- Last closing stock price (price per share)

- P/E ratio (current price per share divided by annualized earnings per share)

- Dividend yield (annual dividend divided by price)

- Return on Equity ratio (net income available to common stockholders divided by common equity)

- Debt to Equity ratio (total debt divided by common equity)

✔ Percentage change in EPS (earnings per share) from the last quarter (current EPS divided by last quarter's EPS less 1.00)

✔ Earnings growth rate (net income from this year divided by last year's net income less 1.00)

Company solvency ratios include:

✔ Current ratio (current assets divided by current liabilities)

✔ Debt ratio (total debt divided by total assets)

Finding out about subsidiaries, brands, and addresses

Knowing what the company owns and where the company operates is important. This can help investors evaluate the political risk of their investments. For example, during the time of South Africa's apartheid, many individuals boycotted Eastman- Kodak. They protested how Kodak products were used in South Africa.

In this age of social conscience investing, you may not want to own stock in a company that supports initiatives and products that you disagree with or believe are unsuitable. Look for answers to the following questions in this section of the annual report:

✔ Where is the company's headquarters, and in what countries does the company have divisions or subsidiaries?

✔ Does the company make clear what lines and brand names it owns?

✔ Does the company have an international distribution network?

You don't have to be a math whiz to calculate ratios

SPREDGAR Software (www.spredgar.com) is a Microsoft Excel add-in that can convert the text of SEC database reports to your Excel spreadsheet. An avid investor who wanted to find a way to manage awkward or cumbersome public data developed the program. SPREDGAR calculates and graphs 30 standard financial ratios from SEC 10-K and 10-Q filings. You can try a 30-day free trial; the price of the add-in is $49.95.

For more information about U.S. financial and operating ratios, check out Harvard University's Baker Library listing at library.hbs.edu/ratio.htm. This listing shows sources for comparative industry ratios, ratios for specific industries, competitive company ratios, and customized online searches.

Perusing the list of directors and officers

The board of directors listing usually appears on the last page of the annual report. Few reports provide any details about the experience and professional backgrounds of these individuals. (Director biographies are usually included on the company's proxies to assist you in voting for new or incumbent candidates for the board of directors.) Other reports don't provide any details. If you feel that this information is intentionally deleted, you can call the company's investor relations department and ask for a background biography of each director.

Look for the following information in this section of the annual report:

✔ How many *outside* versus *inside* directors are members of the board? (If the board has many outside directors, they can possibly force the company and its founders into an unwanted merger or acquisition.)

✔ Are the directors well-known and respected?

Investigating the stock price history

Evaluating the company's stock price history may provide you with some useful insights. For example, is the current stock price the highest in the history of the company? This section of the annual report should provide answers to the following questions:

✔ What are the company's general stock price trends over time?

✔ On which exchange is the company traded?

✔ What's the company's stock symbol?

✔ What's the company's dividend history?

✔ Has the company had any stock splits?

Utilizing Prepared Online Ratio Analysis

Many organizations provide online annual reports that include ratio analyses, performance statistics, accounting notes, and other relevant information. You can download, print, and save all these reports. Much of the downloaded data is ready for your spreadsheet program and your analytic skills; however, you may need to reformat some data, and some data you can't change into a spreadsheet.

In the following list, I describe two online sources of prepared online ratio analysis and company information:

- **Thomson Investor Net, formerly MarketEdge Reports,** (www.thomsoninvest.net or www.marketedge.com) provides more than 7,000 in-depth company reports updated twice a month. For stock research, the company provides stock quotes, company information, stock screening, a list of the month's top performers, and more. Company reports include comparison of the firm's ratios to industry averages, but you can't download the reports to your spreadsheet. Monthly subscriptions are $9.95 and include 25 in-depth company reports and 25 mutual fund reports. Additional company reports are $2.50 ($1.50 for mutual fund companies).

- **Yahoo Market Guide Report** (yahoo.marketguide.com), shown in Figure 11-4, provides free information on *What's Hot* and *What's Not,* a sector listing, an industry listing, the company of the day, and educational information. This service charges for quick company facts, company profiles, detailed company reports, and specialized reports that include ratio comparisons and a peer group report. Earnings estimates, detailed financial statements, and stock screening are also available. Prices are by report ($1.00 to $7.95) or monthly by report types ($4.95 to $19.95). You can retrieve reports even if they aren't included in your subscription plan, and you can download company reports to your spreadsheet.

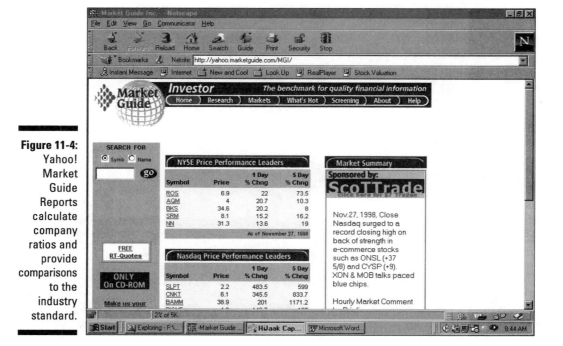

Figure 11-4: Yahoo! Market Guide Reports calculate company ratios and provide comparisons to the industry standard.

Financial statement analysis involves examining the company's annual report and ratio analysis. However, looking beyond the firm's numbers and evaluating changes in accounting procedures that may hide serious problems is also important. For example, how the firm accounts for depreciation and the valuing of inventory can radically vary between similar firms in the same industry. These accounting procedures can result in earnings per share (EPS) that aren't truly representative of the firm's performance, especially when they're compared to the company's previous EPS and the industry standard. An inaccurate EPS number can lead to big surprises toward the end of the year when the company doesn't perform as expected.

Chapter 12

Digging Deeper: Researching Investment Candidates

· ·

· ·

*Y*ou may use an online stock screen (see Chapter 8) to whittle down the number of common stock investment candidates you're considering. Or you may select a few companies because you know something about the products they sell. Maybe you work in the industry or have used the company's products or services over a long period of time.

After you find a few investment candidates, you can use online sources to download the annual reports of the companies that you find interesting (see Chapter 11). You read the financial statements, and you calculate the ratios that are important to investors. You may think that you're done, but you need to do a little more research before you contact your online broker.

The next step involves digging deeper to understand the economic environment in which your investment candidate operates. In this chapter, I help you locate the online sources that you can use to determine where the company stands in its industry and what type of marketing techniques it's using to maintain and increase revenues. I show you where to find out what the experts are saying about your stock pick and where to go online to find analyst earning estimates. I also point out where you can get historical stock price information. After you have all of these hard facts, you can make your investment decision.

Many investors do not have the confidence to select their own stocks. This chapter shows how you can conduct your own online research to find winning investments. Many of the sources I list in this chapter are the same sources that full-service brokers use in their stock analyses.

Turning Your Hunches into Investment Strategies

Every online investor has his or her own research system for investigating investment candidates. What makes any system work is that it's repeatable and that it ensures that you don't make investment decisions based on emotional factors. The following guidelines can assist you in turning your hunches into investment strategies. You begin by gathering all the facts:

1. **Find the candidates that you want to research.**

   Match your hunches about stocks that are positioned to be top performers to your investor profile and use a stock screen or some other method to identify investment candidates. (For more information about researching individual stocks, see Chapter 11. For in-depth coverage of Internet stock screens, refer to Chapter 8.)

2. **Trim your list of candidates.**

   Locate the online annual reports for your short list of stock candidates using the techniques I outline in Chapter 11. Conduct your analysis and reduce the list to several companies

3. **Find out more about each company.**

   Use this background information to put each company into a broader context using the sources I detail in this chapter. For example, is the company a market leader?

   The good news is that the Internet has tons of this type of information, and most of it is free. Here are some examples of sources for this information (I list Internet resources for the following categories of information later in the chapter):

   - **News:** Read the company's press releases and keep current with breaking news. Try to connect isolated news articles to spot trends.

   - **Industry:** Read news articles and industry trade journals to spot patterns that may indicate technological breakthroughs or new products. Does the industry have problems with oversupply, and if so, how does this situation affect the profits of the company you're researching?

   - **Economics:** Note how changes in the national, regional, and local economies affect your investment candidates. Will a rising dollar lower corporate returns? What are the Wall Street economists saying?

- **Market:** What's happening in the stock market? Are prices and trading volume increasing? Are insiders purchasing stock?

- **Analysts' evaluations:** Most publicly traded companies have Wall Street analysts who often provide opinions about the firm. Study what the analysts are saying about the company. What they say may provide you with leads for additional research.

- **Earnings estimates:** Keep current with the earnings estimates of professionals. Are the estimates going up or down?

- **Historical prices:** Sometimes you can tell where a company is going by seeing where it has been. Evaluating a company's past stock prices may provide you with new insights.

4. **Decide whether the company is a low-priced, high-quality stock or a loser.**

   When you put all the facts together, you gain a good understanding of what causes the company's stock price to rise or fall. Additionally, you know what's normal for the company.

5. **Ask yourself "What if?"**

   For example, what if sales drop by 10 percent, like they did five years ago? What if the material the company uses to manufacture its product becomes scarce — would this scarcity cause the cost of goods to increase? Would such a change reduce profits so much that the company couldn't pay its interest expense? Would the company be forced into bankruptcy?

6. **To complete your investment strategy, determine how risky the stock is.**

   Could you lose your entire investment? If so, you need to add a *risk premium* to your required rate of return. This risk premium compensates you for the additional risk of your investment. Should the return be ten times your investment or maybe even 50 times your initial investment? Making this decision can be difficult, because everyone defines risk differently and everyone has a different risk tolerance level. So what's normal anyway?

Conquering Uncertainty with Online Research

You can use the Internet to get background company information by accessing one of the many free and fee-based databases, where you can dig up all kinds of facts and opinions about a company. Some of this information can provide you with new insights, ideas, and leads about additional research.

Overall, this information can provide you with an understanding of how a company works within the economy, how it copes with the competition, and how it ranks within its industry. This information is often critical to your investment decision.

With millions of Web pages on the Internet, finding exactly what you're looking for can be a challenge. However, uncovering one small fact can make the difference between purchasing a mediocre stock and buying a stock that can bring you exceptional returns. As you surf the Internet, you may encounter sites that discuss stocks, markets, online trading, and more. In the following sections, I help you locate the right online sources that can assist you in finding the background information you need to complete your company research.

Gaining new investor insights with breaking news

Daily news and press releases can assist you in keeping current with your investments or investment candidates. These sources often provide the first glimpse of why a stock price is rapidly increasing or falling like a stone. One of the advantages of these online sources is that they have *archives,* where you can check past company events that made news.

Here are a few Internet resources for finding press releases and breaking news:

- **Bloomberg Online** (www.bloomberg.com): This site, shown in Figure 12-1, includes newswire articles, edited columns, audio clips about current market performance, and other information about stocks, bonds, markets, and industry. The site is well organized and provides access to current market statistics, business and financial news, major newspaper stories, Bloomberg columns, and financial analysis tools. (Bloomberg charges a fee for subscribing to its magazine, but you can search its Web site for free.)

  Bloomberg's magazine subscribers ($23.95 for ten issues) can access a special area of the Web site that includes free quotes, company profiles, fundamentals of more than 18,000 stocks and mutual funds, and the capability to analyze and store a portfolio with as many as 50 securities.

- **Commerce Business Daily via the Internet** (www.issinet.com/cbd): This paper covers government procurements, contract awards, foreign government standards, surplus property sales, and other information. Online information is available the day before the printed edition is released. Searchable archives for the last six months are available. *Commerce Business Daily* offers a free 30-day trial. Annual subscriptions and access to past issues are available to individuals for $200 per year.

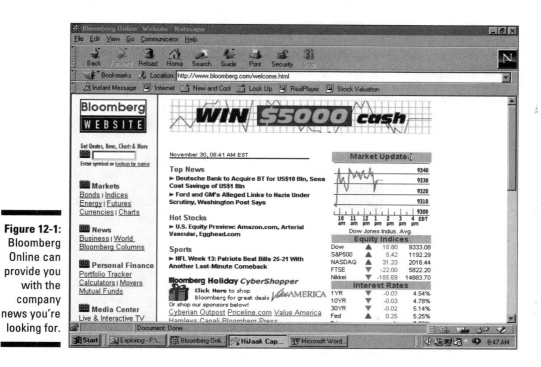

Figure 12-1:
Bloomberg
Online can
provide you
with the
company
news you're
looking for.

✔ **Newspaper Indexes:** You can find comprehensive indexes to the online versions of major newspapers at the Newspaper Association of America (www.infi.net/naa) and Newslink (www.newslink.org).

✔ **The Wall Street Journal Interactive Edition (www.wsj.com):** This interactive site contains recent news, business, and market columns from *The Wall Street Journal.* Articles have links to charts, graphs, and tables. Daily news is continually updated. The site includes closing stock prices and a summary of each day's activities.

Don't forget The Wall Street Journal Interactive Briefing Books. These handy summaries include a company's background, financial overview, stock performance, company news, press releases, and corporate snapshot.

The firm offers a two-week free trial. Subscribers to the print version of *The Wall Street Journal* pay $29 per year for the Internet version of *The Journal.* Other subscribers pay $59 per year. For an additional fee, you can gain access to a much larger database of business research.

✔ **WSRN (www.wsrn.com):** This site provides a good starting place for your search for company information. WSRN has more than 500,000 links to Internet financial sources to help professional and individual investors. The site is divided into eight sections: company information, economic research, market news, news, research publications, mutual funds, broker services, and what's new.

You can start at the "Research a Company" page and use the links to get SEC filings, quotes, graphs or charts, news, earnings estimates, research reports, and summaries.

Locating company profiles and related data

In much the same way as the literary world includes biographies of famous people, the world of finance has *company profiles*. Company profiles include all the events that make a company what it is today. You can keep all of a company's pertinent facts handy by obtaining a company profile. Company profiles are often designed for investors and highlight investor-related information.

Here are a few online sources for obtaining company profiles:

✔ **Companylink (www.companylink.com):** The database sources for this Web site are Cor Tech Database of Technology Companies — Technology Manufacturers and Developers, Demand Research's Executive Desk Register, and Hoover's Online. The site provides company profiles for publicly traded firms plus the largest private companies in the United States. You can use any profiles marked with the *free* symbol without subscribing. Items marked *SUB* are available for unlimited use by subscribers.

Subscribers can also customize the news they receive. Items marked with a dollar sign ($) are premium content, valued individually; subscribers can purchase these items. Companylink offers a free two-week subscription. Subscriptions are $10 per month. Subscribers get $20 worth of premium services for free (if you didn't use the free trial), access to all full-text articles and summary profiles, and the capability to purchase any of the firm's premium content.

✔ **Company Sleuth (www.companysleuth.com):** This Web site features a free service that provides daily e-mail updates on your stocks, investments, competitors, and clients. Follow the activities of your investments to know the next move to make. This information includes patents, trademarks, URLs, insider-trading information, analyst's reports, Yahoo! and Motley Fool message board discussions, Usenet discussion forums, SEC filings, stock quotes, and breaking corporate news.

✔ **Hoover's Online (www.hoovers.com):** This site, shown in Figure 12-2, includes free information about 8,500 companies. You can find ticker symbols, company locations, and sales figures at this Web site. Company profiles include the firm's address, phone numbers, executive names, recent sales figures, and company status. This site has links to stock quotes and SEC financial data. Basic service is free. For $9.95 per month or $99.95 per year, you can obtain in-depth information on more than 3,000 companies.

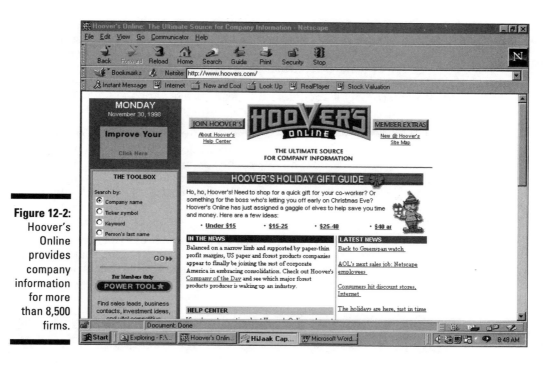

Figure 12-2:
Hoover's
Online
provides
company
information
for more
than 8,500
firms.

Finding industry and statistical information

Annual reports often provide good insights into the forces that drive certain industries. However, this information may not be enough to answer your questions.

Independent research about how a company is doing in its industry is often available from trade associations and periodicals. Market research sites are helpful for determining how the company of your choice stacks up. Here are some online sources for industry and statistical information:

✔ **American Society of Association Executives** (www.asaenet.org): This organization provides links to Web sites for various industries. The Web sites are generally high-quality industry overviews that often include briefings of industry trends, geographic profiles, and statistics for financial performance analysis.

✔ **Fedstats** (www.fedstats.gov): This site allows you to search 14 federal agencies for a specific statistic at the same time. You can also search press releases, regional statistics, or policies.

- **Lexis-Nexis** (www.lexis-nexis.com): Shown in Figure 12-3, this site has a wide variety of business and legal databases. The site recently added a new database of 10- to 20-page market summaries of industry sectors or demographic markets. Additionally, its database includes the *Market Share Reporter* (from 1991 to the present) and *Computer Industry Forecasts*. Pricing for different types of usage varies — if you're interested in this service, contact it for a firm price quote.

- **STAT-USA** (www.stat-usa.gov): Sponsored by the U.S. Department of Commerce, this site provides financial information about economic indicators, statistics, and news. The site also includes data about state and local government bond rates, foreign exchange rates, and daily economic news about trade and business issues. Statistics include interest rates, employment, income, price, productivity, new construction, and home sales.

- **Technometrica Market Research** (www.technometrica.com): Among other things, Technometrica provides business research that includes industry and market features and trends, market share analysis, market potential analysis, and strategic planning.

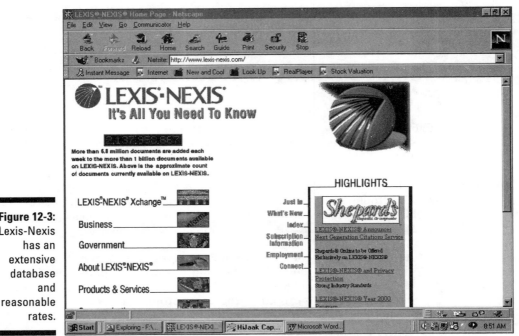

Figure 12-3:
Lexis-Nexis has an extensive database and reasonable rates.

Gathering economic and related data

Many individuals try to predict economic trends, but few (if any) are successful. However, having a good understanding of current economic conditions and where they're headed is vital to your comprehension of the company in its broader context. After all, many companies are sensitive to changes in the economy.

The Internet has many sources for economic information. Here are a few examples:

- **Census Bureau (www.census.gov):** Shown in Figure 12-4, this site provides information about industry, statistics, and general business. *Current Industrial Reports* provides production, shipment, and inventory statistics. *Census of Manufacturers Industry Series* includes industry statistics (some of this information may be outdated). *The Census of Wholesale Trade* contains data about organizations that sell merchandise to retailers, institutions, and other types of wholesalers. The *Survey* provides updates about current and past statistics of monthly sales, inventories, and stock/sales ratios. *Today's Economic Indicator Report* provides information about government and related entities releasing economic reports on industrial production, consumer sentiment, and so on.

- **GSA Government Information Locator Service (www.gsa.gov):** Government agencies are now required to provide and maintain a database of the information they provide to the public. Most agencies are using the Internet to meet this requirement. This site includes many U.S. government agency reports in either full text or abstract forms. Most information resources are cataloged and searchable. Searches can include more than one agency.

- **Internet Federal Reserve sites (www.bog.frb.fed.us/ otherfrb.htm):** This site, shown in Figure 12-5, provides links to all the Fed home pages. Publications by this organization include high-quality statistics, analyses, and forecasts of regional, national, and international economic and financial conditions. Publications include *Economic Trends* (from Cleveland), a monthly report on the GDP (Gross Domestic Product), consumer income, housing starts, producer price index, and consumer price index. *U.S. Financial Data,* published weekly in St. Louis, includes statistics on money supply, interest rates, and securities yields. Regional economic indicators are published in the *Fed Flash.*

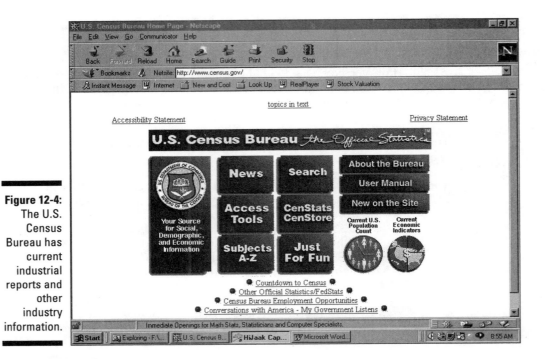

Figure 12-4:
The U.S.
Census
Bureau has
current
industrial
reports and
other
industry
information.

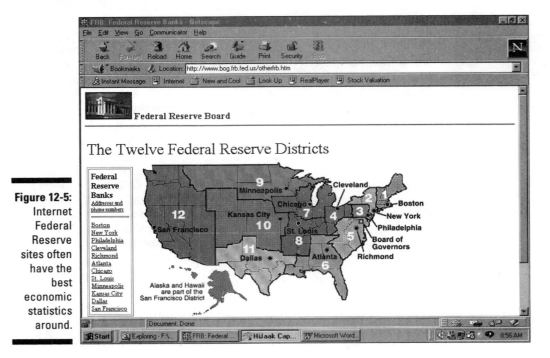

Figure 12-5:
Internet
Federal
Reserve
sites often
have the
best
economic
statistics
around.

Collecting market information

Understanding the current market environment can help you select a stock that can provide you with your required return. You need to know how a company markets its products or services (catalog sales, face-to-face meetings, and so on) and what share of the total market the company commands. This information can give you a better understanding of what drives the company's stock price.

Here are some online sources for market information:

✔ **E-Line** (www.financials.com): This site provides stock ratings and market data, as well as links to DBC (Data Broadcasting Corp.) U.S. Industry Market Summaries, U.S. company stock prices by industry, Griffin Financial Services "Weekly Market Outlook," and Market Vision's "World Markets at a Glance" data about foreign exchange, futures equity, indexes, and U.S. Treasuries.

✔ **Holt Stock Report** (metro.turnpike.net/holt): This online resource provides indexes; averages; information about foreign markets; issues trades; new highs and lows; currency; gold; interest rates; most active issues on the NYSE, NASDAQ, and AMEX; stocks whose trading volume was up by more than 50 percent that day; and stocks that reached new highs and lows.

✔ **Quote.com** (www.quote.com): Shown in Figure 12-6, this site provides free unlimited delayed security quotes from U.S. and Canadian exchanges; limited balance-sheet data; some company profile information; an unlimited number of updates for a portfolio of up to seven securities; daily, weekly, and/or monthly stock price charts; daily market index charts; daily information for major industry groups; and foreign exchange rates.

Basic service is $9.95 a month. Subscribers get all the free services, updates of two portfolios of up to 50 securities each, *Newsbytes News Network* news, any ten historical data files, any ten customized charts that you may want, and annual reports ordering service (for printed copies sent by U.S. mail). Extra service is $24.95 per month, which includes all the basic services plus more historical data, charts, and reports. Premium service and other types of services escalate from there.

✔ **Thomas Register** (www1.thomasregister.com): This site includes buying information for the products and services of more than 155,000 companies, divided into 55,000 categories. The register includes 3,100 online supplier catalogs and is 42,000 pages. After you register and select a password, use of the catalog is free. This site is an excellent source for discovering the chief competitor of a company.

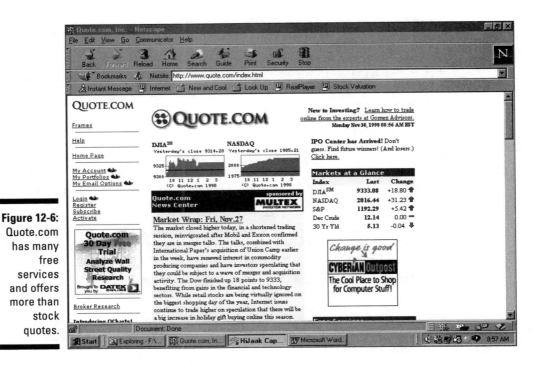

Figure 12-6:
Quote.com
has many
free
services
and offers
more than
stock
quotes.

Checking out analyst evaluations

Often stock prices move because analysts recommend or criticize a company. Although these opinions are "informed," they're still opinions and shouldn't overshadow your good judgment. For example, assume that an analyst suggests buying a stock and forecasts the price to increase to a record high. Over the year, the stock reaches the mark, and then the analyst places a hold on the stock. (A "hold" is a suggestion to investors that they neither sell nor buy the stock.) This hold may look like an unfavorable mark against the stock, but the stock performed just as expected and is currently a good investment.

The Internet now has many analyst reports by individual Wall Street analysts or groups of Wall Street analysts who study a particular stock. However, many of these firms participated in the financing of the companies they're analyzing. Consequently, you rarely see a "sell" recommendation. Additionally, you may see that analysts' opinions vary. Feel free to disagree with their conclusions, but know what the professionals are saying about a company that interests you.

Wall Street Research Network (www.wsrn.com) has links to three analyst evaluation reports:

- ✔ ACE — Analyst Consensus Estimate Reports
- ✔ Standard & Poor's Enhanced Stock Reports
- ✔ Research Investment Reports

For $4.95, Standard & Poor's (www.stockinfo.standardpoor.com) has basic stock reports, industry reports, news stories, and Wall Street Consensus Reports. The Wall Street Consensus Reports include analyst earnings estimates.

Tracking down earnings estimates

The price you pay for a stock is based on its future income stream. If earnings estimates indicate that the earnings per share is dropping, the stock price you pay today may be too high for the true value of the stock.

Here are several Internet sources for earnings estimates:

- ✔ **First Call** (www1.firstcall.com): The First Call database follows more than 7,500 companies and also tracks more than 100 industry groups, several commodities and economic indicators, plus the Dow Jones Industrial Averages and the S&P 500. Products and subscription prices vary. Estimates on Demand cost $1.50 to $3 per document retrieved. Historical information is $25 per report, and the Consensus Guide is $25 per month. Other products are available. See the Web site for details.

- ✔ **NRM Capital** (www.nrmcapital.com): This site provides free earnings announcements, including the company, expected date of the earnings announcement, ticker symbol, estimated amount of the earnings per share (EPS), and last year's EPS.

- ✔ **Reuters Moneynet** (www.moneynet.com): Reuters Moneynet provides an S&P evaluation of the company you are researching. The evaluation includes a dividends rank, average quality opinion, and date of the next expected earnings report. The consensus earnings per share forecast for the next year and statistics about past earnings are included. Figure 12-7 shows one such report.

- ✔ **Stock Smart** (www.stocksmart.com): This site provides earnings estimates for a price. Stock Smart includes a professional portfolio manager, earnings calendar, unlimited stock quotes and graphing, shareholder data, comprehensive research, stock screening, week in review, industry roll-ups, mutual funds, and market information. Subscriptions are $12.95 per month and include a free ten-day test drive.

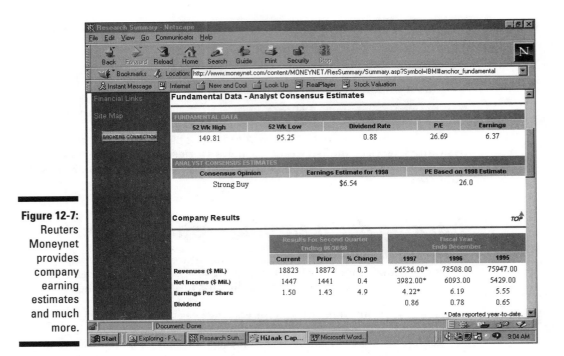

Figure 12-7:
Reuters
Moneynet
provides
company
earning
estimates
and much
more.

✔ **Zacks Investment Research** (www.zacks.com): This site provides estimated earnings reports based on analyst opinions. The site includes a listing of current earnings surprises, recommendations, and the company's annual balance sheet and income statement. This site is linked to WSRN's (www.wsrn.com) company information report.

Researching historical prices

Seeing where a company has been is always important in order to get a feeling about where it's going. Here are a few Internet sources for historical prices:

✔ **Standard & Poor's Stock Screens** (www.stockinfo.standardpoor.com/screens/screen10.htm): The Historical & Projected Industry P/E Ratios Report is one of the most useful pages on the Internet. The report includes P/E ratios for all the major industries for 1995, 1996, 1997, and so on.

✔ **Quote.com** (www.quote.com): This site provides historical data files as an additional service ($1.95) for current subscribers. Four types of historical data are available:

  • U.S. stocks — daily history from October 1988 to the present

  • U.S. commodity futures — daily history from April 1994 to the present

- Indexes and indicators — daily history from October 1988 to the present

- Foreign stocks and commodities — daily history from April 1994 to the present

✔ **Stock Tools** (www.stocktools.com): At the home page, click Reserch. You simply enter the ticker symbol of the company you're researching, and the program automatically retrieves daily data as well as close, high, low, open, and volume data for the last year.

Forecasting earnings and the stock market level

If an investor could accurately forecast a company's earnings, general market conditions, national economic activity, or interest rates, he or she could make extraordinary returns. Over the years, intrepid investors have studied these factors and determined that the most important factor in separating the winners from the losers is profitability and the general stock market level. However, when academics have studied past earnings, they've discovered that historical earning trends were not predictors of future earnings. This information only confirms what investors already know: Past performance does not guarantee future returns.

You can forecast the general stock market level using several methods, but none of them is consistently reliable. For example, the short-term interest ratio theory (the short interest rate for the month divided by the mean daily volume for the same period) theorizes that a very high short-term interest ratio of 2.00 indicates a bull market (up) and a short-term interest ratio of .80 indicates a mildly bearish market (down). When first introduced, this approach was a good way to predict the direction of the market. But over time, this theory hasn't worked well for investors.

Paying the Right Price

You can use several methods to determine the *fair value* of a stock (for a definition and discussion of fair value, see Chapter 7). The following sections illustrate three of the most popular methods of determining the right price for a stock: (1) fundamental analysis, (2) technical analysis, and (3) market timing.

Getting down to fundamentals

Fundamental analysis focuses on the underlying economics of the company being researched. Analysts try to forecast sales, earnings, and expenses, which in turn are used to forecast the company's stock price or returns. All U.S. business schools support this methodology because fundamental analysis seeks to paint the whole economic picture of the company being analyzed.

Fundamental analysis relies on forecasts of the economy, the industry, and the company's commercial prospects. Analysts use fundamental analysis to determine the intrinsic value or fair value of a stock (see Chapter 7 for details). The fair value is compared to market values to determine whether the stock is underpriced or overpriced. In other words, the objective of fundamental analysis is to locate mispriced stocks or undervalued stocks. Fundamental analysis is the most frequently used approach for common stock valuations.

If the stock has higher risk than usual risk (due to past volatility, political turmoil, or other factors), then the investors include a *risk premium* in the required rate of return. This risk premium serves to compensate the investor for the higher than normal risk.

Money.com's "Pay the Right Price for Your Next Stock" (www.pathfinder.com/money/value/), shown in Figure 12-8, is a fundamental online analysis calculator that can assist you in determining the fair value of a stock.

Just enter the company name or ticker symbol and follow the instructions in the worksheet. The Fair Value Worksheet automatically evaluates your investment candidate. Results indicate the fully adjusted price/earnings ratio and this year's estimated per-share earnings. The Web site also includes information about how the system works and how to find investment bargains.

Proceeding with caution

After crunching all the numbers, it's time for a reality check. The fundamental analysis methodology is limited because it often assumes that the investor holds the stock until termination of the company. If the investor holds the stock for a short time, he or she may not get all the expected returns. Additionally, investors and analysts can make errors in dividend projections or may ignore relevant external factors that can result in not valuing the stock correctly. Before you log on to your broker, you need to review your analysis and the data you collected. This is your money and your investment decision. What do you think is going to happen to this company in the future?

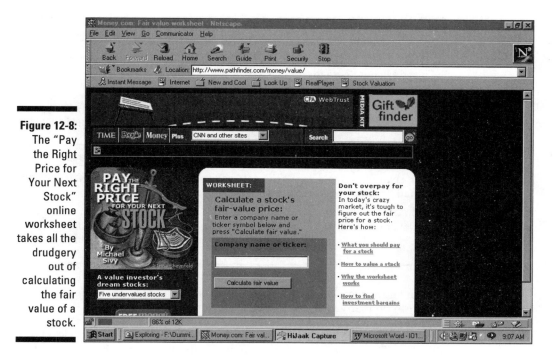

Figure 12-8:
The "Pay the Right Price for Your Next Stock" online worksheet takes all the drudgery out of calculating the fair value of a stock.

Analysis for value shopping

If you're a bargain shopper, you understand how difficult it is to separate the treasure from the trash. This search for value extends to investors who are seeking securities that seem underpriced relative to the fair value or financial prospects. Experts have a variety of opinions about how to decide whether a stock is undervalued (and unloved) or just a loser.

The Leuthold Group at T. Rowe Price at www.troweprice.com has developed one approach. At the T. Rowe Price home page, enter **Value Investing** in the Search Function box and click Go. At the search results screen, click Value Investing.

Table 12-1 shows a snapshot of this methodology. This is one way of separating the winners from the losers. The Leuthold Group suggests that investment candidates meet at least six of the following factors (see Chapter 11 for more information on ratios).

Table 12-1	Value Investing (Spotting the True Bargains)
Factor	*Analysis*
Price/Book Value (1)	Never over 2.0X
Price/Earnings Ratio (2)	Using 5-year average earnings never over 12X

(continued)

Table 12-1 *(continued)*

Factor	Analysis
Ratio of Cash per Share to Price per Share (3)	At least 10%
Dividend Yield	(Dividend yield is equal to the annual dividend divided by the market price) Dividend yield should never be below 3%
Price to Cash Flow	80% or less of the S&P 500 cash flow ratio
Ratio of Long Term Debt (plus Unfunded Pension Liabilities) to Total Capital	The debt equity ratio should be under 50% (include unfunded pension liabilities in the debt)
Financial Strength	Creditworthiness should be at least equal to the industry average. The S&P rating should be at least B-

The following are explanations of the terms used in Table 12-1. (For more information on many of these terms, see Chapter 8.)

Price/Book Ratio (P/BV) (1): Expresses the current selling price divided by book value. If the current selling price of the stock is below this amount, the stock is underpriced. Then again, the company may be on the verge of bankruptcy and that may be why the stock price is depressed.

The Price/Earnings Ratio (P/E Ratio) (2): Reflects how many years of current earning must be earned to purchase one share of stock. For example, if annual earnings are $2.00 and the stock is selling at $30.00, the price/earnings ratio is 15 ($^{30}/_2$). Many investors believe that the higher the P/E ratio, the better. If investors expect earnings to decrease, the P/E ratio will decrease to below the industry average.

Cash Flow per Share (3): Expresses the firm's net income plus depreciation and amortization expenses, divided by the number of outstanding shares.

Many software programs can assist you with your fundamental analysis. One example is Quant IX Stock Analyst (www.quantixsoftware.com/stock.html). This software program is designed to analyze common stocks using a combination of fundamental and quantitative analysis tools to help investors determine the fair value of common stocks, while identifying stocks that are over- or underpriced. The program sells for $39 and has a 30-day money-back guarantee.

Getting technical: Technical analysis

Technical analysis focuses on stock data analysis and stock market statistics. Analysts search for early indicators of pattern changes. As soon as analysts identify the beginnings of a change in a pattern, they use it to predict the future. However, this methodology fails to recognize that stock prices change when the consensus of the investment community's opinion concerning the value of the stock changes. Additionally, market timing is a popular valuation methodology and is similar to technical analysis. This approach uses stock market cycles to gauge when investors should enter or exit the market.

Technical analysis values a stock by tracking price trends of stocks, bonds, commodities, and the market. Technical analysis assumes three things:

- ✔ The past action of the stock market is the best indicator of future performance.

- ✔ 80 percent of the stock's performance is outside of the company's control and 20 percent of the stock price is due to the stock's unique factors.

- ✔ The stock market is based on 85 percent psychology and 15 percent economics.

Although technical analysis consists of many approaches, the most popular approach is the Dow Theory. The Dow theory is based on *The Wall Street Journal* founder Charles H. Dow's methodology for identifying signals of bull and bear markets. The theory suggests that as soon as the market heads in one direction, it stays that course until canceled (stopped) by both the Dow Jones Industrial Average (DJIA) and the Dow Jones Transportation Averages (DJTA). (It takes both averages to indicate that the market has changed its course.)

Technical analysis uses the Dow Theory to analyze individual stocks. However, Dow developed this methodology to predict changes in the general market. He did not expect his theory to be applied to individual stocks. For more on the Dow Theory, see E-Analytics at
www.e-analytics.com/f13.htm.

The Dow Theory maintains that there are three major market movements. First are the daily fluctuations that represent normal activity. Second are intermediate or secondary movements that last about two weeks to a month and point out the long-term trends of the market. Third are long primary trends that indicate either a bull or a bear market.

Stocktrader (`www.stocktrader.com`), shown in Figure 12-9, is a discount brokerage with a Web site that provides links to online technical analysis tools, software programs, and other data. Figure 12-9 shows what a technical analysis chart for the Dow Jones Industrial Averages looks like. If you look closely, you can see the smooth, long primary trend lines and more turbulent secondary trend lines.

For a more detailed explanation of technical analysis techniques, check out Decision Point at `decisionpoint.com/TAcourse/TAcourseMenu.html`.

Technical analysis requires large amounts of information (usually historical price and volume data) that can be manipulated with technical analysis software programs. Some programs are designed for different types of securities and for specific indicators and markets. Additionally, some programs are designed for beginners and others for professionals. The following is a short list of what programs are available:

Equis International (`www.equis.com`): Analysts sometimes refer to this program as the Granddaddy of technical analysis software. MetaStock Professional costs $350. The Web site includes back issues of the Equis newsletter, files of tips, system tests, and custom formulas for use with the software. A downloadable demo is available.

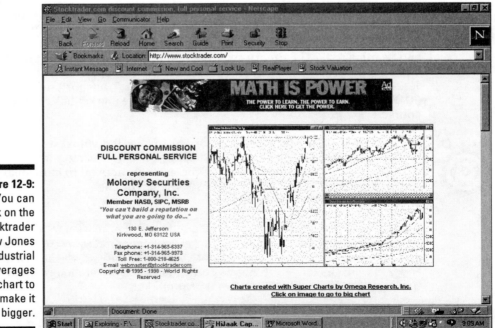

Figure 12-9:
You can click on the Stocktrader Dow Jones Industrial Averages chart to make it bigger.

Insiders TA (www.stockblocks.com): This program uses box charting to highlight each trading period's volume and high and low price. Insider's TA costs $70 and offers a downloadable demo at the Web site.

Stable Technical Graphs (www.winterra.com): This software is a Windows-based product for analyzing stocks, bonds, commodities, mutual funds, indexes, and options. Stable Technical Graphs costs $50 and offers a downloadable evaluation version of the software.

Vector Vest (www.vestorvest.com/stockreport): This program uses fundamental valuation and technical analysis to rank over 6,000 stocks each day. Stocks are ranked for value, safety, and timing. Go to the Web site and sample the program. Just enter the ticker symbol of the company you're analyzing.

Stocks and Commodities (www.traders.com/documentation/survey/98softwr.html) offers reviews of technical analysis software. You can view a survey of the program's features by clicking on the name of the software product.

Market timing

The underlying theory of market timing is that you purchase stocks when prices are low and sell when prices are high. The Market Timing strategy is based on reams of historical data that's used to discover patterns and relationships that affect investment returns. Market timing software uses this data to detect or anticipate changes in market patterns. Market timers note that the market can underperform for long periods of time. This low performance can reduce returns for buy-and-hold investors who decide to go ahead and sell before the next upswing. Market timers point out that their buy-and-hold approach prevents these emotional *sell* reactions by investors.

Statistics indicate that a buy-and-hold strategy can outperform the market timing strategy. See the Syndicate (www.moneypages.com/syndicate/buyholdhtml) article on "A Case for Buy and Hold." The table at this site shows the results of a University of Michigan Study in which the S & P annualized return for 1982 to 1987 was 26.3 percent for the full 1,276 trading days. If the investor is out of the market on ten of the biggest gain days, returns are reduced to 18.3 percent. If the investor is out of the market for 40 of the biggest gain days, returns drop to 4.3 percent.

These percentages point out the biggest problem with market timing: the need to predict when to get into the market and when to get out of the market (in addition to ensuring that the timing strategy will make enough increased returns to offset trading costs). A buy-and-hold strategy makes certain that the investor is in the market for the days with the biggest gains.

For more information about market timing, check out these sites:

First Capital Corporation (www.firstcap.com): This site provides two free newsletters. *Market Timing* presents a short-term technical approach for the stock and bond markets. *Global Viewpoint* provides a weekly technical analysis of world markets that includes interest rates, foreign exchange, spot stock indices, and commodities. You can search back issues online. Both newsletters include recommendations, tips, illustrations, and charts.

Roger Hagan's Market Timing for Mutual funds (www.halcyon.com/rhagan/): This site includes ordering information for a mutual fund timing spreadsheet add-in ($39.95), last week's signal graph, graphs of favorite funds, links to other sites, and who's hot and who's not.

Timely (www.timely.com): This site (see Figure 12-10) posts free charts and quotes on all U.S. and Canadian stocks and indexes. The Web site features include customized charting, company-specific links, indexes that indicate today's market action, and cross-indexed information for locating key market activity.

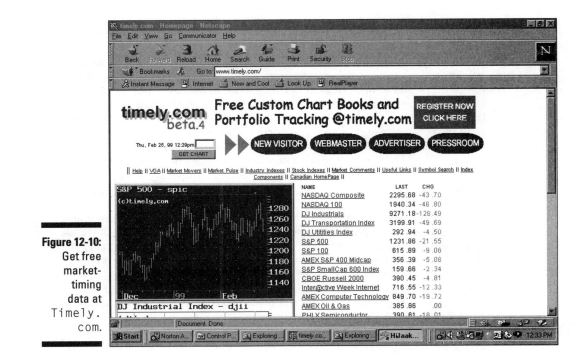

Figure 12-10:
Get free market-timing data at Timely.com.

Chapter 13

Valuing, Buying, and Selling Bonds Online

*I*n this chapter, I show you how to analyze, buy, and sell a variety of fixed-income investments. I explore the benefits of savings bonds, I detail new regulations, and I explain the limitations of this type of investment. I also show you where to find the Savings Bond Wizard, which you can use to determine the exact value of your savings bonds.

This chapter also explains how to purchase Treasury securities without a broker. You can now purchase Treasury securities online or over the phone with *Buy Direct!,* a U.S. Treasury Department sponsored program. In addition, you can access your account online to see your online statement. Other online services include helpful information — for example, dates of government auctions, Treasury yields, auction results, and instructions about how to open your investor's account at Treasury Direct (the master record of the securities you own that is maintained by the federal government).

For online investors interested in paying the right price for a bond, this chapter shows how to value all types of bonds and determine bond yields (returns). Doing so may sound complicated, but with a little practice, you'll be calculating your returns in no time. This chapter also explains where to buy bonds online and it offers a hot strategy that can protect you from interest rate risk.

Nice and Simple: Savings Bonds

For many people, the only way they can save money is by purchasing savings bonds. The United States Treasury Department offers two main types of savings bonds:

- ✔ **Series EE:** You pay half the face value of a Series EE bond at the time of purchase, and you receive the face value when the bond matures. The interest rate isn't fixed, so the maturity term is variable. However, most bonds mature in 18 years and don't accrue any more income after 30 years. The minimum denomination is $50, and the maximum denomination is $10,000.

- ✔ **Series HH:** A Series HH bond pays interest directly to your account at a financial institution every six months. These bonds have fixed interest rates for ten years and earn interest up to 20 years. Series HH bonds are available in denominations of $500, $1,000, $5,000, and $10,000.

Where to buy bonds

About 55 million people own savings bonds, and around $15 billion worth of savings bonds are sold per year. Three sources exist for purchasing savings bonds:

- ✔ **Banks, credit unions, and other financial institutions:** Many financial institutions are qualified as savings bond agents. These agents accept the payments and the purchase orders for the EE bonds and forward the orders to a Federal Reserve bank, where the bonds are inscribed and mailed. Allow 15 days for delivery.

- ✔ **Employer sponsored payroll savings plans:** More than 45,000 employers participate in employer-sponsored payroll savings plans, and some banks offer EE bonds through bond-a-month plans.

- ✔ **Federal Reserve banks:** If you write to your local Federal Reserve bank and ask for an application, you can purchase savings bonds by mail. Figure 13-1 shows the Savings Bond page at the Web site for the Federal Reserve Bank of New York (www.ny.frb.org/pihome/svg_bnds). This site provides the addresses of the 12 regional Federal Reserve banks.

You can get additional information about savings bonds from the following Internet sources:

- ✔ **Market Analysis of Savings Bonds** (www.bondinformer.com): An expert provides a market analysis of savings bonds' short- and long-term interest rates at this Web site.

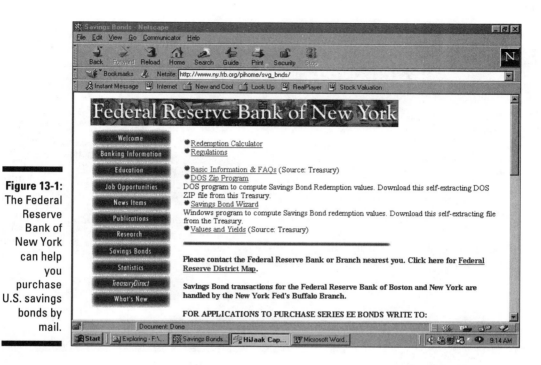

Figure 13-1:
The Federal
Reserve
Bank of
New York
can help
you
purchase
U.S. savings
bonds by
mail.

✔ **The Bureau of Public Debt (**www.publicdebt.Treas.gov/sav/
savbene.htm**):** This site provides information on the benefits of savings
bonds and covers interest rates and maturity periods.

Check for old bonds in your safe-deposit box or among the papers of elderly
relatives. More than $2.3 billion in savings bonds have never been redeemed.

The good and the bad about savings bonds

The returns on savings bonds are so low that they'll never make you rich. In
fact, returns are so low that large pension funds and other big investors don't
purchase savings bonds. However, for many individuals, savings bonds are the
best approach for saving money. Savings bonds offer the following advantages:

✔ **You can save automatically:** Employers who sponsor savings bond
programs can automatically deduct an amount that you designate from
your paychecks. For many people, this program is a painless way to
save money.

✔ **You can diversify your risk:** If you already have investments in stocks
and bonds, you may want to invest in savings bonds and thus add a no-
risk element to your portfolio.

Downloading the savings bond wizard

Savings bonds have always been easy to purchase and are popular gifts for new parents and grandchildren. But as easy as these financial instruments are to buy, they are equally difficult to value. This difficulty can be especially troublesome if you need to cash in a bond before it matures. Additionally, bondholders may have problems keeping an accurate inventory of the savings bonds they have on hand.

Recognizing this problem, the federal government developed a nifty program that does all the work for you. The accompanying figure shows a page from the Web site of the Bureau of Public Debt at `www.publicdebt.Treas.gov/sav/savwizar.htm`. This site contains the Savings Bond Wizard, a free savings bond software program. To download the program, just click on the appropriate link.

One)¶ the Savings Bond Wizard's features allows you to print a copy of your bond inventory. (After a flood or fire, this inventory is an invaluable record of the bondholder's investment.)

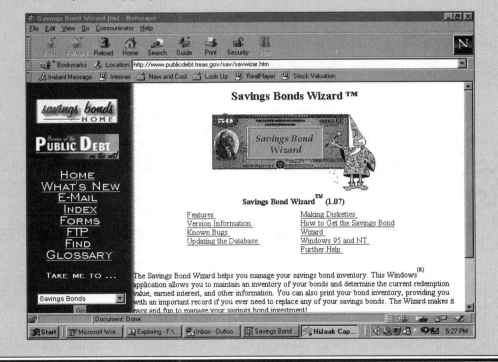

✔ **Your investment is safe:** In exchange for a low return, savings bonds offer absolute safety of principal — they're no-risk investments.

✔ **You don't pay any sales commissions:** Savings bonds don't require the services of a broker to help you purchase them, and thus you pay no sales commissions.

✔ **Your minimum investment is low:** The minimum investment in savings bonds is $25, and employer-sponsored plans can make the minimum even lower per week.

✔ **You pay no or low taxes:** The difference between the purchase price and the redemption value of EE bonds and the payments made on HH bonds comes in the form of interest. This interest income is subject to federal income tax, but not state or local income taxes. You can defer paying federal income tax on the interest until you cash in the bonds.

✔ **You gain education tax benefits:** For EE bonds purchased after 1989 and cashed to pay tuition and post-secondary education fees, the interest earned is not subject to federal income taxes.

EE bonds don't pay accrued interest in periodic cash payments as do HH bonds. An alternative investment exists for people who are about to retire and want an investment that pays interest in cash: Sell the savings bonds, pay the tax, and use the proceeds to purchase 20-year Treasury securities. The Treasury securities pay interest in cash so that retirees can use it for living expenses. *Note:* If selling your E and EE bonds puts you in a higher tax bracket, sell them over a two-year period.

Just Uncle Sam, Treasury Securities, and You

The federal government sells Treasury securities to the public to pay off maturing debt and raise the cash needed to operate the federal government. These securities are sold at 150 auctions throughout the year. There are three types of Treasury securities. All Treasury securities have a minimum purchase of $1,000 and additional purchase increments of $1,000. The chief difference between Treasury securities is the life of the obligation.

✔ **Treasury bills (T-bills)** mature in three months, six months, or one year. Treasury bills are purchased at a discount, so interest is actually paid. You'll write a check for $10,000 and the government refunds the discount (which equals the interest rate determined at auction). In other words, your return is the difference between the purchase price and the maturity value.

- **Treasury Notes** are considered intermediate-term securities and mature in two to ten years. They provide state and local tax-exempt interest payments to noteholders.

- **Treasury Bonds** are long-term securities that have maturities that range from 10 years to 30 years. Interest paid to bondholders is exempt from state and local taxes.

Buying Treasury securities via the Internet

Treasury securities may not look very lucrative if you're used to double-digit returns, but they're excellent investments for investors who can't tolerate risk. In other words, if you're a conservative investor, U.S. Treasury securities may be your type of investment. You can now purchase Treasury securities over the Internet or by telephone.

The Internet purchase program is called, *Buy Direct!,* and you can submit a noncompetitive bid (which I explain later in this section) via the Internet (or by calling 1-800-943-6864). The price of the security is debited from the account you previously designated to receive Treasury Direct payments. (This is called a Treasury Direct account. I show you how to open your own account later in this section.) Tender forms and payments may also be submitted electronically through your financial institution or government securities broker or dealer.

Opening your account

Treasury Direct is a book-entry system that is managed by the federal government. After you open a Treasury Direct account, you can purchase bonds from the government without a broker. Treasury Direct provides a statement of account whenever you make a change to your account (for example, when you buy more Treasury securities, sell your securities, or reinvest earnings).

If you purchase Treasury securities directly from the federal government, they are issued in a book-entry form that is held in the Department of the Public Debt's *Treasury Direct* system. The securities are issued to your individual account. In contrast, if you purchase Treasury securities using a broker, they are issued in a commercial book-entry form, which means that the securities are held in the name of your broker or dealer. The broker then maintains records of each individual investor's Treasury securities.

You can see your account balance online at www.publicdebt.Treas.gov/sec/sectdes.htm. Just go to Virtual Lobby, type in your Treasury Direct account number, and click Enter the Lobby.

Maintenance charges are $25 per year for each $100,000 in your account. Treasury Direct provides information about how to open and maintain a Treasury Direct Investor Account at `www.publicdebt.treas.gov/sec/secacct.htm`.

You can request that an account be set up before you purchase your first Treasury security by submitting a New Account Request form. Just print the form located at `www.publicdebt.treas.gov/sec.sectrdir.htm`. Fill in all the required information and mail the form to your local Federal Reserve bank. Don't send any cash; it's free.

How to buy 'em

Figure 13-2 shows the calendar of upcoming auction dates at the Bureau of Public Debt. The Bureau of Public Debt (`www.publicdebt.treas.gov/of/ofaucrt.htm`) provides a constantly updated three-month calendar of tentative auction dates so that you can plan ahead. Official auction dates are announced about seven days before the securities are offered. Treasury bills, notes, and bonds are sold through competitive and noncompetitive bidding:

- ✔ **Noncompetitive bid:** You agree to accept a rate determined by the auction, and in return you're guaranteed that your bid successfully results in purchasing the security you desire. Most individual investors submit noncompetitive bids. Noncompetitive bids from individual investors can't exceed $5 million for the same offering of Treasury notes or bonds.

- ✔ **Competitive bid:** For a bill auction, the investor submits an offer — or *tender* — specifying a discount rate to two decimal places (for example 5.12 percent). For a note or bond auction, the investor submits a tender specifying a yield to three decimal places (for example, 5.123 percent). Common fractions may not be used. If the bid falls within the range accepted at the auction, the investor is awarded the security. If the bid is at the high rate or yield, the investor may not be awarded the full amount bid. Most financial institutions (banks, insurance companies, brokerages, and so on) submit competitive bids.

You can obtain all the order forms, instructions, auction dates, auction results, and other related information you'll need to purchase Treasury securities at the Bureau of the Public Debt Web site (`www.publicdebt.treas.gov`). You can download and print forms, send e-mail requests for forms, or have forms mailed to you. This site also provides details about how to purchase Treasury securities without a broker (a great money-saving feature for investors).

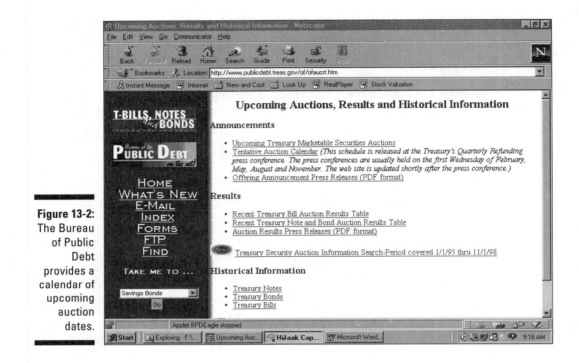

Figure 13-2:
The Bureau
of Public
Debt
provides a
calendar of
upcoming
auction
dates.

Don't let the jargon of Treasury securities make purchasing seem more complex than it really is. A noncompetitive bid is similar to a market order (you definitely get the security, but you don't know what price you receive), whereas a competitive bid is similar to a limit order (you know what price you get, but you don't know whether you definitely get the security).

You may want to consider accumulating cash in a money market account (for any purpose other than education). The interest rate paid is often as good or better than an investment in Treasuries and you have much more liquidity (you don't have to wait three months to five years to get your money back).

Tendering your offer

Select the issue you want to bid on and complete the correct *Treasury Direct Tender Information* form at www.publicdebt.treas.gov/sec/secform.htm. Finish the form by making either a competitive or noncompetitive bid, which is called a *tender*. State how many securities you want to buy, the maturity term, and include full payment payable to your local Federal Reserve bank. You can make payments by direct deposit, certified check, matured Treasury obligation, personal check for notes and bonds, and U.S. currency if presented in person.

When completing the Treasury Direct Tender Information form, you must decide whether you want to send in a competitive or a noncompetitive bid. (Institutional investors always submit competitive bids.) A noncompetitive tender specifies the discount rate with two decimal places that you're willing to pay (for example, 6.12 percent). If your bid is too high and the issue is purchased at a lower rate, you may not get the securities you want.

Detailed directions about how to complete the Treasury Direct Tender Information form and acceptable ways to pay for the Treasuries are available at www.pueblo.gsa and at the Bureau of the Public Debt at www.publicdebt.treas.gov/sec/sectndr.htm.

Cashing in or rolling over your Treasury securities

Treasury bills mature in 13, 26, or 52 weeks. When your Treasury bill matures you have two choices. First, you can roll over your investment and reinvest in the face value of another T-bill (with the same or a different maturity). Second, you can cash in and have the proceeds deposited to your Treasury Direct account. For example, say that your $15,000 Treasury bill with a maturity term of 13 weeks matures. You can elect to reinvest in another $15,000 Treasury bill for 13, 26, or 52 weeks (with a noncompetitive bid). If you do not elect to reinvest your $15,000 at maturity, your Treasury Direct Account is credited with $15,000, or a check for $15,000 is sent to your home.

Selling your Treasury securities

The good news is that you can sell your Treasury securities before they mature, without a broker or with a broker. The first approach is to let the federal government sell your Treasury securities. The second approach is to sell your Treasury securities through a broker. The bad news is that both approaches cost you extra money.

If you need to sell your Treasury security, the federal government will help you. You can sell directly through Treasury Direct — you don't need a broker. The government will get quotes from different dealers and you get the best price offered. The fee is $34 for each security sold. You can even have the proceeds from the sale of the Treasury security deposited directly to your checking account, less the transaction fee. For additional information, see www.publicdebt.treas.gov/sec/secbsr.htm.

In a secondary market for Treasury securities, investors can sell Treasury securities before they mature through a brokerage. For instance, let's say that you purchased a six-month Treasury bill. Three months later, you decide to sell. Other investors will purchase the Treasury bill at a slightly higher price than what you paid because it is closer to maturity. Brokerage fees vary for these services, so shop around for the best price.

You can also purchase Treasury securities in the secondary market if you want to have securities (money) come due on a specific date to meet a financial objective.

Online sources for more information

Information provided by the government is written in a way that makes purchasing Treasuries seem more difficult and complex than they really are, but don't get discouraged. For more information about understanding and purchasing Treasury securities, refer to the following online resources:

- ✔ **Economeister:** The Economeister Web site, located at www.economeister.com, provides auction dates and news about Treasury securities.

- ✔ **GovPX:** This site, located at www.govpx.com, provides quotations of U.S. government securities. The site also provides active lists of Treasury bonds, notes, and bills with each financial instrument's account (CUSIP — Computerized Uniform Securities Identification Program) number, coupon rate, and maturity date. Lists include buyers' bid prices, sellers' asking prices, changes from the prior trading day, and yields.

- ✔ **Quote.com Street Pricing:** This site, located at www.quote.com, provides quotes for Treasury securities and government agency securities. Specific information includes interest rates and spreads, quotes on active Treasuries, and quotes on government agency securities. Cost is $9.95 per month for the basic service.

- ✔ **Zero Coupon Bonds and Strips:** You can get an explanation of these more sophisticated Treasury securities from the Federal Reserve Bank of New York at www.ny.frb.org/pihome/fedpoint/fed41.html.

The Math of Bonds

The bond market is dominated by institutional investors (insurance companies, pension funds, mutual funds, and so on) who account for 80 to 85 percent of all trading. Individual investors tend to purchase municipal and corporate bonds because of their lower denominations (around $1,000) and tax-exempt features. However, the impact of individual investors can also be felt through the purchases of mutual funds that specialize in bonds.

The following section shows the valuation process of bonds and the relationship of interest rate changes to the value of bonds. I provide several easy to use approaches that take the mystery out of determining your bond yield.

Calculating bond values

A bond issued by a corporation is called a *debt instrument*. The bond states how the debtholder (investor) is repaid. Generally, these terms are normal debt arrangements. The borrower makes interest payments and then pays the principal at a predetermined date. Several issues make bonds complicated, such as provisions to convert the bonds to common stocks at a predetermined stock value or terms that allow the bond issuer to retire the bond before maturity.

Treasury securities, and government agency and municipal bonds are valued in the same way as corporate bonds. However, this doesn't show the entire picture. Treasury securities are subject to federal taxes but are exempt from state and local taxes. Government agency securities are generally taxable for federal, state, and local purposes, but some exceptions exist. Municipal bonds are generally tax-free (from federal, state, and local taxes). Therefore, when you value corporate bonds, the calculated rate of return is somewhat overstated because it doesn't take the impact of taxes into consideration.

The value of the bond is based on the investor's assessment of the bond's value. The receipt of future interest payments, the repayment of principal, and the credit rating or riskiness of the bond usually temper these assessments. You aren't obligated to hold a bond until maturity, and bonds are traded freely in the marketplace.

Calculating the value of a bond involves determining the present value of the interest payments and the eventual recovery of the principal. *Present value* means discounting the future cash flow to calculate how much you're willing to pay today for these future receipts.

At times calculating the yield on bonds can seem more complicated than it really is. For example, if you purchase a one-year Treasury bill for $9,500 and redeem it in 12 months at full face value ($10,000), your gain is $500 (subject to federal income tax but exempt from state and local taxes). To determine your yield, use the following formula if your holding period is one year:

Face Value – Price / Price = Annual Return

$10,000 – $9,500 / $9,500 = 0.526 or 5.26%

See the section "The easy way to value your bond returns" later in this chapter, where I show you how to calculate the yield for a bond that has a maturity term that is greater than one year.

Creating yield curves

A yield curve is a diagram that illustrates the relationship of bond yields to maturities on a specific day. Yield curves can be used to decide which type of bond is best for your financial objectives. Bond yields and maturities are posted daily at the Wall Street Journal Interactive Web site (www.wsj.com).

On a piece of graph paper on the horizontal axis, plot the maturities of Treasury securities from left to right starting with the shortest maturity of 30-days to the longest maturity of 30-years. Then on the vertical axis, plot the yield of each Treasury security. Next, connect the dots to make a yield curve. See the curve descriptions in the following list to find out what your results indicate:

- ✔ If the short-term rates are higher than the long-term rates, then the yield curve becomes *inverted,* or has a downward swing to it, which tells you that this situation tends to be *bearish* for the market. In this situation, monetary policy is likely to be tight and the Federal Reserve is pushing up short-term rates.

- ✔ If the short-term rates are lower than the long-term rates, then the yield curve is *positive,* or has an upward swing to it, which usually indicates that investors are willing to tie up their money in long-term commitments to reap higher rewards.

- ✔ If the short rates and the long-term rates are the same (or nearly the same), then the yield curve appears to be flat, like a line.

The yield curve approach also works for other types of bonds, such as government agency, municipal, or corporate bonds. Remember that you need to include in the curve only bonds with the same level of risk, such as all AA-rated corporate bonds.

The easy way to value your bond returns

Bonds are often quoted at prices that differ from their stated (or *par*) values, a situation that can be troublesome for investors who want to determine the yield of the bond. Many ways exist to calculate the yield value of a bond. In my opinion, the *approximate yield to maturity* method provides the easiest way to determine a bond's current yield.

To calculate the approximate yield to maturity (YTM), you need the following information:

- ✔ Annual interest payment (I)
- ✔ Principal payment (P)

   ✔ Price of the bond (B)

   ✔ Number of years to maturity (M)

Using these values, you calculate the approximate yield to maturity by using the following formula:

$$YTM = (I + ((P - B) \div M)) \div ((0.6 \times B) + (0.4 \times P))$$

For example, what is the yield to maturity on a 12-year, 7 percent annual coupon, $1,000 par value bond that sells at a discount for $942.21? Here are the calculations:

$$YTM = (70 + (($1,000 - $942.21) \div 12)) \div ((0.6 \times $942.21) + (0.4 \times $1,000))$$

$$YTM = (70 + (57.79 \div 12)) \div (565.33 + 400)$$

$$YTM = (70 + 4.82) \div 965.33$$

$$YTM = 74.82 \div 965.33$$

$$YTM = 0.0775$$

$$YTM = 7.75\%$$

If your required rate of return is 8 percent, you should *not* purchase the bond because the approximate yield to maturity (7.75 percent) doesn't meet your financial requirements (an 8 percent return). Conversely, if the bond has a return that is equal to or *greater* than 8 percent, the bond meets your objectives and is a "buy" candidate.

Note: If the value of the bond is discounted (that is, sells below its par value — in this case, below $1,000), the yield to maturity (YTM) is greater than the 7 percent coupon rate.

More Online Bond News, Rates of Return, and Advice

For more information about bond markets, commentary, rates, and news, see the following online resources:

   ✔ **Capital Markets Commentary** (www.indata.com/whatsnew.htm) is a weekly fixed-income (bond) market review provided by Interactive Data Corporation, a Financial Times company. The Capital Markets Commentary includes market information about U.S. government agency bonds, U.S. corporate bonds, international bonds, U.S. municipals, and commercial mortgage-backed bonds.

✔ **Smart Money** (`www.smartmoney.com`) shown in Figure 13-3 provides key interest rates, bond market updates, a bond calculator, and glossary. Educational articles include bond strategies, short-term bond investing, bond allocation, and a bond primer.

✔ **Tucker Anthony: Yield Alert** (`www.tucker-anthony.com/yield.htm`) is a financial advisor that assists investors by providing various market rates for Treasury securities, government agency securities, corporate bonds, municipal bonds, and zero-coupon bonds. These comparisons are helpful for benchmarking the performance of your bond portfolio.

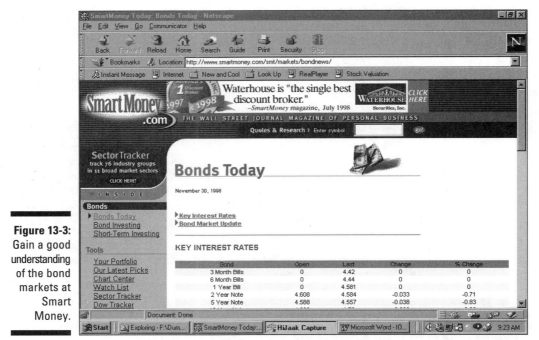

Figure 13-3: Gain a good understanding of the bond markets at Smart Money.

SmartMoney is a joint venture of Hearst Communication Inc. and Dow Jones & Company, Inc.

A hot, no-fuss bond strategy

More Americans have invested in bonds than in any other security. Some of the advantages of bonds are that they offer regular interest payments that are higher than money market accounts, they can be tax-exempt, and they offer a way to stay ahead of inflation.

Some of the limitations of investing in bonds are interest rate risk (if interest rates go up, the value of your bond goes down) and credit rating risk (if your bond gets downgraded, its value goes down). Additionally, unless you own a Treasury security, your principal investment isn't guaranteed by the government the way bank deposits are protected by the Federal Deposit Insurance Corporation (FDIC).

Tucker Anthony, an investment counselor, suggests one way to reduce your exposure to interest rate risk. He suggests creating a *bond ladder*. Each rung of the bond ladder consists of a different bond maturity. For example, the first rung of the bond ladder may consist of bonds that mature in one year; the second rung may consist of bonds that mature in two years, and so on, for ten years.

The yield of the ten-year bond ladder is less than 20-year bonds, but the ladder provides diversification. As each rung matures, you can reinvest the funds in the same or better ways to conserve your principal. The benefits of this approach are some protection from declining interest rates and low maintenance on your part.

If this bond ladder scheme seems too complex, you can always invest in a bond mutual fund. But keep in mind that bond mutual funds rarely "beat the market" and tend to have more risk than individual bonds. Some aggresively managed bond funds include risky investing strategies that can be a real gamble. On the other hand, one of the advantages of a bond mutual fund is that you often get to own a share of bonds that are $50,000, $100,000, or $250,000 each — something that you may not be able to achieve as an individual investor.

Chapter 14

Looking for the Next Big Thing: IPOs, DPOs, and DRIPs

- -

In This Chapter

▶ Evaluating initial public offerings (IPOs)

▶ Getting in early with direct public offerings (DPOs)

▶ Bypassing broker fees to buy shares directly from the company

▶ Using dividend reinvestment plans (DRIPs) to increase your personal wealth

- -

*E*veryone has heard stories about someone who got rich because he or she purchased the right stock at the right time. Looking back at these stories, the type of stock these individuals usually purchased was an initial public offering — called an IPO for short. In this chapter, I show how you can evaluate these types of stocks, determine what their limitations are, locate online sources of IPO news and research, and know which brokers specialize in IPOs or the mutual funds that include this type of financial asset.

An even grander opportunity is a direct public offering, or DPO. Even more speculative than IPOs, shares in these companies are comparable to investments by venture capitalists. This chapter explains the limitations of DPOs, how to purchase DPOs, and where to find online DPO research and information. Additionally, you find out how you can purchase your shares directly from the company, as well as participate in dividend reinvestment plans (DRIPs).

Looking for Investment Opportunities: IPOs

When a company sells stock that trades publicly for the first time, that event is called an *initial public offering* (IPO). These IPO company issuers sell shares to an underwriter. The underwriter, in turn, resells shares to investors at a prearranged offering price. Underwriters often underprice issues by 5 to 10 percent to ensure adequate demand. Generally, shares begin trading immediately on a stock exchange or *over the counter* through the NASDAQ stock market. About one week after issue, due to market efficiency, these excess returns disappear. This indicates that the best time to purchase an IPO is on initial distribution from the underwriting syndicate (which include investment bankers, dealers, and brokers).

Every year, development companies and companies just starting to generate revenues seek additional capital for business expansions. Investors purchase shares so that they can reap the short-term rewards of price swings or share in the long-term prosperity of being in early for a new investment opportunity.

The investment in an IPO is speculative. These companies often have no proven strategies for success and no track record of marketing success or corporate earnings. Many of these companies crash and burn, and only a few endure to become big-time financial success stories. Keep in mind that for every Intel or Microsoft, 50 companies go bankrupt. (Studies show that about 50% of IPO firms are in business five years after their initial offerings.) In other words, the success rate of IPOs is one out of every two.

Understanding the basics of IPOs, performing fundamental research, and knowing how to be an early shareholder can increase your chances of success. Figure 14-1 shows Dun & Bradstreet's CompaniesOnline at www.companiesonline.com. CompaniesOnline and other reporting agencies can assist you in checking the financial backgrounds and disclosures of the companies you're researching. The site requires your free registration and charges $20 for each company's Background Business Report.

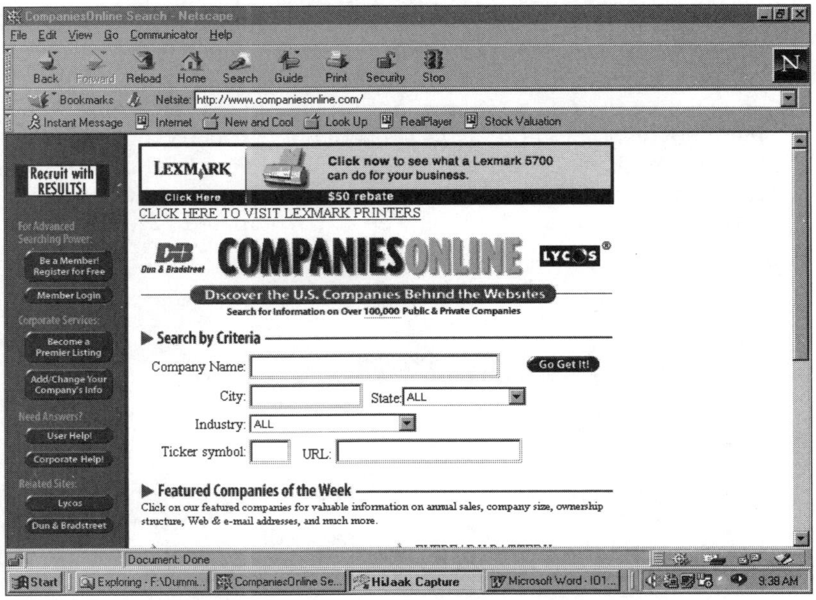

Figure 14-1: Dun & Bradstreet's Companies-Online can assist you in checking out an investment candidate.

Getting the scoop on IPOs

The following guidelines may help you select a winner out of the thousands of companies that have initial public offerings each year:

1. **Read the prospectus.**

   Read the preliminary prospectus *(red herring)* to find out about the company's expected growth. The red herring (a preliminary prospectus that provides information but is not an offer to sell the security and does not include any offering prices) includes a description of the issuer's business, the names and addresses of key corporate officers, the ownership amounts of the key officers, any litigation problems, the company's current capitalization, and how the company plans to use the new funds from the offering.

2. **Perform fundamental analysis.**

   Evaluate the company's financial performance by using fundamental analysis, just like you would for any other stock. (Fundamental analysis is a form of security valuation that seeks to determine the intrinsic value of a stock based on the stock's underlying economics. You then compare the intrinsic value to the asking price. For more details about how to perform a fundamental analysis, see Chapter 12, "Digging Deeper.")

3. **Check out the company's management.**

   Examine the backgrounds of the firm's management. What is their executive management experience and education? Do they have work experience in their current jobs?

4. **Read the mission statement.**

   Investigate the firm's strategy. Is it realistic? How large is the company's market? Who is the competition? If the company plans to gain less than 25 percent of the total market, the firm may not be a long-term success.

5. **Investigate the planned use of funds.**

   Determine why raising a certain amount of capital is so critical to the company's success. If the money is used to pay down debt, the company may be headed for problems. A positive sign is using the money for expansion.

6. **Compare IPO prices.**

   Compare expected IPO prices in the red herring to the final prospectus. If the price is higher in the later prospectus, the underwriters are enthusiastic about the offering. Lower prices indicate a lack of interest by the investment community.

7. **Determine whether it's your kind of company.**

   Decide whether you want to own stock in the company you're researching. Maybe it's a great financial opportunity, but you have reservations
   about the product or service. (For example, do you really want to be
   part owner in a company that kills frogs?)

8. **Estimate your planned holding period.**

   Decide how long you plan to keep the shares. If the IPO is going to be
   successful, it will be a better long-term investment than short-term
   investment because IPO stock prices tend to move up or down with the
   stock market.

For more information on IPOs, see `www.invest-faq.com/articles/`
`stock-ipo.html`. This article includes educational materials about IPOs,
the mechanics of IPO offerings, the underwriting process, and IPOs in the
real world.

Understanding the limitations of IPOs

If your goal is to create massive wealth or enjoy a comfortable lifestyle,
making the most of your money takes time and vigilance. You always need to
be on the lookout for new opportunities and new ways to invest your
savings. To many online investors, an IPO may seem like the perfect investment. However, if the IPO you select is going to be a good investment, then
with luck, it could pay off over the long term. Your investment will grow as
the company expands and becomes profitable. But a high level of risk exists.
IPOs are speculative investments. Many promising firms go bust. The
following shows some of the limitations of IPOs:

- ✔ Many IPOs lose much of their value after the first day of trading.

- ✔ Many positive-looking IPOs are offered only to the "best" clients of large
  brokerage firms, pension plans, and institutions. However, you can
  always gain access to an IPO when it starts trading on the secondary
  market. (The stock begins trading on the secondary market when an
  investor purchases it from the investment-banking firm in the primary
  market and begins to sell it on a stock exchange.) The performances of
  these stocks are similar to the performances of small cap stocks and
  are very volatile.

- ✔ After three to six months, IPOs may underperform some small cap
  stocks. The source of this problem may be employees selling their
  shares and forcing the stock price to decline.

- ✔ After three to six months, the popularity of a strong IPO often fades.

Before you invest in an IPO, take the time to find out about the regulations
governing an IPO. Figure 14-2 shows a useful page (`www.moneypages.com/`
`syndicate/stocks/ipo.html`) from The Syndicate Web site.

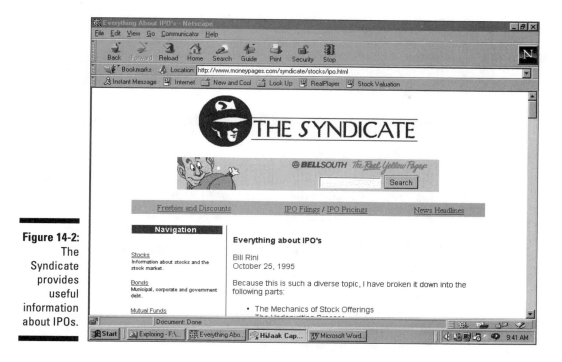

Figure 14-2:
The
Syndicate
provides
useful
information
about IPOs.

Finding IPO news and research on the Internet

You can access various sources for IPO-related news and information on the Internet. A few of these sources follow companies from the initial filing to their performance after the issue becomes public. Many of these sites provide news, commentary, and quotes. Other information includes Securities and Exchange Commission (SEC) recent filings, scheduled pricing, and registration information. Additionally, some sites include statistics on aftermarket performance, IPO ratings, and company performance data.

The following Internet sites track IPOs:

- **Alert-IPO!** (www.ostman.com/alert-ipo) provides complete IPO information. Its system searches the SEC's EDGAR database for new issues. The site includes data on more than 1,664 IPO filings and 1,364 underwriters.

- **IPO Central** (www.ipocentral.com), sponsored by Hoovers (www.hoovers.com), provides the most recent IPO filings, weekly pricing, commentary, and informative articles.

- ✔ **IPO.Com** (`www.ipo.com`) has IPO pricings for companies listed on the NASDAQ, AMEX, and NYSE exchanges, a review of the most recent IPO filings, an IPO calendar that provides a look at IPOs that are about to be priced and traded, news about which companies have withdrawn or postponed their offerings, and research articles, reviews, and information about how to locate other online financial sources.

- ✔ **IPO Daily Report** (`cbs.marketwatch.com/news/current/IPO_rep.htx`) offers daily IPO news from CBS MarketWatch.

- ✔ **IPO Data Systems** (`www.ipodata.com`) is a subscription service that includes an IPO calendar, company profiles, listings of top performers, IPOs by underwriter, and online information about IPOs. At the time of this writing, fees are $15 per month or $150 per year.

- ✔ **IPO Focus** (`www.bloomberg.com/fun/bbco/ipofocus/ipofocus1.html`) is IPO news from the Bloomberg news service.

- ✔ **IPO Interactive** (`www.fedfil.com/ipo/index.html`) shows Federal Filings Business News reports. These reports contain information on all IPOs that exceed $10 million in net proceeds. The reports include actual and pro forma financial results, operational histories, liquidity, and company backgrounds.

- ✔ **IPO Maven** (`www.IPOmaven.com`) is a great source for IPO news, information, and commentary.

- ✔ **IPO Monitor** (`www.ipomonitor.com`) is a fee-based notification service for information and events associated with IPOs. Subscriptions are $29 per month or $290 per year.

- ✔ **TechInvestor** (`www.techweb.com/investor/ipowatch/iposwatch.html`) lists technology-oriented IPOs and pending registrations.

- ✔ **The Online Investor** (`www.investhelp.com`) provides educational information and investing data. Updated daily, this site has weekly articles and special sections on stock splits, IPOs, stock buybacks, analysts' upgrades and downgrades, and more.

- ✔ **Yahoo! IPO News** (`biz.yahoo.com/reports/ipo.html`) is IPO news from Yahoo! (Yahoo! started as a type of topic-specific search engine, and has expanded into different areas such as the IPO News.)

Finding online brokers that specialize in IPOs

After researching IPOs, you may decide that you want a broker who specializes in this type of security. The Internet can assist you in locating the right broker. Here are a couple of examples:

✔ **Schwab** (www.schwab.com) provides its best customers with offerings underwritten by Credit Suisse, First Boston, Hambrecht & Ouist, and J.P. Morgan Securities, Inc.

✔ **Wit Capital** (www.witcapital.com) provides IPO offerings to customers on a first-come, first-served basis. You can view IPOs, purchase shares, read about the rules for investing in IPOs, find out about the risks of IPOs, and check out FAQs about IPOs. Other new issue information includes secondary, follow-on, or combinations offerings managed by major underwriters, private placements for early stage companies (accredited investors only), and public venture capital that allows small investors to take positions in early stage companies.

Including IPOs in mutual funds

Several large mutual funds include IPOs. However, participation in IPOs shouldn't be the only reason you purchase a mutual fund. Before making your investment decision, you still need to carefully read the fund's prospectus and compare it to other mutual funds and your overall financial objectives.

Here are a few examples of mutual funds that include IPOs:

✔ Govett Smaller Companies (GSCQX)

✔ Janus Olympus (JAOLX)

✔ PBHG Emerging Growth (PBEGX)

✔ USAA Aggressive Growth (USAUX)

✔ Warburg Pincus Post-Venture (WPVCX)

For more details, use the ticker symbol lookup feature at Morningstar (www.morningstar.net).

Be Your Own Broker with Direct Public Offerings (DPOs)

Historically, small companies have had a difficult time finding capital to expand their businesses. Traditional lenders are frequently unwilling to take risks with untried companies, venture capitalists negotiate tough deals that often force company founders out of key management roles, and traditional IPOs require a minimum of $15 million in annual revenue.

If you take an initial public offering (IPO) and cut out the underwriter, what you have left is a direct public offering (DPO). DPOs have been around for more than 20 years. For example, Ben & Jerry's used a DPO to raise capital for the ice cream company. However, the offering was limited to its home state of Vermont.

In October 1995, the SEC fueled DPOs with a ruling that makes electronic delivery of a prospectus okay. Consequently, companies can raise needed capital by selling their shares directly to the public via the Internet. These DPOs have the following advantages for small companies:

- ✔ **Cost and time savings:** The company saves thousands of dollars in underwriting expenses.

- ✔ **Regulation of Internet IPOs:** Issuers can file faster, turnaround times are quicker, filing is less expensive, fewer restrictions exist on the sales process, and issuers can announce planned offerings.

- ✔ **Management remains focused:** Management isn't drawn away from the company's day-to-day business needs and customers.

- ✔ **Investors can get in really early:** Investors have access to venture capital-types of investments.

- ✔ **No broker commissions:** Investors don't have to pay high broker commissions.

Recognizing the limitations of DPOs

Many companies are offering a DPO instead of an initial public offering (IPO). For many online investors, a DPO is the best way to get in on the ground floor and share in a company's success. Investors can purchase shares directly from the companies that they want to be part owners of. However, DPOs have some limitations:

- ✔ **Blue sky laws:** Issuing companies must be registered with the SEC and the states where they offer securities, but new legislation allows companies to use the Internet to present initial public offerings. This new legislation is inconsistent with regulations passed in 1911. The 1911 rule requires that issuers register in the states where they offer stocks, but the Internet has no boundaries and thus offers worldwide distribution of stock offerings. Does this mean that issuers don't have to register in each state that uses the Internet? Some issuers register in all 50 states before offering shares. However, one state, Pennsylvania, only requires companies to clearly indicate where they are registered and who may purchase securities.

- ✔ **Fraud and abuse:** Stock issues are highly regulated, but the Internet is an unregulated environment. The enforcement of registration issues on the Internet is keeping the SEC more than busy. The result may be fraudulent solicitations on the Internet.

For information about the SEC rules and regulations for offering stocks, see Bowne Publishing at `publs.bowne/pdf0307/fullmenu.htm`. The reports are free, but you need to use your Adobe Acrobat Reader (included on this book's CD) to view and print the files.

Buying DPOs

DPO issues often open in a blaze of glory due to strong public interest. Then the share prices settle down to a consistent trading range. During the stock's initial period of volatility, the stock price may double or triple. Cashing in at this point can be very profitable and may compensate you for many of your earlier investment mistakes.

DPOs are speculative and definitely for aggressive investors. In other words, if you can't afford to lose all your investment, then you shouldn't be in this market. That said, even the most aggressive investors should only invest between 5 and 10 percent of their total portfolio in this type of financial asset.

To purchase shares, obtain a subscription agreement for the DPO. The subscription agreements are usually included in the last page of the prospectus. If you can't find the form, request one by e-mail or through the U.S. mail. Send the completed agreement and a check for the appropriate amount to the company. The company sends a confirmation letter within five days and the stock certificate within 30 days. (I suggest making a duplicate copy of your check and subscription agreement for your records and sending the originals by registered mail.)

The following list offers some online sources for DPOs:

- ✔ **Direct IPO** (`www.directipo.com`) provides investor resources, information about traditional IPOs and DPOs, an industry spotlight, an IPO contest, a newsroom, and more.

- ✔ **The Direct Public Offering Council** (`isp.mousetrap.net/dpo/home.html`) is a not-for-profit organization that is dedicated to the advancement of the direct public offerings industry. The organization provides a discussion forum, research, forms, and case studies; recommends attorneys and marketing organizations; and more.

- ✔ **Netstock Direct** (`www.netstockdirect.com`), shown in Figure 14-3, is one of the best DPO sites on the Internet. Netstock Direct is an online source for direct investing, statistics, and materials related to direct stock plans. Netstock's search functions can assist you in creating a short list of DPO investment candidates.

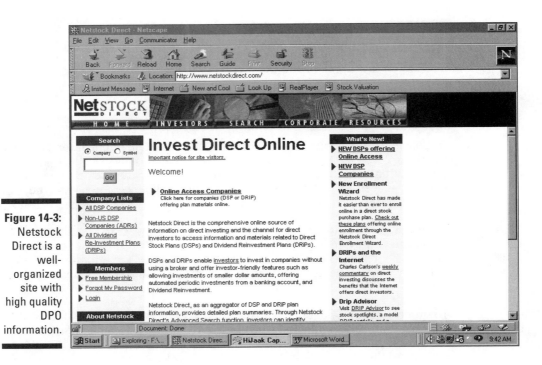

Figure 14-3:
Netstock
Direct is a
well-
organized
site with
high quality
DPO
information.

✔ **Scor Report** (www.scor-report.com) provides information about SCOR direct public offerings and links to related sites.

✔ **SCOR-NET** (www.direct-stock-market.com) is a site for DPOs, quarterly filings, and trading.

✔ **Virtual Wall Street** (www.virtualwallstreet.com) provides a variety of educational materials for consumers. For companies that need to raise funds, Virtual Wall Street provides financial, legal, and online services.

Trading direct public offerings online

The Internet provides several sites that allow small investors to view direct public offering materials and to interact with small and medium-sized companies' offering shares. These sites do not function as stock exchanges but include many of the same elements.

✔ **The Direct Stock Market** (www.dsm.com), shown in Figure 14-4, provides a central online location from which companies that are issuing DPOs can distribute their prospectuses and documents. This opportunity is ideal for companies that may not have many buyers and sellers actively trading their shares. The site is subject to regulatory approval.

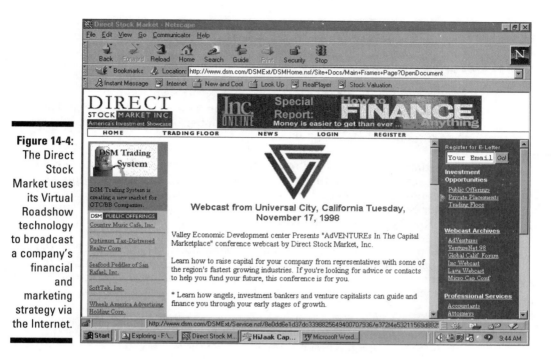

Figure 14-4:
The Direct
Stock
Market uses
its Virtual
Roadshow
technology
to broadcast
a company's
financial
and
marketing
strategy via
the Internet.

✔ **Internet Capital Exchange** (www.inetcapital.com) is designed to bring companies and investors together to generate funding capital and investment opportunities. Companies that are already public can allow their stock to be traded by investors using an interactive trading system.

✔ **The SM Investment Listing Exchange — SMILEX** (www.smilex.com) facilitates member company offerings or performs as a company's investor relations department. Smilex interacts with investors to exchange cash and securities or other agreed upon compensation. Designed for small investors with limited risk capital, investors can search for DPOs in various categories. Depending on their SM assigned investor level, individuals are allowed to view deals only in states where the company has registered the offering and the investor is a resident.

Find out more about DPOs at Virtual Wall Street's Web site (www.virtualwallstreet.com). Educational materials include a comparison chart of a DPO and an IPO, definition of a DPO, information about the DPO process, online resources, DPO and securities laws, and state regulations.

Buying Stock in a Direct Purchase Plan (DPP)

The Securities and Exchange Commission eased regulations in 1994 so that companies can comfortably offer their shares directly to the public. This change has caused a small boom in the number of companies that allow investors to buy shares directly.

Sometimes direct purchase plans (DPPs) are so-called *no-load* stock plans. These plans allow you to join their direct purchase plans (which includes dividend reinvestment features) without first purchasing a share through a broker. Some corporations with DPPs sell shares only to corporate customers, and others are open to all investors.

In the past, utilities were the main companies that had DPPs. In 1996, 150 companies sold their stock directly to the public. In 1997, more than 300 companies offered DPPs. In the coming years, as many as 1,500 companies may sell their stock directly to the public.

About one million individuals purchase their stocks directly. Minimum investments can be as small as $50 a month for IBM shares. Some of the DPPs include dividend reinvestment plans (DRIPs), tax-deferred IRA investments, and loans against stock holdings. A few companies even sell shares below market price. Currently, you can't purchase shares over the Internet, but that's expected to change soon.

The Internet provides many sources for DPP information and education. A few examples follow:

- **Direct Purchase Plans** (cnnfn.com/yourmoney/9707/15/ yomo_direct) is an article from CNNfn about direct purchase plans.

- **Direct Stock Buying** (www.businessweek.com/1997/24/ b3531156.htm) is an excellent article on direct stock purchases.

- **Directions** (www.ndir.com/stocks.drips.html) provides an overview of DRIPs and a listing of Canadian companies that have DRIP programs.

- **Mike's Page** (mk.ml.org/noload) provides a list of 183 no-load stocks.

Buying That First DPP Share

Ford, IBM, British Telecommunications, and many other companies have direct purchase plans (DPPs). All you have to do is contact the firm via the Internet, telephone, or U.S. mail. Direct your request to the Investor Relations Department and ask whether they have a direct purchase plan and an application. Complete the application form and include a check for your initial investment. Make a copy of these items for your records. Send the signed application and check to the company by registered mail.

In more than half of the DPPs, the minimum investment is $250 or less, and as little as $10 thereafter. The plans are designed for long-term investors who plan to hold their shares for at least three to five years. Processing your order is slower than going through a broker; it usually takes about a week. You can make subsequent stock purchases with cash payments and reinvested dividends.

However, purchasing DPPs is proof that there's no such thing as a free lunch, because these so-called no-load stocks are not cost-free. You still have to pay a few fees. You often pay a one-time enrollment fee of $5 to $15, a per-transaction fee of up to $10 plus $0.01 to $0.10 per share, and higher fees when you sell. Some plans charge an annual account management fee. To reinvest your dividend, you may have to pay up to $5 per quarter.

When comparing the fees of some DPPs to the low rates that online brokers charge (between $10 and $30 per transaction), you don't appear to be saving much by buying shares directly from the company. However, the SEC is continuing to relax its regulations about DPPs. Soon companies will be able to advertise their programs at their Web sites. As the market for DPPs heats up, fees are likely to decrease, and you may be able to charge your DPP purchase to your credit card via the Internet.

Profiting with Dividend Reinvestment Plans (DRIPs)

Dividend reinvestment plans (DRIPs) are sometimes called *shareholder investment programs* (SIPs). These plans are an easy, low-cost way to purchase stocks and reinvest your dividend income. About 1,000 companies and closed-end mutual funds sponsor DRIPs.

Most plans require you to purchase your first share through a broker, the National Association of Investors Corporation (NAIC) buying club, or some other method. A share purchased in a DRIP is like any other stock share. You have voting rights and stock splits, and your uninvested dividends are taxed when you sell your shares.

Shares must be registered in your name. You can purchase subsequent shares directly from the company, often at discounted prices and with no broker commissions. Most plans allow investors to make voluntary payments to the DRIP to purchase more shares. In other words, the advantages of DRIPs include:

- ✔ No brokerage commissions and few fees for purchasing stock through the DRIP.

- ✔ Frequent discounts of 3 to 5 percent off the current stock price.

- ✔ Optional cash payment plans (OCPs). These plans are often part of DRIPs. Usually after the first dividend has been reinvested, the investor can send voluntary cash payments directly to the company to purchase more shares. Amounts can be as small as $10 to $25. (This option allows investors to own fractions of stocks.) For example, General Electric allows OCPs of $10 to $10,000 every month.

Many of the nation's premier corporations have DRIPs, including most of the companies in the Dow Jones Industrial Average. The InvestorGuide page on DRIPs and DPPs (www.investorguide.com) has a public directory with links to the corporate home pages of many companies that have dividend reinvestment plans. For more information, contact each company you're interested in and ask for a DRIP prospectus. At the corporate home page, you can e-mail your request. If the company doesn't have a Web site, use Stock Smart, at www.stocksmart.com, to locate the corporation's address and telephone number.

Additional features of DRIPs

One of the benefits of DRIPs is their (often free) certificate safekeeping service. This service eliminates the need for paying for a safe-deposit box and the possibility of your stock certificates becoming lost or stolen.

DRIPs often have gift-giving programs. For example, Texaco lets you open an investor services plan in another person's name, and the company provides you with a gift certificate to give to the recipient.

Not all DRIPs are alike

Each company has its own plan. With some firms, you can pay for additional shares with cash; some allow partial redemption of shares; and some have termination fees. However, the plan may only purchase shares once a month, and if you want to sell your shares, completing the transaction may take five to ten days.

Some plans allow you to buy shares one at a time. However, some companies have a minimum purchase amount. For example, Bristol-Myers Squibb requires a minimum purchase of 50 shares. Bristol-Myers Squibb also charges a fee of 4 percent of the dollar amount of dividends being reinvested (a maximum of $5 per share). In general, plans differ from one another in the following ways:

✔ Some companies allow (and some companies don't allow) the reinvestment of preferred dividends for common shares.

✔ Some companies allow partial reinvestment of dividends.

✔ The amount of optional cash payments (OCPs) varies from company to company.

✔ Fees for participating in the DRIP vary from company to company.

How to get your first DRIP share

Sometimes, getting started is the hardest part of investing. Many ways exist to go about getting your first share for a DRIP. Here are five different approaches — one of these methods may be right for you:

✔ **Find a brokerage that charges special rates for single shares:** Several brokerages charge special commission rates to current accountholders for the purchase of single shares. A.G. Edwards charges a flat 16 percent of the share price. Dean Witter charges a flat 10 percent of the share price.

✔ **Join a special investment club:** First Share Buying Club can assist you in getting your first share so that you can participate in a DRIP. Annual membership is $18 a year ($30 for two years). Members receive a handbook about DPPs and DRIPs, transferring shares, and the registration of shares.

For individuals who don't want to join the club, you can buy one share in one company for a flat fee of $20. If you want to purchase more than one share, becoming a member is more cost-effective. You can request any number of shares in any number of companies. For more information, call 800-683-0743.

✔ **Share the cost with a friend:** You can use a buddy system to reduce the cost of purchasing your first share. You and a friend pay the brokerage to purchase two shares. Have both shares registered to one person and join the company's DRIP. After you've joined, transfer one share to your friend and split the cost of the fees.

✔ **Join the NAIC:** The National Association of Investors Corporation (NAIC) enrolls people in any of more than 100 DRIPs via its Low Cost Investment Plan. The NAIC enrolls its members in a company for a $7 per company fee. Membership in the NAIC is $39 for individuals and $35 for an investment club plus $14 per member of the club. See the NAIC Web site at www.better-investing.org or telephone 801-583-6242 for details.

✔ **Use a deep-discount online broker:** Sometimes, the simplest way to purchase your first share is to go through a deep-discount broker. Online brokerage costs vary from free to $40. To participate in the DRIP, you need the stock registered in your name. To get the stock registered in your name (rather than in the brokerage's default street name), you may have to pay an additional fee.

Selecting the right DRIP

DRIPs have many advantages, but you shouldn't let one characteristic be your sole criterion for purchasing the stock. Regardless of how attractive the DRIP program is, you still need to make certain that the stock fits in with your overall investment strategy. In other words, don't select a stock just because it has a DRIP.

Here are two online resources for finding out more about dividend reinvestment plans:

✔ **DRIP Investor** (www.dripinvestor.com) is a guide to buying stocks without a broker by using dividend reinvestment plans.

✔ **Investment FAQ** (invest-faq.com/articles/trade-drips.html) provides an article that shows how investors can use buying clubs (see the section, "How to get your first DRIP share" earlier in this chapter) to purchase their first share.

Part IV
Making More Money on the Internet

The 5th Wave
By Rich Tennant

"I've never seen an adjustment to a fluctuating stock market made with a paperweight before."

In this part . . .

The chapters in this part of the book show you how to monitor, buy, and sell securities online to increase your returns. This part of the book also shows you how to use online and PC-based portfolio management programs to track your investments and how to get daily updates sent to your e-mailbox free of charge. See how to manage your checking account electronically. Identify the best savings rates and certificate of deposit rates online.

Chapter 15

Brokers and Online Trading

● ●

In This Chapter

▶ Checking out online brokerages

▶ Finding the type of brokerage that meets your needs

▶ Opening your electronic brokerage account

▶ Increasing your profits by choosing the right trading techniques

▶ Understanding day trading

● ●

*I*n this chapter, I show you how to save money on trades, gain unlimited control over your investments, and enter trades from your computer 24 hours a day, 7 days a week. You just need to get the hang of a few online trading basics and the risks that any investor faces.

This chapter describes three types of brokers: full-service, discount, and deep-discount. Each type of broker offers a different range of services. Internet deep-discount brokers are generally the least expensive, but they offer bare-bones services. However, not all brokers are alike. Occasionally, an inexpensive broker costs you more money. For example, if you require real-time stock quotes and subscribe to an online service, the cost is about $30 per month. If you select a broker who has a commission rate that's higher than some others but includes free online securities quotes, you may save money. This chapter also describes some of the additional features of brokerages. This information can help you decide which brokerage is right for you.

Online trading accounts require you to complete an application form and to open and maintain a minimum cash account balance. While your electronic brokerage is processing your account (which takes two to three weeks), you can turn to this chapter to find out where you can practice trading online and how to increase your profits by using the right trading strategies. This chapter concludes with a section that explains the dangers of day trading for beginning investors. Discover what gear day traders need, how much cash, what they look for, and how they trade.

Finding a Brokerage Firm

For each trade, you pay commissions ranging from a few dollars to hundreds of dollars per order. Commissions can take a large bite out of your profits. For example, assume that you invest $2,000 and pay a $200 commission to a full-service broker. Your securities must increase to $2,200 for you to break even. One way to avoid high commissions is to use a discount broker or a deep-discount broker.

A full-service broker researches many companies and securities, helps you organize your goals, and gives you advice on specific securities that match your financial goals. These firms often use a *commission grid* to calculate the fees that they charge their customers. For example, if you purchase 10 shares of a stock that costs $47 per share, the commission may be $47 (a commission rate of 10 percent). If you purchase two shares of a stock that costs $75 per share, the commission may be $35 (a commission rate of about 23 percent).

All brokers physically handle your securities, maintain a history of your transactions, and calculate your gains (or losses). (But most do not provide you with the performance reports.) Additionally, they track how many shares you own, when the stock splits, and when dividends are paid.

As a general rule, full-service brokers provide recommendations and inform you of initial public offerings (IPOs), insider trading, and legal concerns about your investments. For example, if you own stock in a firm that is a takeover target, a full-service broker notifies you and provides you with any relevant information regarding offers to buy your stock. When you want to buy or sell securities, the full-service broker decides what type of order to place and oversees its implementation.

In the past, discount brokers offered no advice and conducted no research. Today, many discount brokers, such as Quick and Reilley, Fidelity, and Schwab, offer "full-service" advice, IPO information, and research to customers who desire that type of service. Consumers have the option of seeking advice for special transactions or placing orders directly. The discount broker receives your touch-tone telephone order and relays it to the firm's floor broker, who in turn contacts the individual who executes your order. The discount broker then confirms that your order has been completed.

Deep-discount brokers are electronic brokerages in every sense of the word; contact with a human broker is rare and may cost you more money. Deep-discount brokerages often start as subdivisions of discount or full-service brokerages. They may offer lower prices by automatically accepting touch-tone telephone orders and Internet-based stock orders. A recent innovation to online trading is the full-service online brokerage. These companies often provide discount pricing, 24-hour phone service, branch offices throughout the nation, and high quality online research. For example, Charles Schwab & Co., Inc. (www.schwab.com) offers free research from Morningstar, Hambrecht & Quist, and Credit Suisse/First Boston.

You can easily locate a broker via the World Wide Web. For a good alphabetical list of licensed brokers, see the Invest-FAQ at invest-faq.com/links/trading.html.

Checking Out Prospective Brokers

The Securities Investor Protection Corporation (SIPC) insures brokerage accounts in a way that's similar to how the Federal Deposit Insurance Corporation (FDIC) insures bank accounts. Each customer's account is insured to $500,000, and some brokerages have additional insurance. If your brokerage firm goes belly-up, you're covered. However, if you make poor investment selections, you can lose all your money.

As an investor, you're wise to look into the background of a brokerage firm before investing. The Central Registration Depository (CRD) — a registration and licensing database used by regulators throughout the securities industry to collect data about securities firms and their brokers — is available at your state securities agency or the National Association of Securities Dealers (www.nasdr.com/2000.htm). Additionally, each month the New York Stock Exchange releases a disciplinary action list at www.nyse.com.

Your state securities regulator can tell you whether the broker you're considering is registered, and some state securities commissions provide cautionary lists at their Web sites. Good examples are at the Oklahoma Securities Commission site at www.state.ok.us/~osc and at the Illinois secretary of state's office at www.sos.state.il.us/pubs/securities/invguide/contents.html.

Getting Online Trading Services for Less

As I mention at the beginning of this chapter, no two brokerages are alike. Furthermore, individual brokerages may change their services and fees to keep pace with their competitors. To find the online broker that best meets your needs, you must investigate the prices, services, and features that various brokers offer.

Make certain that your brokerage doesn't charge you for services that are free elsewhere. For example, say that an online brokerage charges a flat fee of $15 for your trade. If the brokerage adds a postage and handling fee of $4 for your transaction, your transaction actually costs $19. That's 27 percent higher than you expected. Other hidden fees may include:

✔ Higher fees for accepting odd lot orders (less than one hundred shares)

✔ Higher fees for certain types of orders (see "Increasing Profits with Simple Order Specification Techniques" later in this chapter)

✔ Fees for sending out certificates (some firms charge $50 per certificate)

✔ Fees to close your account

✔ Fees to withdraw funds from your trading account

Trading online for $15 or less

Before 1975, the only type of stockbroker available was a full-service broker. All brokerages charged the same fees and commissions. Regulatory changes in 1975 allowed brokerage firms to start competing with one another on the basis of price, and the discount broker was born. Discount brokers' commissions were typically 50 to 75 percent lower than those of full-service brokers. This change helped make Fidelity, Charles Schwab & Co., Inc., and Waterhouse Securities the leading discount brokers they are today.

The rapid growth of the Internet and more brokerage evolution has led to the deep-discount brokers. Generally, all Internet brokers can handle any type of basic transaction with a minimum of human contact. This evolution has lowered the cost of doing business and fueled a fierce price war. Many reputable online brokerages can complete your trade for $15 or less. Table 15-1 lists several examples of these deep-discount brokerages.

Table 15-1	**You Can Trade Online for $15 or Less**	
Brokerage Name	*Web Address*	*Commission Structure*
Ameritrade	www.ameritrade.com	$8 flat rate + $5 for limit orders
Burke, Christensen & Lewis	www.bclnet.com	$18 to 1,000 shares, + $0.02 thereafter; $13 market order to 1,000, + $0.02 thereafter
Charles Schwab & Co., Inc.	www.schwab.com	$29.95 to 1,000 shares (plus special discounts for active traders)
CompuTEL Securities	www.computel.com	$14 market orders of 1,000 to 5,000 shares; $14 market orders of less than 1,000; $19 limit orders; + $2.50 postage and handling

Brokerage Name	Web Address	Commission Structure
Datek Securities	www.datek.com	$9.99 to 5,000 shares
DLJDirect (Formerly PCFN)	www.dljdirect.com	$20 to 1,000 shares + $0.02 thereafter
Empire Financial Group	www.lowfees.com	$0 on at least 1,000 @$5; $15 on market orders less than 1,000 @$5; $20 on limit orders for NASDAQ, less than 5,000; $20 + $0.01 for limit orders over 5,000 shares
E*Trade	www.etrade.com	$14.95 market trades to 5,000, + $0.01 thereafter; $19.95 limit orders to 5,000, + $0.01 thereafter
Farsight Financial Services	www.farsight.com	$10 flat rate
Fidelity Investments	personal.fidelity.com	$14.95 for active traders to 5,000 shares + $0.03 thereafter; $25 for online traders to 1,000 shares, + $0.03 to 5,000 shares, over 5,000 shares + $0.02
ForbesNET	www.forbesnet.com	$12.95 for up to 5,000, + $0.01 thereafter
Freedom Investments	www.freedom-investments.com	$15 flat rate
Investex	www.investexpress.com	$13.95 market orders; $17.95 limit orders; $17.95 for up to 5,000, + $0.05 thereafter
Investrade Discount	www.investrade.com	$13.95 flat rate
J.B. Oxford & Company	www.jboxford.com	$15.00 up to 3,000 shares, + $0.01 thereafter
Pacific Brokerage Services	www.tradepbs.com	$15 flat rate (all market and limit orders)
ProTrade	www.protrade.com	$5 for 1,000 shares or more, market orders; $12 for less than 1,000 shares and limit orders

(continued)

Table 15-1 *(continued)*

Brokerage Name	Web Address	Commission Structure
Quick & Reilly	www.quick-reilly.com	$14.95 market orders; orders; + $0.02 for over $19.95 limit 1,000 shares
Scottsdale Securities	www.scottrade.com	$7 flat rate
Stocks4Less	www.stocks4less.com	$10 market orders; $15 limit orders; + $2.50 postage and handling
SureTrade.com	www.suretrade.com	$7.95 flat rate
Trade Fast	www.tradefast.com	$15 minimum for market or limit orders + $0.03 per share
Trading Direct	www.tradingdirect.com	$9.95 for up to 5,000 shares, + $0.01 thereafter
Waterhouse Securities	www.webbroker.com	$12 for up to 5,000 shares, + $0.01 thereafter

Note: The brokerage commission structures listed in the preceding table use notations such as the following: 0 on at least 1,000 @$5; $15 on market orders less than 1,000 @$5; $20 on limit orders for NASDAQ, less than 5,000; $20 + $0.01 for limit orders over 5,000 shares. Here's what this notation means:

- The commission fee is $0 on a minimum order of 1,000 shares that are priced at $5 or more. (Total cost $0.)

- The commission fee is $15 on *market orders* (instructions for the broker to immediately buy or sell a security for the best available price) of 1,000 shares that are priced at $5 or more. (Total cost $15.)

- The commission fee is $20 on *limit orders* (trading orders that specify a certain price at which the broker is to execute the order) for the NASDAQ (an automated nationwide communications network operated by the National Association of Securities Dealers that connects brokers and dealers in the over-the-counter market) of less than 5,000 shares. (Total cost $20.)

- The commission fee is $20 plus $0.01 (a penny) for limit orders of 5,000 shares or more. For example, if you want a limit order for 6,000 shares, the fee is $20 for 5,000 shares plus $10 for the quantity over 5,000 ($0.01 × 1,000) for a total cost of $30.

How poorly executed orders can cost you big bucks

Beginning investors are often not aware of the price disparities between the primary exchanges, like the New York Stock Exchange (NYSE) and the "third market." The third marketplace is defined as trading between dealers and institutional investors, through the over-the-counter market, of NYSE-listed stocks. Many low-cost online brokerages automatically route orders to the third market. This isn't "wrong," but it can cost you more money. Say that you decide to purchase 2,000 shares of a NYSE listed stock. The stock has a current spread of $15 to $15¼. Your trade is executed on the third market for $15¼. However, if the trade was executed at the NYSE,

you could have gone between the bid and ask price and paid $15⅛ — a savings of $250.00.

Some online brokerages won't trade on the primary exchanges even if you ask them. Check your confirmations. If your confirmation doesn't state that your order was filled on the NYSE, then it was executed in the third market. What can you do? Compare the service of two brokerages by asking them both to make the same trade on a stock and see which one gets you the better price. For example, Charles Schwab & Co., Inc. (www.schwab.com) has an electronic system that "works the order" to get you a better price.

Finding online brokers with no or low initial account minimums

One of the things that many investors may find prohibitive about online trading is the initial minimum deposit required for opening a cash account. This requirement means that the broker already has your money when you request a trade. However, this requirement is changing, just like everything else on the Internet. Table 15-2 lists several online brokerages that offer cash accounts with no minimum deposit or a low minimum deposit.

Table 15-2   Minimum Amounts to Open Trading Accounts with Online Brokers

Online Brokerage	Web Address	Account Minimum
Burke, Christensen & Lewis	www.bclnet.com	$0
Charles Schwab & Co., Inc.	www.schwab.com	$0
CompassWeb Brokerage	broker.compassweb.com	$0
DLJDirect (Formerly PCFN)	www.dljdirect.com	$0
Empire Financial Group	www.lowfees.com	$0

(continued)

Table 15-2 *(continued)*

Online Brokerage	Web Address	Account Minimum
Investex	www.investexpress.com	$0
Muriel Siebert & Company	www.msiebert.com	$0
Quick & Reilly	www.quick-reilly.com	$0
SureTrade.com	www.suretrade.com	$0
Trade Fast	www.tradefast.com	$0
E*Trade	www.etrade.com	$1,000
American Express Financial Direct	www.americanexpress.com/direct	$2,000
Ameritrade	www.ameritrade.com	$2,000
Datek Securities	www.datek.com	$2,000
Investrade Discount	www.investrade.com	$2,000
ProTrade	www.protrade.com	$2,000
Waterhouse Securities	www.webbroker.com	$2,000

Checking Out Online Broker Special Features

Commission structures change radically from firm to firm. One reason for this wide range is that some Internet brokers include special or additional features. When deciding which broker is best for you, factoring in some or all of the features that I list in this section is probably wise. First, consider whether each broker offers the following features in your cash account:

- ✔ Low minimum amount required to open an account
- ✔ Low monthly fees with minimum equity balance
- ✔ No additional charges for postage and handling
- ✔ A summary of cash balances
- ✔ A summary of order status
- ✔ A summary of your portfolio's value
- ✔ Confirmation of trades (via e-mail, phone, or U.S. mail)
- ✔ A historical review of your trading activities

✔ No charges for retirement account maintenance

✔ Consolidation of your money market, investments, checking, and savings accounts

When comparing brokers, consider whether each broker offers the following account features:

✔ Unlimited check-writing privileges

✔ Dividend collection and reinvestment

✔ Debit cards for ATM access

✔ Interest earned on cash balances

✔ Wire transfers accepted

✔ No IRA inactivity fees

You should ascertain which of the following types of investments the broker enables you to trade:

✔ Stocks (foreign or domestic)

✔ Options

✔ Bonds (corporate or agency)

✔ Treasury securities

✔ Zero coupon bonds

✔ Certificates of deposit

✔ Precious metals

✔ Mutual funds

✔ Investment trusts

Finally, you need to determine whether the brokerage offers the following analytical and research features:

✔ Real-time online quotes

✔ Reports on insider trading

✔ Economic forecasts

✔ Company profiles and breaking news

✔ Earnings forecasts

✔ End-of-the-day prices automatically sent to you

One feature that's of interest to frequent traders is real-time quotes. Some brokerage firms offer real-time quotes for free, other firms offer a limited number for free when you open an account or make a trade, and several firms charge $30 a month for nonprofessional, real-time quotes.

Rating Online Brokers

Gomez Advisors (www.gomezadvisors.com) is a Boston-based independent rating agency that specializes in online investing. This firm has developed a quarterly Internet Broker Scorecard to help investors select the online broker that's right for them.

Online brokerage rankings are based on ease of use, customer confidence, on-site resources, relationship services, and overall cost. Individual factors within these categories are scored and averaged. Scores range from one to ten, with ten indicating the best quality. Table 15-3 shows the Internet Broker Scorecard for the third quarter of 1998 for the top ten online brokerages.

Table 15-3	Internet Broker Scorecard — Third Quarter of 1998					
OB	**OS**	**E of U**	**CC**	**OR**	**RS**	**OC**
1. E*Trade	7.47	8.52	8.06	7.86	6.71	6.20
2. DLJ Direct	7.04	8.11	7.61	8.61	4.79	6.06
3. Discover	6.85	6.37	8.62	7.48	5.48	6.32
4. Waterhouse	6.62	4.92	9.31	5.38	5.48	8.02
5. Datek Online	6.38	6.25	7.45	5.34	3.84	9.04
6. Lindner FarSight	6.36	6.93	4.90	5.71	4.25	10.0
7. Web Street	6.30	7.17	6.92	6.30	3.29	7.83
8. Quick & Reilly	6.20	5.12	7.53	8.10	3.70	6.57
9. National Discount Brokerage	6.20	5.68	8.22	7.18	3.56	6.36
10. Schwab	6.16	4.17	8.87	7.20	6.58	3.97

Key: OB = Online Brokerage; OS = Overall Score; E of U = Ease of Use; CC = Customer Confidence; OR = On-Site Resources; RS = Relationship Services; OC = Overall Cost

Deep-discount brokers offer investors more power over their portfolios and lower transaction fees. One limitation of online brokerages is that your broker may not protect you from speculating with your life savings. You need to take responsibility for analyzing your financial goals, creating a plan to achieve those goals, and building a portfolio that's as risk-free and diversified as possible to reach those goals. You have to be disciplined and able to take responsibility for your own trading successes and mistakes.

How to Open Your Online Brokerage Account

Internet brokerage firms are basically cash-and-carry enterprises. They all require investors to open an account before trading — a process that takes from two to three weeks to complete. Account minimums vary from $0 to $10,000.

When you place an order, your Internet broker withdraws money from your cash account to cover your trade. If you sell stock or receive a dividend, the Internet broker adds money to your cash account. If you develop a good history, your Internet broker may allow you to place trades without funds in your cash account if you settle within three days.

All Internet brokers require that you complete an application form that includes your name, address, social security number, work history, and a personal check, certified check, or money order for the minimum amount needed to open an account. Some brokers accept wire transfers or securities of equal value. All brokerages are required by law to have your signature on file. Figure 15-1 shows the online application form for CompuTEL Securities (www.computel.com).

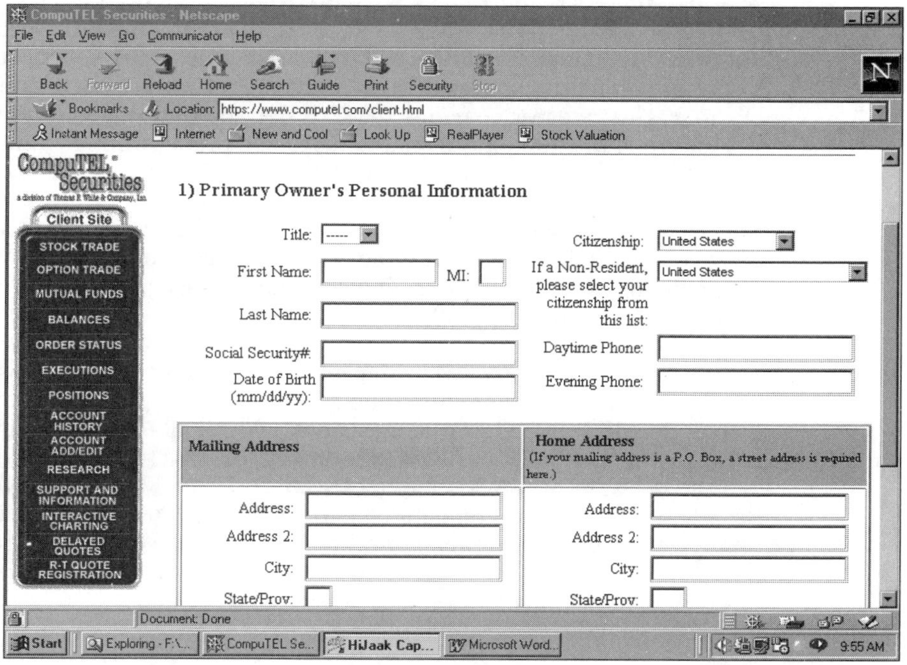

Figure 15-1: The online application form for CompuTEL Securities.

To speed up the application process, you can complete application forms online or fax them to the Internet broker. You must then follow up by sending the completed, written, and signed forms via U.S. mail within 15 days or the account is canceled. The Internet broker then verifies all the information on the form and opens your account. Investors receive a personal identification number (PIN) by mail. After you receive your PIN, you're ready to begin trading.

Increasing Profits with Simple Order Specification Techniques

In the past, brokers recommended the order specifications for your stock transactions and confirmed that your transaction was completed. Specifying security execution orders was one of the expert services that brokers used to justify their fees. Order specifications define how your request is completed. One type of order specification is called a *day order*. Day orders are good only on the day you place the order.

Another type of order is the Good Till Canceled (GTC) order. The investor decides when the order expires but is uncertain about the order being executed. In other words, if no one in the market takes the order within the specified time (which can be anywhere from several hours to several years to several decades), the order is canceled. In other words, the order lasts until the customer cancels the order. For example, an investor wants to buy a certain company's shares, but not until the shares are a few dollars cheaper. The investor specifies a GTC order and determines when the order will expire. If the company's shares reach the predetermined limit (today, tomorrow, next year, or next decade), the order is filled.

Figure 15-2 shows an online order form from SureTrade.com (www.suretrade. com/QRS/homeOUT.html). Trading online means that you are now in charge of specifying your stock order. Knowing how to designate the terms of your order can increase your profits.

As you look over your online order form, you'll notice different ways of specifying how the order should be executed. In the past, your full-service broker decided which approach was best. With online trading, you select the method you feel is best. Many online brokerages (for example, Charles Schwab & Co., Inc. at www.schwab.com and DLJ Direct at www.dljdirect.com) have handy online trading demos that can assist you in practicing trading online. The four most popular ways to specify your stock order are as follows:

✔ **Limit orders:** Any order in which the buyer or seller specifies the top price he or she is willing to pay. For sell orders, the *limit* specified is the minimum price at which the investor is willing to sell. For buy orders, the limit is the maximum price that the investor is willing to pay.

✔ **Market orders:** Any order (buy or sell) to be executed immediately at the *best effort* price available. In other words, the investor wants to buy or sell a stated number of shares at the best price at the time the order is placed.

✔ **Stop:** After a security reaches the price set by the investor, the order becomes active. When the order is activated, that investor is guaranteed that the order will be executed. However, the investor isn't guaranteed the execution price.

✔ **Stop-limit orders:** After a security reaches the investor's predetermined price, the order is activated. The order can only be executed at the set price or better, so the order may not be completed.

You may want to use a *limit order* when purchasing or selling *odd lots* (less than 100 shares of any one stock). This type of order can increase your profits. Odd lots rarely get the best price because they must be bundled with other orders. The following example shows how you can get, if not the best price, at least a better price by using a limit order.

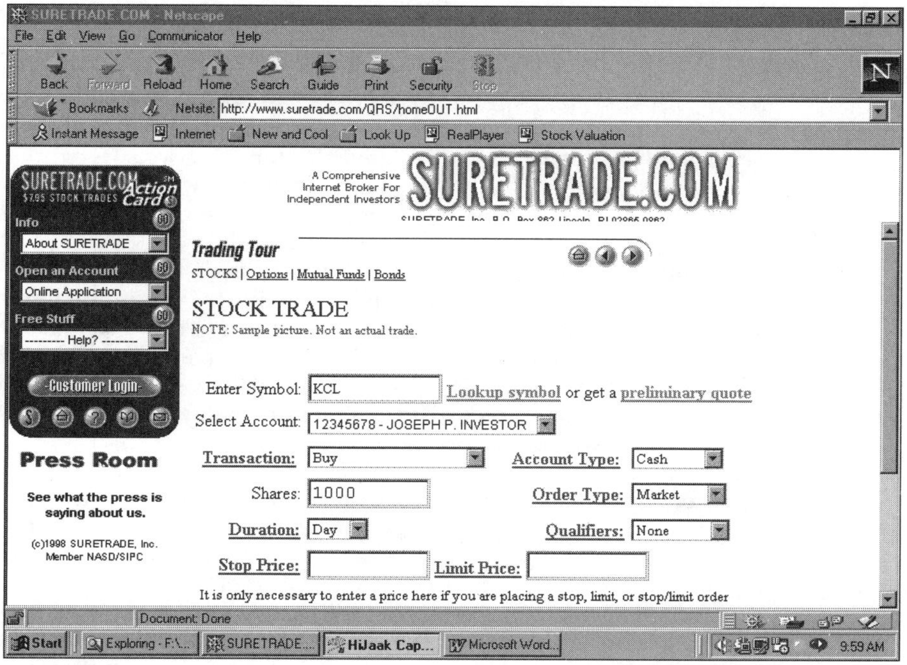

Figure 15-2:
The
SureTrade
.com online
order form.

Assume that the stock you want is offered by the specialist (someone who specializes in selling a certain firm's stock) at $25\frac{5}{8}$ (the asking price), and the bid price is $25. You should place a limit order of $25\frac{1}{4}$ so that you have a chance of paying less than the market order price of $25\frac{5}{8}$.

Someone other than the specialist is likely to take this order ($25\frac{1}{4}$) because it's more than the specialist's bid price of $25. (They get a better deal.)

Note: This strategy only works if a $\frac{1}{4}$ ($0.25) or greater spread exists between the bid and asking price.

The Dangers of Day Trading

Lower trading commissions, improved technology, and changes in government regulations make day trading possible. After the crash of October 1987, NASDAQ mandated the development and implementation of the Small Order Execution System (SOES). SOES is designed to protect small investors and is a forced execution system for orders up to 1,000 shares. The NASDAQ computer automatically executes the SOES order without any hesitation, which allows day traders (sometimes called SOES bandits) to immediately enter and exit transactions when they see changes in a stock.

In August 1996, SEC regulators determined that NASDAQ market makers had to fill or broadcast a customer's limit order to all other market makers on the NASDAQ system if it improved the inside price (the difference between current bid and ask prices). The new rules also stated that their private prices had to be posted on Electronic Communications Networks (ECN). In other words, dealers can't make more profits by waiting until they can collect the entire spread (the difference between the bid and offer prices).

Day trading involves buying and selling stocks on the NASDAQ and NYSE for your own account. Traders buy and then sell stocks within minutes, profiting by market changes. It's not unusual for a day trader to make over 175 trades per day. Traders buy and sell stocks in an effort to profit $0.125, $0.25, or $0.50 per share. Day traders primarily use the NASDAQ because it's twice as volatile as the NYSE (meaning that traders have twice as many opportunities to make short-term profits).

This section on day trading is for educational purposes. Day trading is not recommended for beginning investors. Keep these things in mind as you read this section: (1) Studies indicate that day trading has proven to be riskier and less successful than long-term trading; (2) Day trading is for experienced investors who can afford to lose all of their investment; (3) Day trading at your home or office often requires an initial investment of $5,000 or more for communications equipment, financial information services, and software.

Day trading appears to be a simple process. For example, say that you, as a day trader, purchase 1,000 shares of Dell at $86 per share for a total cost of $86,000 from a market maker. You then sell the same shares for $86,250. The stock would then be worth $86.25 per share. The difference is $250 less a commission of $50 ($25 to buy and $25 to sell) for a gain of $200. In this example, the profit is $200.

What is day trading?

One of the first steps in understanding day trading to is define the players. What day traders really focus on are the activities of market makers. A *market maker* represents an institution (such as Lehman Brothers, Merrill Lynch & Co., Prudential Securities, and so on) that wants to *make a market* in a particular NASDAQ stock. The market maker is a specialist on an exchange or dealer in the over-the-counter market who buys and sells stocks, creating an inventory for temporary holding. He or she provides liquidity by buying and selling at any time. However, he or she isn't under any obligation to buy or sell at a price other than the published bid and ask prices.

The downside of being a market maker is that you are obligated to purchase stocks when no one wants them. The upside of being a market maker is that you get to pocket the profits of a spread. A *spread* is the difference between a bid and ask price. For example, a stock with a bid and ask price of $15 \times 15^1/_4$ has a spread of $^1/_4$. The bid price is $15 and the sell price is $15.25. If the market maker sells 1,000 shares at $15.25, he or she profits by $250.

Spreads are often just a few cents for each stock. However, these pennies quickly become dollars due to high trading volume. Last year, NASDAQ market makers earned $2 billion from spreads. Day traders have sliced into some of these profits. Recent reports indicate that market maker spreads are down by 30 percent.

The existence of several kinds of spreads has caused some confusion. The following list defines some of these spreads.

- **Dealer spread:** The quote of the individual market maker. A market maker never earns the entire spread. The market maker needs to be competitive on either the bid or offer side of the market. The dealer is unlikely to be at the best price (the highest price if selling and the lowest price if buying) on both sides of the market at the same time.

- **Inside spread:** The highest bid and lowest offer being quoted among all of the market makers competing in a stock. Because the quote is a combined quote, it's narrower than an individual dealer quote.

- **Actual spreads paid:** The narrowest measure of a spread, because it's based on actual trade prices. The actual spreads paid is calculated by measuring actual trade prices against the inside quote at the time of the trade.

Spotting the Signals for Day Trading

Day traders can spot many buy-and-sell signals. Stocks that are good day-trading candidates have "a surprise in earnings" (earnings reports that are above or below analysts expectations) or are the subjects of buyout rumors. Day trading software programs connected to electronic communication networks can help day traders target changes in inside quotes or track stock candidates. Some programs create real-time line graphs for trend analysis and comparison to other stocks or indexes (such as the Dow Jones Industrial Average). Charts are created for different time periods (intraday, daily, or yearly). Day traders use these charts to look for buy, sell, and exit signals.

Day trading is the ultimate in market timing. Not only does the day trader have to pick the "right time" to enter the market, but also the "right time" to exit. The frequency of this decision-making is also a factor. Successful day traders have to pick the "right time" 150 to 200 times in one day.

Having What It Takes to Be a Day Trader

Besides a stoic nature, day traders need large amounts of cash (that they can afford to lose) and lots of time. Experienced day traders suggest that it takes about $100,000 to get into the business of day trading. Such an amount serves as risk capital that the day trader must be able to afford to lose. Day trading is a full-time job that requires the day trader to be ready to act each weekday from 9:00 a.m. to 4:00 p.m.

Day traders have to be good winners and good losers, as well. Inexperienced traders can easily lose between $3,000 and $4,000 per day (or even more). Some traders leverage their capital by trading on margin, which means that the brokerage establishes credit for its customer/trader. For example, $100,000 of capital can support $200,000 of security purchases. This credit arrangement is called *leveraging* and provides an opportunity to gain — or lose — big money.

Many brokerage and investment advisors offer one-day to five-day seminars on day trading that can cost anywhere from $900 to $2,500. See Swift Trade Securities, Inc. (www.swifttrade.com) for information on its seminar.

Gearing Up for Day Trading

Currently, about 3,000 professional day traders are up and running in the nation. Most day traders work when the market opens until it closes (from 9:00 a.m. to 4:00 p.m.). Traders can average 175 trades per day and rarely hold stocks for overnight or longer. Day traders can trade from home, office, or specialized brokerage trading floors, such as Broadway Trading (www.broadwaytrading.com) in New York, NY.

The day trading puzzle contains many pieces. Some individuals like remote trading at home or in an office. Others want to telephone their SOES brokers with their limit orders. New software enables day traders do one stop shopping by combining a decision support system with real-time live quotes and an electronic clearing network. The type of hardware and software you select depends upon your personal day-trading system. And as the industry introduces new products and services or if regulations change, you may need to revise and update your approach.

Getting ready (to day trade)

The following lists the hardware needed to get started in day trading. Installation of the Internet connection may take time, so plan ahead:

- **Computer workstations:** Day trading requires a computer with a Pentium processor or equivalent (minimum of 200 MHz/64MB of RAM). The modem should have a baud rate of at least 28.8 bps.

- **Direct Internet connection:** Day traders often need a permanent Internet address for high level data exchanges and fast connectivity (in this business seconds mean dollars). Cable and telephone companies provide this service for between $40 to $500 per month. (The cable company service I use charges $40 per month.)

Getting set (to make the investment decision)

NASDAQ Level II real-time quotes show, for each stock listed, how many shares each market maker wants to buy or sell; the quotes also indicate changes as orders are processed and filled. This assists day traders in forecasting when a stock will move and in what direction.

NASDAQ Level II real-time quotes show *the depth of the market.* Day traders need NASDAQ Level II real-time quotes to be effective.

Some organizations, like the Data Broadcasting Corporation (www.dbc.com), offer wireless, portable, real-time NASDAQ Level II quotes for about $150 to $200 per month. Many brokerages offer NASDAQ Level II quotes free to customers who make over 100 trades per month. Some day-trading broker-ages even provide this information free to their customers.

Day Traders can use stock monitoring decision-support software with a computer, modem, and data connection. These computer programs are often connected to day-trader brokerages (which are different than Web-based online brokerages) to provide access to Electronic Communications Networks. (Connectivity can cost up to $2,000 and is usually paid by the brokerage.) Day traders who aren't electronically connected must telephone their limit orders to their SOES brokers. The SOES broker then enters the order into an ECN.

In addition to the hardware day traders need, they may also use day-trading decision-support software. Some day-trading decision-support software includes real-time quotes to improve investment judgments. The software in the following list is used to assist day traders in making investment decisions:

- **Attain (**www.attain.com**):** Direct market access for fast executions and confirmations, and real-time Level II quotes. You also get point-and-click order submissions to the Attain ECN. Multiple NASDAQ Level II screens, charting, graphs, and analysis are available. Monthly service is $250 and is waived upon execution of 200 orders per month. An online demonstration of the system is provided.

- **CyBerTrader (**www.cyber-corp.com**):** This software filters data from 10,000 stocks for alerts, fundamental, technical, and trend analysis. It includes market data in real time. At the home page, click on CyBerTrader. Send an order and receive confirmations. Additional features show position management, account and risk management, your trading status, and more. Check out available market makers at the inside price level. (See Figure 15-3.)

- **KillerKey (**www.castleonline.com**):** Data packages with charts and news, and automated account information. Free NASDAQ Live Level I quotes. NASDAQ Live Level II quotes are $150 per month and waived upon the execution of 100 orders or more per month. Castle Online brokerage commission rates for SOES, Select Net, and Island ECN trades cost $19.95 for up to 10,000 shares. Additional $1.00 charge for partial executions, and $0.15 for ECNs other than Island. $5,000 minimum to open an account. Killer Key and Java Trader software is free and downloadable.

- **NASDAQ Level II (**www.elitetrader.com**):** NASDAQ Level II includes time-of-sales, real-time news, real-time quotes with customizable layouts, intraday and historical charts, options analytics, and more. The firm provides a two-week trial for $25 plus exchange fees of $50 per month for all trades. (To see a free online tutorial, check out Elite Trader at www.elitetrader.com/members/level2b.html.)

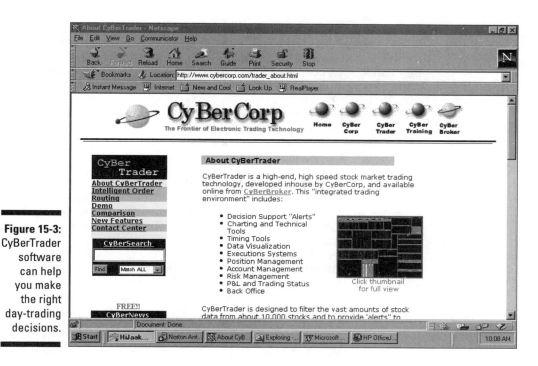

Figure 15-3:
CyBerTrader
software
can help
you make
the right
day-trading
decisions.

✔ **Watcher** (www.broadwaytrading.com/trading.html): Offers an online execution that provides the individual investor with the capability to place orders directly into an order entry system. The Watcher program is free, but the order entry system has a fee. Watcher instantly accesses real-time market data, monitors positions and account activity, and interfaces with Island ECN. Downloadable and free demo available.

Going! (Placing the order)

When placing an order, day traders go to specialized day-trading brokerages. These brokerages are connected to an Electronic Communications Network (ECN).

These SOES and SuperDot brokerages specialize in day trading NASDAQ and NYSE securities. SOES brokerages frequently offer real-time quotes, NASDAQ's small order execution system, and NYSE's SuperDot system to execute quick stock market transactions. The following are a couple of examples of SOES brokerages:

✔ **Block Trading** (www.bloc.com): Available in 11 offices nationwide and doesn't have a set fee schedule. The additional charges (SelectNet, and so on) are normally included in the commission fee, which is not more than $20 per ticket (order) at any office.

- **Trend Trader** (www.trendtrader.com): Specializing in remote electronic order routing, free real-time quotes and charts, order entry routing to the NASDAQ SOES and NYSE DOT systems, online information about open positions, and Level II market maker screens. Commissions are as low as $15.

In 1971, NASDAQ became a true electronic market that allows traders to buy and sell through a network of computers. Market makers could display their best bids, and offers and orders could be executed instantaneously over NASDAQ Level II workstations.

This electronic trading system uses NASDAQ's Select Net, which is an anonymous electronic communication system between the trader and the market maker to buy or sell stock. This system allows the trader to stipulate the desired stock and have the order placed directly to watching market makers.

Beginning in 1997, day traders (customers) could display bids and offers through an alternative system called an ECN (Electronic Communications Network). Electronic Communications Networks are supported and manned by the brokers of day traders.

ECNs allow traders to display their orders to other customers. Trader orders can be matched and traded with other customer orders before they reach the NASDAQ Level II system. This provides individual traders with more of a competitive edge and a higher probability of a successful trade. If a match isn't made through an ECN, the order enters the SOES system and it instantaneously appears on the NASDAQ Level II system. Good examples of ECNs are:

- **Attain** (www.attain.com): Now a SEC-approved electronic clearing network, the Attain ECN is a proprietary system used by subscribers (brokers/dealers) to post bids and offers for their clients (day traders) in a certain over-the-counter security. Attain ECN is an alternative to the traditional market making price quote system on NASDAQ.

- **Island** (www.isld.com): An alternative trading system that matches buy orders with sell offers in NASDAQ stocks. If Island can't find a match, it allows orders to receive direct representation in the marketplace as NASDAQ Level II quotes. Prices vary, so check the Web site for details.

Chapter 16

Online Portfolio Tracking

*P*ortfolio management may sound like busywork, but knowing how much you own in cash, stocks, bonds, and other investments is important. Without portfolio management, how can you determine whether your returns are meeting your financial requirements? Are you missing opportunities by not buying or selling securities at the right time?

This chapter covers three Internet-based approaches to managing your portfolio. The first approach is using free and fee Web-based portfolio tracking tools that can be customized and often provide e-mail alerts on price changes and end-of-the-day quotes. The second approach to portfolio management is using PC-based tools that are free, offer free trials, or cost only a few dollars. These programs use your Internet connection to automatically update portfolio quotes. (If you already have Money 99 Financial Suite or Quicken Deluxe 99, I show you how to use the portfolio feature and update price quotes in just a few clicks.) The third portfolio management approach is using your online broker's free portfolio management program. Your broker knows all about your buying and selling habits. He can automatically update your portfolio, and you don't have to wait until the end of the month to determine the value of your investment decisions. I conclude this chapter by discussing the difficulties of measuring portfolio performance and risk.

Why Manage Your Investments?

You may select the best investments, but if you don't have a way to track your gains and losses, you can lose time and money. Good record keeping is invaluable for calculating your taxes, preparing for retirement, estate planning, and taking advantage of opportunities to increase your personal wealth.

Sources on the Internet can assist you in keeping careful records of every stock, mutual fund, bond, and money market security you own. Setup time can be as little as ten minutes. You can update and monitor your portfolio once a week or once a month. Your investments can be in one portfolio (for example, your retirement fund) or many (say, your retirement fund, an emergency fund, and your children's college fund). You can also track investments that you wish you owned or that you're considering for investment.

The Internet offers programs that automatically update your portfolio with daily price changes and then re-tally your portfolio's value. To sum up, many portfolio management programs can perform the following tasks:

- ✔ Help you determine how much you own in cash, stocks, and bonds
- ✔ Show you how these investments line up with your asset allocation targets
- ✔ Indicate what returns (capital gains or losses) you're receiving
- ✔ Compare returns to your financial requirements
- ✔ Alert you that securities are at the prices at which you want to buy (or sell)

How often do you need to monitor your investments? Once every two or three days is a little aggressive, once a week is average, and some investments only require monitoring once a month.

Tracking the Right Information

If you own more than one investment, you probably want to compare the performance of your investments. The more investments you have, the harder this task is. Many novice investors find it difficult to determine whether they're making money, losing money, or just breaking even. To determine how your investments are performing, you need to look at the following data:

- ✔ **52 week high and low:** The highest and lowest selling price in the previous 365 days
- ✔ **Dividend:** The annual per-share amount of cash payments made to stockholders of the corporations
- ✔ **Dividend yield percent:** The total amount of the dividend paid in the last 12 months divided by the closing price (the price at which the last trade of the day was made)
- ✔ **Growth rate:** How much the dividend increases from one fiscal year to the next

✔ **P/E ratio:** The ratio of the closing price to the last 12 months' earnings per share

✔ **Volume:** The number of shares traded in one day

✔ **High, low, close:** Highest selling price of the day, lowest selling price of the day, and closing selling price

✔ **Net change:** The difference between the day's closing price and the previous day's closing price

You can compare these amounts and ratios to the performance of your other investments, the firm's previous performance, the industry, and the market indexes (for example, the S&P 500).

If you own several securities, how do you keep track of all this data? Once again, the Internet provides an answer. The Internet has hundreds of Web- and PC-based portfolio management programs that are just waiting to assist you. Some of them are free, others are fee-based, and some are automatically set up for you by your online broker.

Your Portfolio Management Options

The Internet offers three types of portfolio management programs:

✔ **Web-based portfolio management programs:** Investor supersites, Internet portals, and large news organizations generally sponsor online portfolio management programs. These programs usually don't require any software downloading, and they constantly update your portfolio. Limitations of these programs are that they don't offer many features, such as customized graphs or charts, fundamental analysis, or tax planning tools.

✔ **PC-based portfolio management programs:** These programs present portfolio tracking as a feature of a personal software program like Quicken (www.intuit.quicken.com) or MS Money (money.msn.com). PC-based portfolio involves tracking with a software program downloaded from the Internet. These programs can be very inexpensive or free. PC-based portfolio tracking programs usually have more choices and functions than Web-based portfolio management programs. Limitations of this approach are that you must download the proprietary software and you may have to *import* (transfer data from one source to another) stock quotes.

✔ **Portfolio management with your online broker:** Portfolio management with your online broker is automatic. Your online broker knows what you traded, so the brokerage can automatically update your portfolio. The advantages of using your broker's portfolio management system are that you don't have to manually add transactions, and your portfolio always reflects the current value of your investments.

In the following sections, I offer examples that detail the features and functions of these three types of portfolio management programs.

Using Web-Based Portfolio Management Programs

Many Web sites provide online portfolio tracking services. Some of these services are free and others are fee-based. The aim of Web-based portfolio management tools is to help you make better investment decisions and thus increase your capital gains. Each Web-based portfolio management program offers something different. In the following sections, I describe just a few examples.

Don't let the fascination of having your portfolio online tempt you into over-trading (buying or selling) your investments.

Investor compilation or supersites provide, among other things, free and fee-based portfolio tracking. Some investor supersites often require your free registration and are supported by advertisers. Other compilation sites provide different levels of services, costing from nothing up to $8 to $10 per month. The benefits of tracking your portfolio at one of these sites is access to the vast repositories of investor information, data, and tools that they offer. That is, if you want to research or analyze something in connection with your portfolio, you don't have to go to several investor sites to get the job done, which can save you time and money if you need to make a quick investment decision. In the following sections, I profile several of these investor compilation sites.

MSN Investor

MSN Investor Portfolio Manager (investor.msn.com), shown in Figure 16-1, uses MSN Investor software that's downloaded in about 5 minutes using a 28.8K modem. This one-time download allows you to automatically track up to 5,000 securities in one or several portfolios. You can enter transactions manually, import personal finance software programs from Money or Quicken, or download accounts directly from your brokerage. You can personalize the portfolio management program to show your annualized gain, current P/E, and market value. If you wish, you can arrange to receive e-mail alerts of stock splits and dividends, late breaking news, and technical price events. MSN subscribers ($9.95 per month) can receive daily e-mail updates either before the market opens or after the market closes.

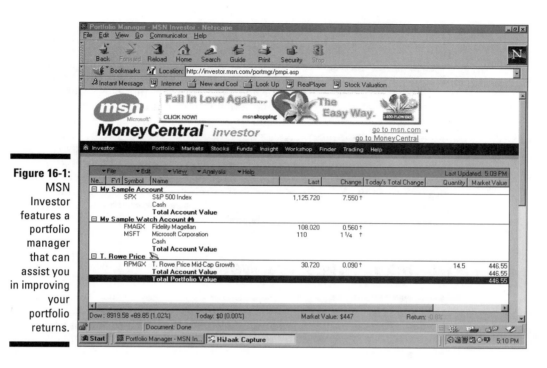

Figure 16-1:
MSN
Investor
features a
portfolio
manager
that can
assist you
in improving
your
portfolio
returns.

Stockpoint

Stockpoint Portfolio Management (www.stockpoint.com) provides a personal portfolio, stock news, and end-of-the-day e-mail portfolio updates. The portfolio management program requires your free registration. Stockpoint Portfolio Management allows you to download current share options in a Quicken software format and handles up to 50 U.S. and Canadian stocks, mutual funds, and stock indexes (so that you can compare the performance of your investment selections). To access the portfolio management Web page from the Stockpoint home page, click Portfolio.

This portfolio management program includes the last traded price, each day's price changes, the percentage of each day's price changes, and the current value of each holding. It calculates the capital gains and losses and the percentage of capital gains and losses from the initial purchase price that you entered when you set up the portfolio. The program provides information about volume and moving averages of several securities at once. You can click on the Export button to download all the portfolio information to Quicken software for additional analysis. Some limitations of Stockpoint's portfolio management program are that it doesn't provide any fundamental analysis or graphing and you must add all stock splits manually.

Telescan Wall Street City

Wall Street City (www.wallstreetcity.com) offers online financial news, information, and analytical tools. Some services are free and others have fees. The portfolio tracking programs and historical quotes are free. At the home page, click Portfolio. When the portfolio screen appears, enter the ticker symbol, number of share purchases, and the purchase price where indicated. The portfolio analysis presents current quotes (delayed 20 minutes) and a news watch of the company, Telescan rankings, news, and price alerts. For technical analysts, the tracking program provides short-term, intermediate, and long-term breakout information. Service costs vary from free to $149.95 per month for a comprehensive financial database, financial analyses, and online research tools. A free 30-day trial is available that allows full access to the Web site.

Thomson Investors Network

Thomson Investors Network (www.thomsoninvest.net) has free and fee-based services. Registered guests have free use of the portfolio-tracking services with end-of-the-day quotes sent to your e-mailbox and limited access to other site services. The Web site is a subsidiary of Thomson Financial Services and includes a wide variety of high-quality investment research, screening tools, and news services (S&P Comstock, CDA/ Wiesenberger, First Call, Institutional Shareholder Services, and more).

Guests are allowed 25 portfolios containing 25 securities each. Figure 16-2 shows the Thomson Investors Network portfolio tracker, which allows up to ten securities in one portfolio. The portfolio displays values in fractions or decimals, account history and tax liability, and commissions. Micro-icons indicate charts, and alerts or breaking news about your investment are available. For example, click the News icon and the news page appears. Articles include company news, changes in credit ratings, and other pertinent information about your investment.

You can create a customized view by following a few online instructions and adjust for stock splits. Additionally, the portfolio tracker includes *flash mail,* which notifies you by e-mail at the end of the business day with news and other information affecting your portfolio. Specifically, the portfolio management function includes the following:

> ✔ **The Today's market view** shows the price for the last trade, change, high and low prices, volume, position, and value. Positions are either long or short. Long positions are the traditional buy-and-hold strategies. A Short position is where the investor borrows stock from a broker and then sells it. When the stock price drops, the investor purchases the original amount of shares and returns them to the broker. The difference from the sales price and the repurchase price are the investor's profit, less broker fees.

✔ **The fundamental view** shows last traded price (delayed 20 minutes), P/E ratio, EPS, Dividend rate, Market Capitalization, 52-Week Highs and Lows, Price/Book Ratio, and Value.

✔ **The graphical view** compares the best and worst performers in the portfolio. If this view shows that a stock is dragging your returns to a lower than acceptable level over a period of time, you may want to consider selling.

✔ **The closed position view** indicates your tax liabilities, which is helpful when tax season rolls around.

Membership is $9.95 per month or $89.95 per year for unlimited access, which includes a *live ticker* that you can detach and use on your computer's desktop for real time indexes and delayed stock quotes. Other membership services include flash mail (reports sent directly to your e-mailbox), 25 mutual fund reports and 25 company reports per month, company and mutual fund screening tools, and intraday updates of market news and analyses. Thomson also includes municipal bond news, bulletin boards, chats with experts, and an education center. Additional company reports cost $2.50, and additional mutual fund reports cost $1.50.

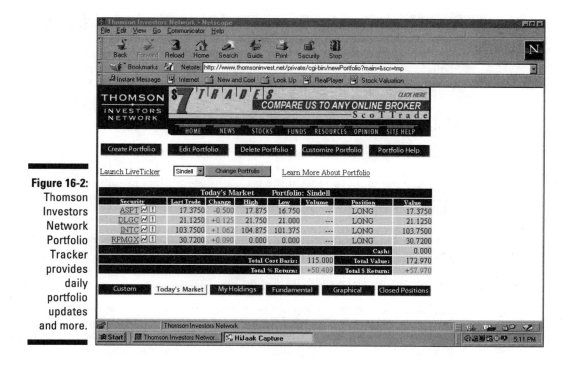

Figure 16-2: Thomson Investors Network Portfolio Tracker provides daily portfolio updates and more.

Reuters Money Network

Moneynet (www.moneynet.com), a Reuters-sponsored investment supersite, features a free, easy-to-use Web-based portfolio management program called Portfolio Tracker. This program can create up to ten customized portfolios for as many as 30 stocks, mutual funds, and options in each portfolio. The easy-to-read grid includes a security symbol, company name, price or NAV (Net Asset Value of a mutual fund), volume, high, low, and date/time stamp.

At the Reuters Moneynet home page, click Portfolio Tracker. To create a portfolio, click Add Securities, enter a portfolio name or multiple portfolio names, and then add investments and the number of shares (optional). After you build a portfolio, the program automatically monitors the market for you.

Alerts you receive include e-mails about current market value and market information. You can select notifications for up to twice a day, weekly, monthly, or quarterly. Click on the investment name and a Quote Detail Report appears that includes 52-week high/low, P/E ratio, EPS (earnings per share) information, and more.

The Wall Street Journal Interactive Edition

The Wall Street Journal Interactive Edition (www.wsj.com), shown in Figure 16-3, offers easy access to your portfolio. Click on the top-right corner of almost any page of the Interactive Edition to access the portfolio program. You can establish five portfolios with as many as 30 securities in each one. Delayed stock prices constantly update the portfolio, which also shows percentage change and gain/loss information.

The grid displays an issue-by-issue breakdown of your investments. Total value (along with your portfolio's current gain/loss and percentage of change) is included at the top of the grid, along with the current value of the Dow Jones Industrial Average. You can download investment information to your favorite spreadsheet program.

If news is available for any company in your portfolio, a flag appears next to the company's name. To access the news, click on the flag. Links to detailed quotes and mutual fund snapshots are also available. These links provide additional performance and background information.

You can download the portfolio by using either comma-delimited text or plain text. To import data to your spreadsheet program, use the comma-delimited format. Use your browser to save the file with .cvs as the file's extension — for example, Stocks.cvs. You can open the file by using any spreadsheet program. If you want to paste the portfolio information into a word-processing file, download it as a plain text (.txt) file — for example, Stocks.txt. The plain text format is best used with a fixed-width font, such as Courier.

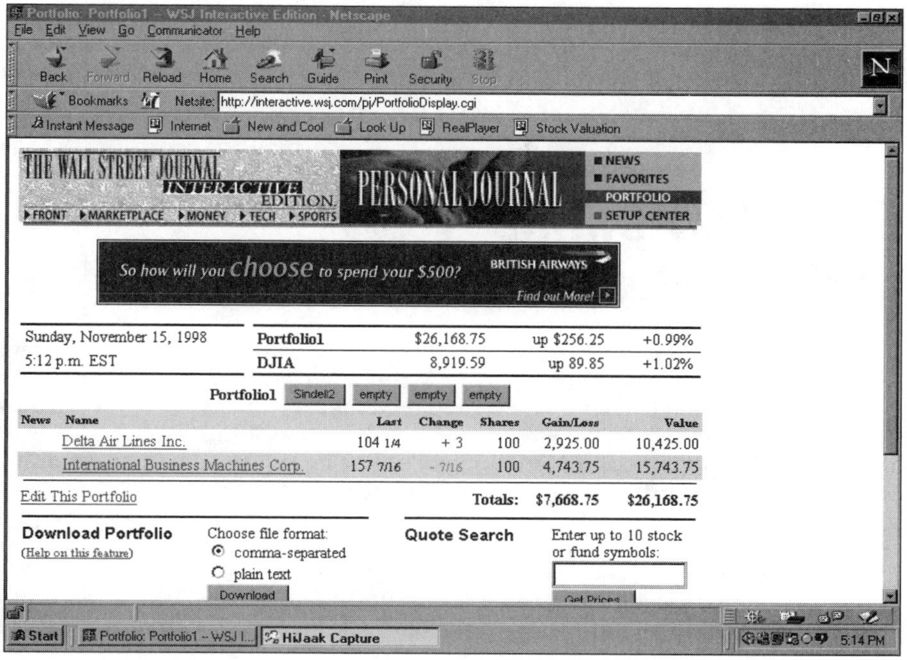

Figure 16-3:
You can access your portfolio on almost any page at The Wall Street Journal Interactive Web Site.

Like many Web-based portfolio management programs, this program doesn't provide any graphs or charts of your portfolio. However, you can perform fundamental analysis by using a spreadsheet program, downloaded portfolio data, and additional information. Annual subscriptions cost $59.

Zack's Investment Research

Zack's Investment Research (www.zacks.com) provides free and fee-based services. Portfolios can include up to 20 stocks in a single portfolio. (Additionally, you can purchase portfolios that go to separate e-mail addresses.) To begin your portfolio, just click Portfolio and provide your e-mail address. On the next screen that appears, enter the ticker symbol and the number of shares you own or wish to own. (As a free service, Zack's provides portfolio alerts that are sent to your e-mailbox.) Portfolio alerts include daily closing prices, changes in prices, and trading volume. Portfolio information also includes Zack's Investment Research scores of your securities (using their own ranking system), analysts earnings per share estimates, and buy/hold/sell recommendations, in addition to reported earnings per share surprises, news, EPS report dates, and declared dividends.

You can use daily alerts for monitoring stocks on your _Watch List_. You can have e-mail alerts sent to you daily or weekly. When you begin your free subscription, Zacks includes a 30-day free trial of news and analyst's reports on the portfolio. The basic subscription gives you up to 35 ticker symbols per report for $19.95 per year. Extended subscriptions provide you with up to 100 ticker symbols per report for $29.95 per year. Plus subscriptions get you up to 200 ticker symbols per report for $59.95 per year.

Following Online News with Portfolio Tracking

Online portfolio tracking tools allow investors to see exactly how their investments are prospering. Many large news organizations provide portfolio-tracking services that can make your portfolio tracking very convenient if you already use one or more of these news sources. The portfolio tracking functions of online news organizations generally require the security's ticker symbol, quantity you purchased, purchase price, and date of purchase. In return, your portfolio tracker shows today's delayed market price, today's change, market value of your shares, the value of your investment, your gain or loss, and the percentage of the return. The following list profiles a few examples of online news organizations' portfolio trackers.

Business news

Many online business news organizations provide portfolio tracking. Getting your investment news and tracking your investments at the same site is like one-stop shopping and can be a real time saver. You can read the news and check on your securities at the same time. For a few examples, check out the following:

ABC News Moneyscope (www.moneyscope.com**)** features a sophisticated, free portfolio-tracking program that tracks, organizes, and graphs individual stocks, indexes, and mutual funds data on one screen. Prices and corporate news are continuously updated. (This program needs to be downloaded.)

CBS MarketWatch (portfolio.marketwatch.com**)**, a free program, allows you to create an unlimited number of portfolios and track up to 200 ticker symbols for options, mutual funds, and stocks on all the major exchanges in each portfolio. You can also customize price and value views to display the data. Prices are automatically updated every five minutes.

New York Times (www.nytimes.com**)**, go to the Business Section and click Your Money. Then click Portfolio to set up or see the status of your portfolio. To set up your portfolio, just enter the securities you own or wish to own by inputting the ticker symbol, amount of shares, commission paid, and date of purchase. The portfolio program does the rest. PC Quote (www.pcquote.com) provides the quotes and the New York Times provides the free service.

Portal portfolio management

Portals are Web sites that are designed to be the Internet user's first window onto the Web — the first page that comes up when the user accesses the Web. Often, portals can be personalized so that the user can get news, sports, current portfolio data, or interest rate information before moving on to other sites. The following two sections profile examples of portals with free portfolio tracking.

Yahoo! portfolio management

Figure 16-4 shows the My Yahoo! personalized portfolio program (my.yahoo.com). To use the free portfolio, you need to set up an account with My Yahoo!. Click the Log In link that appears on the Portfolio line and then click Create an Account. Click the Edit link that appears and enter a portfolio name. Add the ticker symbols of your investments separated by commas where indicated. You can also enter indexes like the S&P 500 (SPX) for comparison purposes. You can use the same ticker symbol to record separate purchases. Enter or edit the number of shares or purchase prices by clicking the Enter More Info button at the bottom of the page.

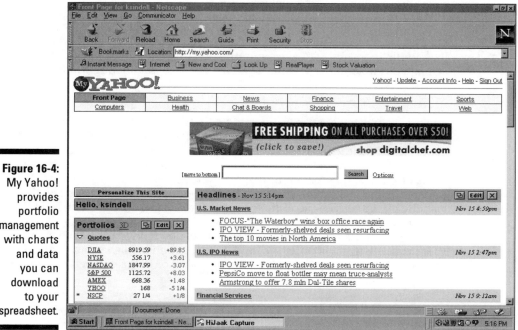

Figure 16-4:
My Yahoo! provides portfolio management with charts and data you can download to your spreadsheet.

Quotes are delayed by 15 minutes for NASDAQ and 20 minutes for other exchanges. Portfolio management information includes company ticker symbol, price at the last trade, amount of price change at last trade, trading volume, number of shares held, the total value of the issue, dollar and percentage of change between the purchase price and the current value, amount paid per share, and dollar capital gain or loss and percentage of capital gain or loss.

The program provides charts, news, research, SEC filings data, and related information. Recent headlines that link to news stories about your portfolio investments appear at the bottom of the page. You can get your information by signing in on any computer (and use the sign-out feature to make certain that others can't pry).

You can select a nontable version of the portfolio's data, choose to have all portfolio data downloaded to a spreadsheet, and retrieve detailed quotes for each investment. You can customize the portfolio by deciding to sort information alphabetically, use a small font, or display the portfolio by using detailed quote information rather than basic quote data.

Detailed quote information includes last trade (date and time), change (dollars and percent), previous closing price, volume, the day's price range, 52-week range, and bid, ask, and open prices. Also included are ex-dividend dates, earnings per share, P/E ratio, last dividend per share amount, and yield. Charts of the security's price for the last three months, year, two years, five years, and maximum number of years are available.

You can view your portfolio in a floating window, which lets you track your portfolio even when you leave My Yahoo!. Just click on the stacked pages icon in the top right-hand corner of the portfolio module. If you get tired of seeing your portfolio, click on the X sign to close the floating window.

Excite

Excite (www.excite.com) is a portal that lets you customize more than any other portal Web site after you enter your ZIP code and e-mail address. You can decide how the page looks, which news stories you want to be listed first, select reminders, choose your favorite links, and more. You can select stocks to track and create multiple portfolios. The first portfolio view shows only the ticker symbol, current price, and percentage of change since the last closing price. The portfolio tracker provides alerts, information on the most active stocks, and a market update. The full portfolio screen shows the ticker symbol, current price, today's change, percentage of change, volume, shares you own, gains or losses, and links to company news and chats. If you need to look up a company's ticker symbol or find a delayed quote, Excite includes the service.

Using PC-Based Portfolio Management Software

If you want more analysis, including graphs of your investments' performance, tax data, and price and volume alerts, you may want to consider a PC-based portfolio manager (a software program that operates on your PC). For example, you can select Money 99 Financial Suite or Quicken Deluxe 99 (which you may already use for your online banking), shareware, or free Internet programs. In the following sections, I describe a few examples of PC-based portfolio management programs.

Personal software programs

Personal finance software programs often offer much more than what you pay for. Personal software programs provide a way to access online banking, organize your personal finances, understand what you have and what you owe, and organize your financial accounts for the tax man. Additionally, portfolio management programs track and analyze your portfolio's performance. In most personal finance software programs, your portfolio's gains and losses are automatically used for your net worth calculations. With many personal finance programs, if you are connected to the Internet, you can automatically update securities prices. Following, I list the two most popular personal finance software programs: Microsoft Money 99 and Quicken 99.

The NAIC portfolio management program and other portfolio management programs allow investors to sort investments by type of industry or company size, then print the reports. This allows investors to make comparisons within their own portfolios. In other words, it's a convenient way to sort out the winners and losers. A limitation of some personal finance software programs is that they do not include this feature. Additionally, personal finance software programs often have trouble with dividend reinvestment plans.

MS Money 99 Financial Suite

MS Money 99 Financial Suite (www.microsoft.com/money) is a personal finance software program that can help you stay organized by tracking activities in your savings and checking accounts, and do your banking and bill-paying online. Manage your investments by downloading quotes and brokerage statements from the Internet. Plan your retirement and more. You can download free 90-day trial versions of Money 99 at microsoft.com/money/about/trial for $5.95. The program costs $65 and includes a free 6-month subscription to MS Investor (investor.msn.com).

MS Money 99's portfolio management function allows investors to view performance, holdings, quotes, fundamentals, positions, and the asset allocation of the portfolio. You can track employee stock options and create a Watchlist of investment candidates. Portfolio information is linked via your hard drive to MSN Investor (investor.msn.com). However, to access MSN Investor you must pay $9.95 per month after a six-month free trial (for MS Money 99 purchasers).

MS Money 99 allows you to download your account statement from over 100 brokerages to your portfolio. MS Money 99 alerts let you know when a stock reaches a high or low price that you specified. The program monitors your Watchlist of investment candidates and market indices to automatically update the price of a security in your portfolio.

To automatically update the price of a security in your portfolio:

1. **Open the portfolio window that holds the security whose price you want to update.**

2. **Click the Update Price button. The Update Price dialog box opens.**

   The program automatically updates all the securities that you checked in the drop-down box and selects the investments whose prices you want to update.

3. **Click the Up Call button. If this is the first time you have used the program, provide your Internet Service Providers required user ID and password.**

   The program automatically updates securities prices.

For more information about Money 99, see *Microsoft Money 99 For Dummies,* by Peter Weverka (IDG Books Worldwide, Inc.).

Quicken Deluxe 99

Quicken Deluxe 99 (www.intuit.com/quicken) is a personal finance software program that can assist you with your home and small business finances, and help you prepare for retirement and educational costs. The Quicken 99 portfolio's table-style format is easy to read and can be organized into customized views. It also tracks tricky financial transactions like stock splits and corporate takeovers. You can download up to five years of stock quotes for trend analysis and record-keeping. Quicken can also help you calculate your capital gains taxes (not an easy task with today's tax laws).

Quicken 99 has a feature called Online Investment Tracking. This feature connects individuals to financial institutions for online banking, online bill paying, and online investment tracking through the Open Financial Exchange Server. The Open Financial Exchange Server software was developed by Microsoft, Intuit, and CheckFree.

Intuit's online Investment Tracking (www.intuit.com/ofs/invest_tracking.html), shown in Figure 16-5, allows participating brokerages to download current account statements directly to individuals, which allows investors to stay up-to-date by seeing recent transactions, holdings, and balances. In other words, investors don't have to wait until the end of the month to see exactly what they own. The Quicken Deluxe 99 program costs $59.

To automatically update securities:

1. **Choose Features➪Investment➪Portfolio View.**

2. **Pull down the Update Prices menus and select Get Online Quotes and News.**

   This page provides the required Internet information (if this is the first time you are using the program). The program assumes that you want to update all the quotes of your securities. If you want to update only a few quotes, click those quotes to check them and make certain that the securities you don't want to update are not checked (check marks would appear next to the security name).

3. **Click Get News For The Last and enter the number of days you want to know about to download any headlines, if you want the latest news on your investment.**

4. **Click Update Now.**

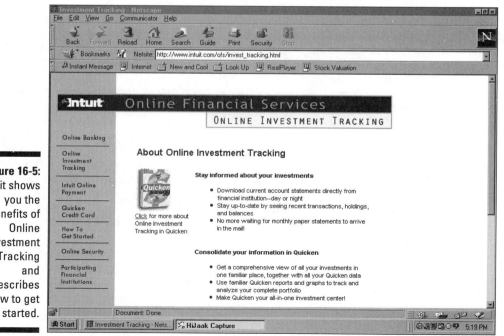

Figure 16-5:
Intuit shows you the benefits of Online Investment Tracking and describes how to get started.

Portfolio management software programs

Several hundred portfolio management programs are available for your investment tracking. The programs vary in price from free to $500. Many of the freeware and shareware portfolio management programs include an amazing amount of features but are somewhat cumbersome to work with. Some brokers give free portfolio management programs to customers who open an account. Financial data providers frequently give free portfolio management programs with a subscription to their services. Other portfolio management programs are components of larger investment analysis applications. To discover what works for you, try some of the free demonstrations or trials that vendors offer. They require no obligations, and after sampling several programs, you can get a good idea of which features you need. Following, I list a few examples of PC-based portfolio management programs:

BB Stock Tool (www.falkor.com) tracks, charts, and analyzes stocks. The program includes charting, technical analysis, portfolio management, market timing, buy/sell signals, profit testing, customized high/low alerts, automatic stock split detection and management, most active volume, and price movement summaries. You can access daily quotes with your modem and Internet access to automatically update your portfolio. Software developer Falkor Technologies Inc. provides an owner's manual and sample data. The BB Stock Tool uses Windows 95 or Windows NT 4.0. You can get a 30-day free trial. The program costs $89 if you decide to keep it.

Captool Individual Investor for Windows (www.wallstreetsoftware.com) includes a portfolio management tool for all types of securities and transactions. You can define security types and groups. You can account for reinvestments, short sales, splits, mergers, return on capital, and more. The program contains over 70 transaction codes to facilitate modeling all situations. It also calculates returns on investments, estimates your tax liabilities, and performs batch valuations (for multiple portfolios). Captool Individual Investor automatically updates security prices with your Internet access. You can also make manual entries. Reports can be customized and graphical reports include valuation versus time, ROI versus time, portfolio growth versus indices, and more. The program uses Windows 3.x, Win 95/98, or Windows NT. The program costs $249 plus shipping and handling.

Fund Manager for Windows 95 (downloadable at rocketdownload.com **or** www.zdnet.co.uk/software/) is a top-rated portfolio management program for stocks and mutual funds for the average individual investor. It takes a short time to get the hang of it, but samples help shorten the learning curve. Fund Manager provides many easy-to-read graphs, charts, and reports that are printable. You can update prices by clicking on Internet. Fund Manager imports from Prodigy, MSN, Quicken, and other sources. Retrieve the latest quotes from AOL, CompuServe, or many international Internet sites. Fund manager tracks your investment performance quickly and easily. The program uses Windows 95. It's free to try, $34 to own, and $5 to upgrade.

NAIC Personal Record Keeper (www.quantixsoftware.com) is the official software offered by the National Association of Investors Corporation (www.better-investing.com) for personal portfolio management. The program tracks investment transactions (buys, sell, income, reinvestment, and so on) for a variety of investments. It also automatically updates prices from online services. Reports can be printed recording the full history of your portfolio or for a specified time period, including industry and company size breakdowns and return calculations. The program generates more than 35 reports and graphs, keeps tax records, indicates diversification, compares portfolio performance to the market, and automatically notifies you if a price alert has been reached. The program uses Windows 3.1 and Win 95/98. Pricing is $95 for NAIC Computer Group members, $99 for NAIC members, $129 for nonmembers, and $45 for the upgrade from DOS or Windows previous versions. A free demo is available for download.

StockTracker is free, downloadable software available at www.stockcenter.com. You need to register and download the software to use this program (downloading takes about five minutes).

StockTracker can automatically update security prices, value the portfolio, and provide price alerts that you predetermine. The program can be connected to the Internet and have access to all the principal U.S. and Canadian markets. You can create up to 12 portfolios. You can also save pricing data and build charts while the program constantly updates your portfolio.

Wall Street Access offers StockTracker free to the investment community in hopes that they will enjoy the product and open an account. The minimum order amount to open an account is $10,000. Placing an order with a trader averages $45. Trades placed electronically average $25.

WinStock Pro (www.download.com or hotfiles.zdnet.com) is a stock market tracking and portfolio management program using your Internet connection. You can set up several portfolios that use the Internet to update prices. The program converts foreign currencies, and features a ticker toolbar and printed reports. You can import or export to Quicken. The program includes e-mail, automatic dial-up, paging, audible alarms, and flexible reporting. WinStock Pro requires Windows 95 and is free to try and $30 if you decide to keep it. (See Figure 16-6.)

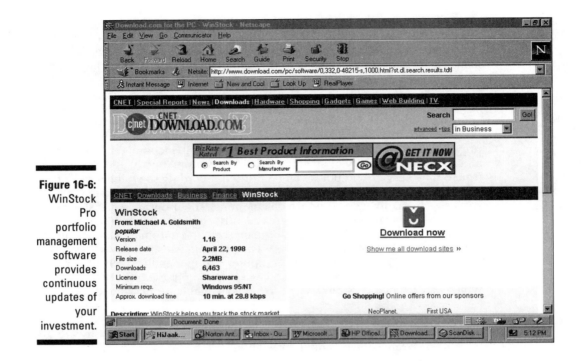

Figure 16-6:
WinStock
Pro
portfolio
management
software
provides
continuous
updates of
your
investment.

Using Online Brokerage-Based Portfolio Tracking

As a general rule, you have to manually update Web-based portfolio management programs when you buy or sell securities, pay a commission, or receive a dividend or stock split. This manual updating is time consuming and the possibility exists that you may make an error. These inconveniences can be especially troublesome for active traders. Using the portfolio management function of your online brokerage is one way to avoid the problem of manually updating your portfolio. The following are several examples of electronic brokerages that provide portfolio management programs.

DLJdirect (www.dljdirect.com) provides its customers with up-to-the-minute personal portfolio information to assist them in making better investment decisions. This information allows you to stay on top of your portfolio performance so that you can react quickly to changing market conditions. Portfolio information includes order status, execution report, cash balances, margin balance, portfolio values, and a 120-day account history. Each night, the portfolio is updated with the day's closing prices. A portfolio demo is available that shows how the firm handles alerts, balances, portfolio holdings, order status, history, cash withdrawals, and profits.

Discover Brokerage (www.discoverbrokerage.com) provides customers with a Balances Portfolio View that gives the real-time value of all the customer's personal accounts. The Balances Portfolio View shows the total net worth of the account, long and short market values, cash, margin calls, and buying power and margin information. Other portfolio screens include views of holdings, the portfolio's asset allocation, activity, and orders. Discover Brokerage provides a demo of their portfolio-tracking program. If you want a figure defined, just click on the heading to bring up an explanation of that figure.

E*Trade (www.etrade.com) provides a portfolio management tool with your free registration. Click on Log-In and the program requests data. Next, click Portfolios and Markets, which automatically updates your portfolio to include trading activity. To create your portfolio, simply enter the name of your portfolio and a description (for example, Retirement Account). Enter the ticker symbol, type of security, quantity, cost, date acquired, and position (long or short) of the securities you own. The portfolio management program displays your portfolio performance. You can manually edit, add, or split investments into multiple portfolios (the college account, the retirement account, and so on).

Charles Schwab (www.schwab.com), shown in Figure 16-7, provides customers with a portfolio management feature. The portfolio shows the ticker symbol of the security, the quantity owned, the name of the security, and the current market value. For company news or charts of the security's performance just click on the appropriate links. Charles Schwab also provides an asset allocation toolkit that shows the current allocation of assets for your trading account. The asset allocation model, which shows conservative, moderately conservative, moderate, moderately aggressive, and aggressive asset allocations, is used for comparative purposes. The analysis can be used to assist you in meeting your financial objectives. Short demonstrations of both the portfolio management and asset allocation features are available.

Keeping the Winners and Selling the Losers: Measuring Performance

Measuring portfolio performance is often difficult. For example, suppose that you invest $2,000 in a mutual fund that returns 15% in the first quarter of the year. In each of the next three-quarters you invest $2,000, but the fund doesn't provide any returns during those months. Your return on the first $2,000 is 15%. Your returns on $6,000 for nine months is zero. The fund reports an annual gain of 15%, not counting dividends and gains distributions. However, these percentages don't mean that you should measure performance on a short-term basis. Market prices vary and returns fluctuate for many reasons. What really counts is the true rate of return, which can't be measured from quarter to quarter.

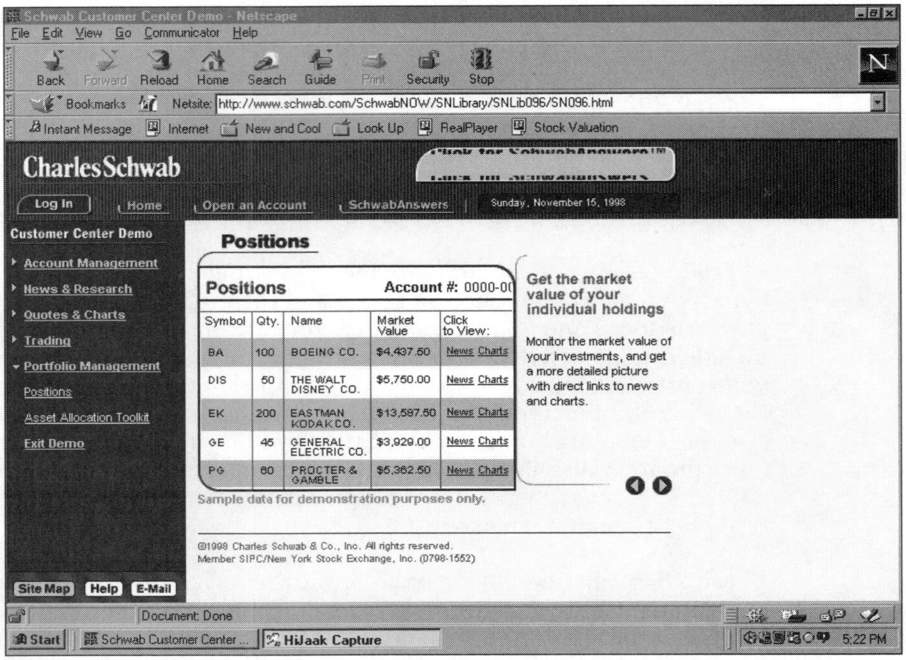

Figure 16-7:
Schwab's
portfolio
tracking
program
helps you
meet your
asset
allocation
goals.

Another problem in measuring portfolio performance is risk. Risk is defined as the variability of returns. In other words, the more the returns vary, the greater the risk. One of the disadvantages of using standard deviation (a measurement of the variability of historical returns around the average return) is that it doesn't take into consideration *good variability*. Good variability means that returns are exceeding expectations. This event increases the stock's volatility and standard deviation. The stock is now considered more *risky* because returns are higher than expected. What this shows is that standard deviation isn't always a good way to judge risk. In other words, standard deviation is just a measurement of volatility. Risk only enters the picture if volatility is *below* the investor's return target.

You can utilize many ways to measure the performance of your portfolio. One way to measure performance is to use benchmarks — that is, comparing the performance of your various investments to top performances and indices. For example:

✔ Divide your stocks into capitalization groups (small cap, mid cap, and large cap) and rank each group by P/E ratio. Compare your investments to top performing stocks in each capitalization group daily and weekly.

✔ Divide your fixed income (bonds and Treasury securities) investments by quality rating and then rank each group by yield. Compare your investments to the top performing bonds in each asset allocation class.

Doing this type of work by hand is time consuming. Figure 16-8 shows Riskview (www.riskview.com), a free Web site where individual and professional investors can:

✔ **Track historical equity performance:** Analyze stocks to determine their price/return ratio, risk/return over a period of time with risk/return graphs.

✔ **Conduct risk/return analyses:** Risk/return analysis, historical risk, risk/return table, and return versus risk comparisons.

✔ **Forecast volatilities:** Volatilities and correlation, introduction to correlation, limits of correlation, and sensitivity graphs.

✔ **Perform personal portfolio performance analyses:** Portfolio returns analysis, portfolio/benchmark analysis and graphs, daily portfolio returns, and the distribution of daily returns.

✔ **Conduct customized risk management analyses:** Portfolio risk analysis, introduction to volatility, forecast of risk estimates, daily risk estimates, and risk adjusted returns.

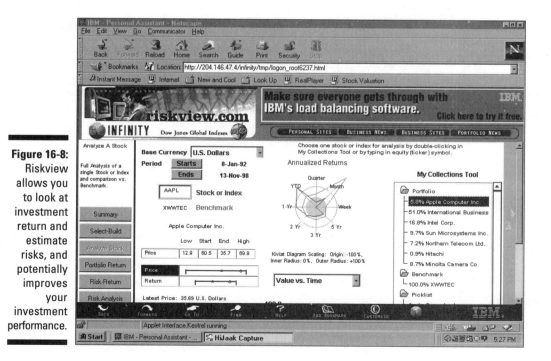

Figure 16-8: Riskview allows you to look at investment return and estimate risks, and potentially improves your investment performance.

Developed by Infinity Financial Technologies, Riskview is a free, single-source tool you can use to monitor total returns on individual equities or indexes and perform *what if* risk scenarios using over five years of daily historical data. The site provides daily updates to stocks and indexes and Value-at-Risk (VaR) analyses based on Infinity's EquityMetrics, a full set of return volatility and correlation estimates.

Riskview's database includes the Dow Jones Global Indexes (DJGI) and its underlying stocks (which represent more than 80 percent of the total stock market value in 29 countries), and provides over 3,000 indexes for tracking stocks in 29 countries, 9 geographic regions, 9 economic sectors, and 121 industry groups.

Part V
The Part of Tens

The 5th Wave   By Rich Tennant

"Who added my portrait of Elvis to my retirement portfolio?"

In this part . . .

In The Part of Tens, I tell you the ten sell signals and how to spot the ten green flags for buying.

Chapter 17

Ten Signals to Sell

*I*ndividual investors routinely sell winners too early and ride losers too long. Knowing which stocks to sell and when to sell them is the hallmark of a savvy investor. From the time that you purchase a stock, you want to be considering the right time to sell and reap your rewards.

If you're pondering a sale, don't focus on only the sale price. Take the time to ask several questions and research the Internet for answers about the security's future.

When you purchase a security, you anticipate a certain rate of return. To examine your investment selection's performance, calculate what you have gained by holding the security.

> ✔ **For bonds,** measure the current yield by taking the annual interest payment and dividing it by the current price of the bond. (For details, see Chapter 13.)

> ✔ **For stocks and mutual funds,** calculate the investment's total return (ending value less beginning value plus income divided by beginning value). (See Chapter 4 for more information.)

To check the quality rating of all bonds, read the appropriate annual reports and fund statements for your stocks and mutual funds. Remember that no scientific formulas exist to guide your selling decisions. Knowing some general rules and the kinds of questions to ask, however, can help you become a more successful investor.

The selling system that's best is the one that locks in gains and protects you if the value of your assets drop. Your personal selling system needs to work well with your investment time frame, investment style, and risk-tolerance level.

Know When to Fold

The following are general examples of selling rules that beginning investors may find valuable. Veteran investors may have the same selling rules or quite different ones. Regardless of which category you fall into, both new and experienced investors needs to choose a personal system and stick to it.

A sure way to lose big money is to hang on to an investment that's losing money. Try not to emotionally involve yourself with your investment selections. One way to lower the likelihood of holding on to an investment for too long is to develop a few personal selling rules. Write your personal selling rules in your investment plan and store the plan on your computer's hard disk. Your personal selling rules may state, for example, that you're to sell the stock if any of the following conditions occur:

- The stock drops below your predetermined trading range.
- Market experts call the company "steady," or dividend increases are behind the general market.
- You discover that the company's sales growth, profitability, or financial health is in trouble.
- You discover that the industry is in a serious decline.
- The company loses its competitive edge and market share is declining.
- The stock's trading volume increases but the stock price doesn't rise.

Don't hold on to any securities that you don't believe are investment candidates.

 FundAlarm (www.fundalarmc.com) is a free, noncommercial Web site that provides objective information to help individual investors make mutual fund sell decisions. FundAlarm compares your mutual fund to an appropriate benchmark and tracks its performance. If the fund consistently under performs, you should consider selling.

Set Profit-Taking Goals

Realizing your profit is what investing is all about. Paper profits may look good, but money in the bank is what pays for your child's education or enables you to retire early. If your stock is selling for a high price and is now a large part of your portfolio, you may want to sell.

What's more, if you're contemplating selling the stock, you don't want to sell before the stock reaches its peak. In other words, you want to sell at the best price and before the stock starts to decline. What should you do? The following list gives you some ideas:

- ✔ Say that your stock is currently selling for 50 percent more than your purchase price. Take the money and run if the stock is not likely to go any higher.

- ✔ Set a target price that may not be your sell price but a benchmark. If your stock reaches the benchmark price, reevaluate your investment plan. Make certain that you check similar companies to see whether they're selling at the same level or higher. If so, you may want to raise your target price.

- ✔ Consider selling if a stock starts showing up on brokerage buy lists, gets included in many mutual funds, or receives a lot of favorable press.

- ✔ If a winner now represents more than 10 percent of your portfolio, you may want to sell part of your holdings. That way, you lock in part of the profit and still benefit if the stock keeps rising.

- ✔ Don't try to sell at the stock's top price. You didn't buy at the bottom, so don't expect to sell at the very top. Even after all your analyses, you still need to rely on your gut feelings about the right time to sell.

Remember that you must pay taxes on your capital gains. To get a handle on your tax liability, see the Wells Fargo Securities Special Report on the Web at `wellsfargo.com/investing/srtra/`.

You Can't Be Right All the Time

Selling a loser is often harder than selling a winner. If you purchase a stock with a certain expectation, but the company never lives up to your expectations, you should sell. The following list provides a few examples of such situations:

- ✔ Sell a stock if it declines 20 percent in a down market and 10 percent in an up market. If a stock drops 15 percent in a flat market, reevaluate.
- ✔ The company's growth rate and earnings trends peak and then fall.
- ✔ The company cuts its dividend or stops dividend payments entirely.

If you sell a loser, note exactly why it didn't turn out as expected and include these notes in your investment plan. Such documentation helps you avoid making similar mistakes in the future.

Everyone expects strong performers to keep up the pace. Past performance however, doesn't guarantee future performance. For more information, see the article "Do Past Winners Repeat?" at the Investor Home Web site (www.investorhome.com/mutual.htm#do).

If the Stock Is Going Nowhere, Get Going

If the stock or fund in which you invested is a mediocre performer, you need to replace it. You may not want to rush to judgment, however. Give the company about a year to make any needed changes to bring its performance up to speed. Then sell it if you don't see any improvement at all.

You can tell whether you have a nowhere stock by comparing it to the appropriate index. (See the section, "What Does the S & P 500 Have to Do with Anything?" in Chapter 7.) If the index is consistently matching your nowhere stock, you may want to consider selling. Doing so frees up funds for you to use in purchasing better performers. If you don't have any great investment candidates, think about spreading the proceeds among your portfolio's best existing ideas. Or, better yet, just hang in there — a good investment opportunity is likely to appear sooner or later.

Get some help to beat the crowd from The Online Investor at www.investhelp.com.

Don't Be Fooled by P/E Spurts

Be suspicious of sudden jumps in the P/E (price/earnings) ratio. Such spurts may mean that it's headed for a fall. Soaring P/E ratios and depressed dividend yields can be signs that market prices are unstable. Consider selling if the P/E ratio rises more than 30 percent higher than its annual average for the last ten years. Say that the P/E ratio for the last ten years is 20, for example, and then it suddenly climbs to 26. Consider selling the stock. (On the other hand, don't sell stocks that are in a temporary sinking spell.)

Watch Interest Rates

Bond investors must anticipate the turns and directions of interest rates. If interest rates increase, bonds and bond fund prices decrease because buyers are less willing to purchase investments with lower rates than those stated on new bond issues. Bonds with longer maturity terms lose more value if interest rates continue to climb. Bonds are subject to inflationary expectations, monetary demand, and changes in short-term interest rate expectations. Thirty-year bonds purchased in the '70s, for example, lost approximately 45 percent of their value after interest rates increased in the '80s (for details, see Chapter 9). Keep in mind the following principles for a personal selling system:

- Rising interest rates tend to divert money from the stock market and depress stock prices.

- Low interest rates usually indicate a good time to own stocks, because the economy grows as a result, and stock prices are sure to increase.

- Declining interest rates indicate less fear of inflation.

- Income stocks often are more sensitive to changes in interest rates than are other types of stocks.

Keep an Eye on Economic Indicators

Until recently, inflation has averaged 3 percent a year since 1926. Investments like certificates of deposit, Treasury securities, agency bonds, and corporate bonds are fixed-income investments. Their yields don't vary regardless of the inflation rate. Over the long term, therefore, low-yielding fixed-income securities can lose out to inflation.

Stock market declines often precede economic recessions. Indications of an economic slump may suggest to you that you want to get out of the market. Stock prices often rebound at the end of a recession, however, which argues against selling during a recession.

For more information about what to look for in economic data, see the CBS MarketWatch Web site (cbs.marketwatch.com/news/primer/stocks/econ_primer.htx?source=htx/http2_mw).

Watch What the Insiders Are Doing

Do you want an inside tip? Watch what insiders do with the stocks for their own companies. The SEC requires that officers, directors, and shareholders owning 10 percent or more of the company's stock report their trades. These reports are readily accessible on the Internet.

Insiders trade shares so that they can purchase shares by using the options that they receive as part of their employment contracts. Additionally, if the stock's value is significantly different than its selling price (either higher or lower), you see a lot of insider trading activity. High sales activity by insiders may foreshadow a financial debacle. Consider selling your own shares if such trading occurs (especially if the sale price is decreasing).

For a daily report of insider trading, see CNET Investor (`www.news.com/ investor/frontdoor/`). Bloomberg powers this handy daily report.

If the Company or Fund Changes

The company in which you own stock may have changed its core business since your purchase or the fund changed its objectives or increased fees. You need to think about the original reasons why you purchased a company's stock or a mutual fund. If the investments no longer meet these criteria, you're best off to move on.

Similarly, if your own financial situation changes, you may want to sell some or all of your investments. A good reason to do so is if your risk-tolerance level changes; for example, you're getting close to retirement, or your child is about ready to start college.

Have you witnessed a material change in the company? For the latest news, see CBS MarketWatch (`cbsmarketwatch.com`) or Yahoo! Finance (`quote.yahoo.com`).

Chapter 18
Ten Green Flags for Buying

*T*he exit poll for the 1994 election indicated that 24 percent of all Americans have investments. More recent studies by the National Association of Investors Corporation (www.better-investing.org) show that more than 51 million individuals invest in the New York Stock Exchange. Furthermore, if you have a pension, you're likely to have at least half your pension funds currently invested in the stock market. Despite all this popularity, however, equities (stocks) have a serious drawback: They don't offer the security of interest-bearing investments (market funds, CDs, and fixed-income securities).

Interest-bearing securities offer consistent returns. In contrast, stock price fluctuations just "happen." Every stock investor can count on market increases and decreases. These fluctuations aren't company specific, but that fact doesn't offer much comfort. Over time, stock investments tend to reward patient investors with good, inflation-beating returns that are greater than those of any other type of investment. For many individuals, investing is the only way that they can reach their financial goals.

Over the years, avid investors have developed many methods to help others decide which stocks to buy and when to purchase them. No hard-and-fast rules exist. The approach that's best is the one that works for you. The following sections offer a collection of investor wisdom that can assist you in maximizing your personal wealth.

Buy If the Stock Is at Its Lowest Price

This principle is simpler said than done. Excellent investment candidates are stocks that are selling at their lowest price in three to five years (assuming that the company's financial position hasn't deteriorated). Wait for the price to stop declining and the company to show some strength, however, before you put your money down.

You must condition yourself to work against the crowd. The time to sell your stock is whenever it's "hot," its prices are high, and everyone wants to own it. For free, delayed quotes and online company reports, see Zacks Investment Research at www.zacks.com.

Check Out the Earnings Forecast

People use *earnings forecasts* in fundamental analyses to determine the fair value of a stock. If this fair value is less than the stock's current price, the stock is overpriced. If the fair value is more than the current price, the stock may be underpriced and a bargain.

Financial software developers and most brokerages have analysts that develop earnings forecast for companies. Prices for these reports vary from free to several hundred dollars. The Internet provides many sources for earnings forecast reports. The following are a few examples.

Investor's Forecast (mrbig.crt.net/I4C/) delivers collective investor forecasting. You enter your forecast and receive a collective forecast chart for the Dow Jones Industrial Average and the company in which you're interested. Additionally, with your free registration, you're entered into a weekly contest. Each week, the investor whose guess comes the closest to the Friday closing amount of the DJIA wins $100.

Financial Web (www.wallstreetguru.com/dailyguru) provides free earnings upgrade and downgrade information in addition to other related information.

Stock Wiz Links (www.i-soft.com) provides a links page for company information. Just enter the ticker symbol of the company you're researching, and you have your choice of hyperlinks to quotes, news, broker recommendations, research analysts' earning estimates (and actuals), company profiles and fundamentals, SEC filings, and intraday charts.

Watch for Stocks That Are Trading under Book Value

Book value is the company's net-asset value — that is, assets minus liabilities divided by the number of outstanding shares. This amount appears in the company's annual report. See Securities and Exchange Commission (www.sec.gov) and Zacks Company Reports (www.zacks.com). Companies that sell below their book value (if they don't have serious problems) are often bargains.

Beware of Firms with High Long-Term Debt

Usually, the lower the debt ratio is, the safer is the company. Beware of companies that aggressively borrow but never earn a high return on their new capital. Compare the company you're researching to similar firms. Companies that have paid down their debt over the last two or three years, however, may be worth your serious consideration.

Get an industry report from Hoover's (www.hoovers.com) and discover the average debt ratio for the industry. Compare this average to the debt ratio of the firm you're researching. To discover which firms have low debt ratios, use the online stock screens at Quicken (www.quicken.com) or Morningstar (www.morningstar.net).

Invest in Entrepreneurial Companies

Locate a rising company in a rising market. Small and midsized companies tend to be hungrier and more innovative than their older and bigger brothers. A company needs something new to create a startling increase in stock price, and these companies may have that something.

Successes in American industry come from a major new product or service, new management, or an important change for the better in the conditions of a particular industry.

Select companies with entrepreneurial management — rather than caretakers who discourage innovation — that take risks and keep up with the times. Companies with managing executives who own a meaningful share of the outstanding stock are generally good investment candidates.

Bigger is not always better. If you're choosing between two stocks, and one has 10 million shares outstanding and the other has 60 million shares outstanding, select the smaller company. All things being equal (that well-used economics' expression), the smaller company is going to be a better performer.

To find out where the entrepreneurial companies are, see *The Wall Street Journal* (www.wsj.com), annual subscription, $59; *CNN Financial Network* (www.cnnfn.com), free; the *Investor's Business Daily* (www.investors.com), which requires your free registration for most of its content; or the *ABC News* business section (www.abcnews.com/sections/business).

Invest in Industry Leaders

If you investigate a company in a specific industry, determine which companies are growing the fastest in that industry and which are the industry leaders. By focusing on just these two elements, you're likely to reduce the number of investment candidates for your consideration in this industry by 80 percent. You also discover the following information:

- ✔ Many companies in the industry have no growth or display lackluster growth.
- ✔ Older companies have slower growth rates than do younger companies.

Remember that investing in industry laggards seldom pays, even if they're amazingly cheap. Look for the market leader and make certain that you have a good reason to invest in the industry in the first place. Additionally, be aware that all industries have their own cycles of growth, and you want to invest in an industry that's in an upswing. For industry surveys and reports, see Value Line Investment Surveys (www.valueline.com).

Buy Good Performers

Try to buy for value and not price. Select companies that regularly outperformed their competition in the last three to five years. Invest in companies that have consistent rather than flashy returns. Take into consideration the following guidelines:

- ✔ Check the company's stability and examine its five-year earnings record.
- ✔ Keep in mind that an annual percentage increase is desirable but so is stability and consistency over the past five-year's earnings.

✔ You may want to consider not including a company's one time extraordinary gains in your calculations.

✔ Determine whether the company's annual growth rate is between 25 percent and 50 percent for the last four or five years. If so, it may be a winner.

Don't try to chase after last year's high performer; it could be this year's loser. For company reports, see Standard & Poors Wealthbuilder (www.wealthbuidler.com) or Standard & Poors Stock Reports (www.standardandpoorsinfo.com).

Select Your P/E Ratio Strategy

Any analysis of investment candidates generally includes P/E (price/earnings) ratios. The importance of these ratios varies from analyst to analyst. The following subsections describe two strategies that are worthwhile to consider. Select the one that works best for you. (See Chapter 12 for additional information about P/E ratios.)

Low P/E and high dividend approach

Long-term investors often employ the "7 and 7" approach — that is, they purchase stock in companies with a P/E ratio of 7 or less and a dividend yield greater than 7. Additionally, if the company's P/E ratio is lower than 10 and the earnings are rising, you may have found a winner. Make certain, however, that no major long-term problems exist that can drive the P/E to 4 or lower by investigating the security. (See Chapter 12 for details.)

High P/E ratios are worth the price

The following example shows that you often get what you pay for. From 1953 to 1985, the average P/E ratio for the best-performing emerging stocks was 20. The Dow Jones Industrial's P/E at the same time averaged 15. If you weren't willing to pay for the stocks that were trading over the average, you eliminated most of the best investments available.

For more information about how to use P/E ratios in your stock buying analyses, visit the Investor Home Web site (www.investorhome.com).

Look for Strong Dividend Pay-Out Records

If you're risk adverse, your time horizon for investments is shorter than that of many investors, or you believe that the market is heading for a downturn, you may want to invest in companies with consistent records of paying generous dividends. These *income stocks* tend to hold their value in volatile markets because investors are confident that they're going to continue to receive sizable dividends. The disadvantage of these companies is that, because they pay out such a large proportion of earnings, they may not retain enough capital to grow the company. This failure to invest in their own growth may cause the stock prices of these companies to drag. Additionally, income stocks are more sensitive to changes in interest rates than are other stock types. To find companies that investors categorize as income stocks, see Vector Vest (a software developer), at www.vectorvest.com/safegro.htm, for a weekly report.

Appendix
About the CD

Here's some of what you can find on the *Investing Online For Dummies,* 2nd Edition, CD-ROM:

- MindSpring, a popular Internet service.
- An easy-to-navigate, electronic version of the book's Internet Directory so you can quickly jump to the Internet sites you need for selecting, buying, selling, and tracking your investments online.
- Free, high-quality software programs to assist you with a variety of investor tasks.
- Shareware and freeware programs for financial planning and analysis, portfolio management, and other essential investor activities.
- Demonstration versions and free trials of invaluable software tools for online investors.

System Requirements

Make sure that your computer meets the minimum system requirements listed below.

- A PC with a 486 or faster processor.
- Microsoft Windows 3.1 or later.
- At least 8MB of total RAM installed on your computer. For best performance, we recommend that Windows 95-equipped PCs have at least 16MB of RAM installed.
- At least 100MB of hard drive space available to install all the software from this CD. (You need less space if you don't install every program.)
- A CD-ROM drive — double-speed (2x) or faster.
- A sound card for PCs.
- A monitor capable of displaying at least 256 colors or grayscale.
- A modem with a speed of at least 14,400 bps.

If your computer doesn't match up to most of the requirements, you may have problems using the contents of the CD.

If you need more information on the basics, check out *PCs For Dummies,* 6th Edition, by Dan Gookin; *Windows 95 For Dummies,* 2nd Edition, by Andy Rathbone; or *Windows 3.11 For Dummies,* 4th Edition, by Andy Rathbone (all published by IDG Books Worldwide, Inc.).

How to Use the CD Using Microsoft Windows

To install the programs from the CD to your hard drive, follow these steps.

1. **Insert the CD into your computer's CD-ROM drive.**

2. **Windows 3.1 or 3.11 users: From Program Manager, choose File⇨Run.**

   Windows 95 users: Click the Start button and then click Run.

3. **In the dialog box that appears, type** D:\SETUP.EXE

   Most of you probably have your CD-ROM drive listed as drive D under My Computer in Windows 95 or the File Manager in Windows 3.1. Type in the proper drive letter if your CD-ROM drive uses a different letter.

4. **Click OK.**

   A License Agreement window appears.

5. **Because I'm sure that you'll want to use the CD, read through the license agreement, nod your head, and then click the Accept button. After you click Accept, the License Agreement window will never bother you again.**

   From here, the CD interface appears. The CD interface is a little program that shows you what's on the CD and coordinates installing the programs and running the demos. The interface basically lets you click a button or two to make things happen.

6. **The first screen you see is the Welcome screen. Click anywhere on this screen to enter the interface.**

   Now you're getting to the action. This next screen lists categories for the software on the CD.

7. **To view the items within a category, just click the category's name.**

   A list of programs in the category appears.

8. **For more information about a program, click the program's name.**

Be sure to read the information that appears. Sometimes a program requires you to do a few tricks on your computer first, and this screen will tell you where to go for that information, if necessary.

9. **To install the program, click the appropriate Install button. If you don't want to install the program, click the Go Back button to return to the previous screen.**

You can always return to the previous screen by clicking the Go Back button, which allows you to browse the different categories and products and decide what you want to install.

After you click an install button, the CD interface drops to the background while the CD begins installation of the program you choose.

10. **To install other programs, repeat Steps 7, 8, and 9.**

11. **When you finish installing programs, click the Quit button to close the interface.**

You can eject the CD now. Carefully return it to the plastic jacket of the book for safekeeping.

To run some of the programs, you may need to keep the CD inside your CD-ROM drive. This is a Good Thing. Otherwise, the installed program would have required you to install a very large chunk of the program to your hard drive space, which would have kept you from installing other software.

MindSpring Internet Service Provider

In case you don't have a connection to the information superhighway, the CD includes sign-on software for MindSpring Internet Access, an Internet service provider.

If you already have an Internet service provider, be forewarned that downloading the MindSpring Internet Access software may cause you to lose your Internet access with your current provider. The software makes changes to your computer's current Internet configuration and may replace the current settings.

After you are signed on, one of the first places you can check out is the MindSpring Web site at www.mindspring.com. (You do need a credit card to sign up with MindSpring Internet Access.)

An Electronic Version of the Directory

The *Investing Online For Dummies,* 2nd Edition, companion CD-ROM includes a listing of the book's Internet Directory, which lets you quickly go to the Internet sites you want.

The Links Page at `Links.htm` is an HTML page that you can open in your web browser and have point-and-click access to all of the Web sites listed in the Directory section of *Investing Online For Dummies*. To view the links page, open your web browser and use the File⇨Open File command to open the Links.htm document at the root level of the CD-ROM. Click Go Back to return to the previous screen.

Bonus Chapters

Investing Online For Dummies, 2nd Edition, had so much information that I had to put four chapters on the CD. Check out the bonus chapters that, among other things, cover these topics:

✔ Finding investor stuff on the Internet

✔ Taking options

✔ Delving into commodities and financial futures

✔ Getting the most out of online banking

Investing in stock options (Bonus Chapter 2: Taking the Option) can be dangerous to your financial health. There are many new types of options and option strategies that are constantly introduced to the marketplace. These new stock option financial products and option strategies can include risks that do not become apparent until they have been tested over a period of time. This means that investors can be exposed to more risks and potential losses than they expect. Additionally, not all option strategies are suitable for all investors. These proven but high-risk strategies (such as writing "naked calls"), expose investors to excessive levels of potential loss. For more details about the risks of option holders and writers, go to The Options Clearing Corporation (CCC) at `www.optionsclearing.com/publications/riskstoc.htm` and check out the online booklet titled, "Characteristics and Risks of Listed Options," Chapter 10, "Principal Risks of Options Positions."

To access these chapters, install and start Adobe Acrobat Reader (included on this CD) and open the files by clicking on File⇨Open; then type in D:\CHAPTERS\CHAPTER1.PDF (or CHAPTER2 or 3 or 4, for that matter).

What Investor Software You'll Find

This section is a summary of the software on this book's companion CD-ROM. The CD interface can help you install the software easily. (If you have no idea what I'm talking about when I say "CD Interface," see the section, "How to Use the CD Using Microsoft Windows" in this appendix.)

Free investor software programs

If you love getting something for free, these programs are just what you're looking for. The following shows what you can expect on the _Investing Online For Dummies_ companion CD-ROM.

Acrobat Reader 3.02

Web pages may be great-looking, but some publishers aren't happy with having to change the original page layout to an HTML design. (HTML is the computer language that Web pages are written in.) To avoid having to use HTML, some publishers use the Adobe Acrobat format, which preserves the page layout and lets you see pages in their original glory. For details about Acrobat Reader, see www.adobe.com/prodindex/acrobat/readstep.html.

Internet Explorer 4.0

Internet Explorer 4.0 is a powerful World Wide Web browser. Plus it's free, which makes it a true bargain. Internet Explorer 4.0 brings you Web browsing features that provide an easy, consistent, and organized way to explore the Web. The integration into Windows makes it easy to find the information you need, whether it's on your computer's hard drive, a local area network, or the Internet. For more on Internet Explorer 4.0, refer to microsoft.com/windows/ie/default.htm.

Investor's Advantage

Now you can chart your favorite stocks and general market trends on your PC computer using proven technical market indicators. Investor's Advantage for Windows also provides a weekly report of all the stocks being tracked, sorted strongest to weakest by a strength rating. This rating is calculated based on the price performance of each individual stock. The more stocks you track, the better your chances of including the strongest stocks in your portfolio. For more information, see www.sacc.com/iawin/iawin.htm.

myTrack

myTrack, from Track Data, is an Internet-based personal investment tool with free basic service. Check out myTrack for continually updated quotes, breaking company news, trade-by-trade log, charting, and proprietary library of intraday market statistics. Delayed quotes are free, and real-time quotes start at $20/month. The Track Data Web site is at www.mytrack.com/new.htm. (*Note:* myTrack works with Windows 95 and later only.)

Netscape Communicator 4.04

While the Netscape folks are working on Netscape Communicator 5.0, others in the organization have been improving the 4.0 version. Netscape Communicator 4.04 adds several new features to satisfy corporate customers, brings its mail and graphics capabilities up-to-date, and makes it easier for you to stay in touch with your friends. For details, see home.netscape.com/comprod/mirror/index.html.

Options Toolbox for Windows

Designed for both beginners and experts, this software can help you with the fundamentals of options trading. The program includes an options position-modeling feature that simulates the performance of your planned strategy under a variety of conditions. Use this software to test before you invest. For more information, see www.cboe.com/education/toolbox.htm.

(*Note:* Before you use the Options Toolbox software, you have to accept the terms of the License Agreement that appears on the screen. If you don't accept the terms of the License Agreement, you can't use the software.)

Shareware and freeware financial management programs

Shareware programs are not free. Shareware programs are free to try but cost a few dollars to keep, which allows software developers to distribute their programs inexpensively. Shareware programs use an honor system. If you don't like the program, you delete it from your computer. If you keep the program, you pay by registering the program, which entitles you to upgrades, information, and other goodies from the software developer. In contrast, freeware programs are yours to keep at no charge.

The Internet provides many downloadable financial shareware and freeware programs for PC and Macintosh computers. The book's companion CD-ROM includes some of the best shareware and freeware programs available. The following outlines what you'll find on the CD-ROM for personal financial management.

Financial Authority for Windows

Designed for financial planning, this program tracks loans, annuities, retirement savings, Series EEE bond appreciation, mutual fund performance, and more. Visit www.halcyon.com/cbutton/welcome for all the details.

Stock Wiz Pro 98

This investment tracking program uses historical data from over 8,000 public companies (one-day delayed). Check out www.stockwiz.com for more information.

EEBond

This savings bond analysis shareware can help you determine what your savings bonds are worth at any point in time. For details, see MMR Software at www.mmrsoft.com.

Quote Ticker Bar for Windows

This shareware program can access stocks, mutual funds, or index prices from any of nine different online quote servers. You can even set an audio alarm to notify you if your preset price is reached. Check it out at Starfire Software (www.starfire-inc.com).

Freeware and shareware portfolio management programs

The Internet provides many freeware and shareware portfolio programs that can assist you in monitoring the performance of your investments. The *Investing Online For Dummies,* 2nd Edition, companion CD-ROM provides many of the latest and best investor shareware programs available. The following outlines what you'll find on the CD-ROM for portfolio management:

Fund Manager

Fund Manager is a full-featured portfolio management application for the individual investor. Fund Manager is designed to help investors monitor and analyze their stocks, mutual funds, and other investments with a wide variety of easy-to-use graphs and reports. This shareware program is ideal for stocks but is especially well suited for managing your mutual funds portfolio. For more information, see www.beiley.com/fundman/.

Capital Gainz for Windows

This popular shareware program is terrific for handling stocks, bonds, and mutual funds. Record your purchases, sales, dividends, capital gains, and other transactions. Calculate your gains or losses, and print reports and tax forms. Visit www.localweb.com/alleycatsw/ for details.

NetStock

NetStock is a fast, easy way to keep track of your stocks and mutual fund investments via the Internet. Primarily, the software is a simple stock and mutual fund quote retrieval program. For a set of stocks, NetStock displays a variety of data, including the current price, P/E ratio, yield, value, daily high, daily low, 52 week high, 52 week low, and more. Quotes can be imported into the Intuit Quicken program. For details, see www.splitcycle.com/pages/netstock.html.

Market Watcher for Windows

Market Watcher for Windows is an Internet interactive software program for tracking your portfolio. Visit www.marketwatcher.com for more information. (*Note:* This program works with Windows 95/98 only.)

Personal Stock Monitor

Personal Stock Monitor is a portfolio management program that retrieves stock quotes from a variety of free online quote servers. For details, see www.personaltools.com/psm.

Investor demonstration programs

The Internet provides many downloadable demonstration programs for PC computers. These demonstration programs are often just like the full editions, but they have a limited life. The *Investing Online For Dummies* companion CD-ROM includes the best of these investor demonstration programs. This section outlines what you can find.

Power Optimizer, Ramcap, Xpress, ScanData, and Analytics

These downloadable demonstration copies of asset allocations programs help you get organized and get going. Here's a brief description of each. (For more details, see Wilson International at www.wilsonintl.com.)

- ✔ The **Power Optimizer** program provides interactive computer models to analyze the risk and return characteristics of existing or proposed investments.

- ✔ **Ramcap** is an entry-level asset allocation package that offers an easy-to-use alternative to the Power Center programs. If you're restrained by budget limitations, Ramcap may be the program for you.

- ✔ The **Xpress** program is an entry-level asset allocation package designed primarily for point-of-sales presentations. The program includes an internal questionnaire to establish your risk/return parameters and limited asset allocation (optimization) capabilities.

- ✔ **ScanData** is a tool for sorting and reviewing information on asset classes, mutual funds, stocks, variable annuities, and closed-end funds.

- ✔ The **Analytics** program permits users to review and analyze asset classes, mutual funds, stocks, variable annuities, and closed-end funds.

OptionVue5

Gain a unique understanding of the special qualities of options and why traders love 'em. This 10-minute demo presentation gives you an overview of the OptionVue5 software features. OptionVue offers a fully functional 30-day trial version of the software for $49. For details, go to `www.optionvue.com`.

Stock Vue

Track financial information on the Internet with Stock Vue. For details, see `www.stockvue.com`.

First Finance

First Finance is demonstration software for financial planning and financial management calculations. Visit `www.what.com/firstfin` for details.

MetaStock

MetaStock is a demonstration program for sophisticated investment analysis software. For additional information, see `www.metastock.com`.

If You've Got Problems (Of the CD Kind)

I tried my best to compile programs that work on most computers with the minimum system requirements. Alas, your computer may differ, and some programs may not work properly for some reason.

The two likeliest problems causing these programs not to work on your computer are that you don't have enough memory (RAM) for the programs you want to use or you have other programs running that are affecting installation or running of a program. If you get error messages such as `Not enough memory` or `Setup cannot continue`, try one or more of these methods and then try using the software again:

- ✔ Turn off any antivirus software that you have on your computer. Installers sometimes mimic virus activity and may make your computer believe incorrectly that a virus is infecting it.

- ✔ Close all running programs. The more programs you're running, the less memory is available to other programs. Installers also typically update files and programs. So if you keep other programs running, installation may not work properly.

> ✔ Have your local computer store add more RAM to your computer, which is, admittedly, a drastic and somewhat expensive step. However, if you have a Windows 95 PC with a PowerPC chip, adding more memory can really help the speed of your computer and allow more programs to run at the same time. This may include closing the CD interface and running a product's installation program from Windows Explorer.

If you still have trouble installing the programs from the CD, please call the IDG Books Worldwide Customer Service phone number: 800-762-2974 (outside the U.S.: 317-596-5430).

Index

• C •

Order EEBond today!
Get your free upgrade featuring the latest values and newest enhancements

It's easy. Just fill out and return the coupon below and you will receive one free EEBond upgrade. The upgrade has the most recent savings bond redemption tables and values and includes all the latest program enhancements. A valid email address is **required** for the free upgrade.

If you'd like the program immediately, email the information listed on the coupon to:
freeupgrade@mmrsoft.com
Upon receipt we will email you the download instructions.

Or, if you do not have access to email and would still like the upgrade, send $10 to the address below (checks payable to MMR Software) and the disks will be mailed.

Please print

FREE *EEBond Upgrade Coupon*

Mail coupon to:

MMR Software
Franklin Leibsly
P.O. Box 34916
Bethesda, MD 20827

Email address _____

Name _____

Address _____

City _____ State _____ Zip _____

Phone (_____) _____

Please check out our other fine products at: http://www.mmrsoft.com

What the press is saying about EEBond:

Kiplinger's Personal Finance Magazine, "What's my savings bond worth?
The answer is only a few keystrokes away using a quick and easy on-line calculator on the World Wide Web. At a Web site sponsored by MMR Software (http://www.mmrsoft.com), all you have to do to get the current value of your series EE bond is type in its face value and the month and year it was issued. In about 5 seconds the calculator can tell you the value. Savings Bond values are updated every six months, when the government issues new redemption tables. MMR Software also publishes EEBond, a $20 program that calculates savings bond values and prints reports.

Milwaukee Sentinel
Calculating the value of your U.S. savings bonds can be difficult and time consuming, but there is help available. A new software program, EEBond, has been developed by Frank Leibsly and is available through MMR Software.

CPA Technology Report
Ever tried computing savings bond values manually? It's a chore, and estimates can be off by hundreds of dollars. Rather than wade through the Tables of Redemption Values, you -- or a client -- can use a $20 utility called EEBond to streamline the task. EEBond comes with a database of Series EE and Series E bond and Savings Notes -- and computes the value of bonds up to six months in advance. All you do is enter the serial number and date of purchase, and EEBond determines the worth.

Computer Craft
EEBond is an inexpensive computer program from MMR Software that you can use to compute the value of Series EE Savings Bonds up to 6 months in advance. The program maintains a database of Series EE and Series E Bonds and Savings Notes. All you do is enter the serial number and date of purchase, and the program takes it from there, automatically determining the worth of your bonds for the next six months.

Compuserve Magazine
Bonds Away - Latest version of Franklin Leibsly's popular U.S. savings bond value calculator, for IBM and compatible computers, computing interest on Series E and EE bonds and U.S. savings notes. Now has Windows-like enstronment, scrollable screen reports and powerful database engine.

Managing your Money BETTER
Finding out how much your US savings are worth usually isn't easy. And short of going to your local bank or picking up a copy of the Tables of Redemption Values from the Bureau of the Public Debt, there was no easy way to know the interest your bond earned, until now. EEBond is an easy to use product from MMR Software that shows you the value of your bonds. It also prints reports of your savings bond holdings, and offers insights, information and advice about bonds.

FREE EEBond Upgrade
See the free upgrade coupon and mail it in today!

Playing games is really fun... The Dummies Way™!

Pressman®
©1998 Pressman Toy Corporation, New York, NY 10010

Crosswords For Dummies™ Game

You don't have to know how to spell to have a great time. Place a word strip on the board so that it overlaps another word or creates a new one. Special squares add to the fun. The first player to use up all their word strips wins!

For 2 to 4 players.

Trivia For Dummies™ Game

You're guaranteed to have an answer every time! Each player gets 10 cards that contain the answer to every question. Act quickly and be the first player to throw down the correct answer and move closer to the finish line!

For 3 or 4 players.

Charades For Dummies™ Game

Act out one-word charades: when other players guess them, they move ahead. The special cards keep the game full of surprises. The first player around the board wins.

For 3 or 4 players.

...For Dummies and The Dummies Way are trademarks or registered trademarks of IDG Books Worldwide, Inc.

IDG Books Worldwide, Inc.,
End-User License Agreement

READ THIS. You should carefully read these terms and conditions before opening the software packet(s) included with this book ("Book"). This is a license agreement ("Agreement") between you and IDG Books Worldwide, Inc. ("IDGB"). By opening the accompanying software packet(s), you acknowledge that you have read and accept the following terms and conditions. If you do not agree and do not want to be bound by such terms and conditions, promptly return the Book and the unopened software packet(s) to the place you obtained them for a full refund.

1. **License Grant.** IDGB grants to you (either an individual or entity) a nonexclusive license to use one copy of the enclosed software program(s) (collectively, the "Software") solely for your own personal or business purposes on a single computer (whether a standard computer or a workstation component of a multiuser network). The Software is in use on a computer when it is loaded into temporary memory (RAM) or installed into permanent memory (hard disk, CD-ROM, or other storage device). IDGB reserves all rights not expressly granted herein.

2. **Ownership.** IDGB is the owner of all right, title, and interest, including copyright, in and to the compilation of the Software recorded on the disk(s) or CD-ROM ("Software Media"). Copyright to the individual programs recorded on the Software Media is owned by the author or other authorized copyright owner of each program. Ownership of the Software and all proprietary rights relating thereto remain with IDGB and its licensers.

3. **Restrictions on Use and Transfer.**

   (a) You may only (i) make one copy of the Software for backup or archival purposes, or (ii) transfer the Software to a single hard disk, provided that you keep the original for backup or archival purposes. You may not (i) rent or lease the Software, (ii) copy or reproduce the Software through a LAN or other network system or through any computer subscriber system or bulletin-board system, or (iii) modify, adapt, or create derivative works based on the Software.

   (b) You may not reverse engineer, decompile, or disassemble the Software. You may transfer the Software and user documentation on a permanent basis, provided that the transferee agrees to accept the terms and conditions of this Agreement and you retain no copies. If the Software is an update or has been updated, any transfer must include the most recent update and all prior versions.

4. **Restrictions on Use of Individual Programs.** You must follow the individual requirements and restrictions detailed for each individual program in the "About the CD" appendix of this Book. These limitations are also contained in the individual license agreements recorded on the Software Media. These limitations may include a requirement that after using the program for a specified period of time, the user must pay a registration fee or discontinue use. By opening the Software packet(s), you will be agreeing to abide by the licenses and restrictions for these individual programs that are detailed in the "About the CD" appendix and on the Software Media. None of the material on this Software Media or listed in this Book may ever be redistributed, in original or modified form, for commercial purposes.

5. Limited Warranty.

(a) IDGB warrants that the Software and Software Media are free from defects in materials and workmanship under normal use for a period of sixty (60) days from the date of purchase of this Book. If IDGB receives notification within the warranty period of defects in materials or workmanship, IDGB will replace the defective Software Media.

(b) IDGB AND THE AUTHOR OF THE BOOK DISCLAIM ALL OTHER WARRANTIES, EXPRESS OR IMPLIED, INCLUDING WITHOUT LIMITATION IMPLIED WARRANTIES OF MERCHANTABILITY AND FITNESS FOR A PARTICULAR PURPOSE, WITH RESPECT TO THE SOFTWARE, THE PROGRAMS, THE SOURCE CODE CONTAINED THEREIN, AND/OR THE TECHNIQUES DESCRIBED IN THIS BOOK. IDGB DOES NOT WARRANT THAT THE FUNCTIONS CONTAINED IN THE SOFTWARE WILL MEET YOUR REQUIREMENTS OR THAT THE OPERATION OF THE SOFTWARE WILL BE ERROR FREE.

(c) This limited warranty gives you specific legal rights, and you may have other rights that vary from jurisdiction to jurisdiction.

6. Remedies.

(a) IDGB's entire liability and your exclusive remedy for defects in materials and workmanship shall be limited to replacement of the Software Media, which may be returned to IDGB with a copy of your receipt at the following address: Software Media Fulfillment Department, Attn.: *Investing Online For Dummies,* 2nd Edition, IDG Books Worldwide, Inc., 7260 Shadeland Station, Ste. 100, Indianapolis, IN 46256, or call 800-762-2974. Please allow three to four weeks for delivery. This Limited Warranty is void if failure of the Software Media has resulted from accident, abuse, or misapplication. Any replacement Software Media will be warranted for the remainder of the original warranty period or thirty (30) days, whichever is longer.

(b) In no event shall IDGB or the author be liable for any damages whatsoever (including without limitation damages for loss of business profits, business interruption, loss of business information, or any other pecuniary loss) arising from the use of or inability to use the Book or the Software, even if IDGB has been advised of the possibility of such damages.

(c) Because some jurisdictions do not allow the exclusion or limitation of liability for consequential or incidental damages, the above limitation or exclusion may not apply to you.

7. U.S. Government Restricted Rights. Use, duplication, or disclosure of the Software by the U.S. Government is subject to restrictions stated in paragraph (c)(1)(ii) of the Rights in Technical Data and Computer Software clause of DFARS 252.227-7013, and in subparagraphs (a) through (d) of the Commercial Computer–Restricted Rights clause at FAR 52.227-19, and in similar clauses in the NASA FAR supplement, when applicable.

8. General. This Agreement constitutes the entire understanding of the parties and revokes and supersedes all prior agreements, oral or written, between them and may not be modified or amended except in a writing signed by both parties hereto that specifically refers to this Agreement. This Agreement shall take precedence over any other documents that may be in conflict herewith. If any one or more provisions contained in this Agreement are held by any court or tribunal to be invalid, illegal, or otherwise unenforceable, each and every other provision shall remain in full force and effect.

Installation Instructions

The *Investing Online For Dummies,* 2nd Edition, CD-ROM contains some of the most useful Internet investment software tools available for investors. Here's a quick overview of the tools you can install from the book's companion CD:

- An electronic version of the book's Internet Directory
- Shareware and freeware programs for financial planning and analysis, portfolio management, and other investor tasks
- Demonstration versions of software tools for online investors

For details about the contents of the CD and instructions for installing the software from the CD, see the "About the CD" appendix in this book.

IDG BOOKS WORLDWIDE BOOK REGISTRATION

We want to hear from you!

Visit **http://my2cents.dummies.com** to register this book and tell us how you liked it!

- Get entered in our monthly prize giveaway.

- Give us feedback about this book — tell us what you like best, what you like least, or maybe what you'd like to ask the author and us to change!

- Let us know any other *...For Dummies*® topics that interest you.

Your feedback helps us determine what books to publish, tells us what coverage to add as we revise our books, and lets us know whether we're meeting your needs as a *...For Dummies* reader. You're our most valuable resource, and what you have to say is important to us!

Not on the Web yet? It's easy to get started with *Dummies 101*®*: The Internet For Windows*® *98* or *The Internet For Dummies*,® 5th Edition, at local retailers everywhere.

Or let us know what you think by sending us a letter at the following address:

...For Dummies Book Registration
Dummies Press
7260 Shadeland Station, Suite 100
Indianapolis, IN 46256-3945
Fax 317-596-5498

BESTSELLING
BOOK SERIES